MW00810130

The Goldilocks Challenge

THE GOLDILOCKS CHALLENGE

Right-Fit Evidence for the Social Sector

Mary Kay Gugerty

and

Dean Karlan

OXFORD
UNIVERSITY PRESS

Oxford University Press is a department of the University of Oxford. It furthers
the University's objective of excellence in research, scholarship, and education
by publishing worldwide. Oxford is a registered trade mark of Oxford University
Press in the UK and certain other countries.

Published in the United States of America by Oxford University Press
198 Madison Avenue, New York, NY 10016, United States of America.

Library of Congress Cataloging-in-Publication Data
Names: Gugerty, Mary Kay, author. | Karlan, Dean S., author.
Title: The Goldilocks challenge : right-fit evidence for the social sector /
Mary Kay Gugerty and Dean Karlan.
Description: New York, NY : Oxford University Press, [2018] |
Includes bibliographical references.
Identifiers: LCCN 2017043942| ISBN 9780199366088 (hardcover : alk. paper) |
ISBN 9780199366101 (epub) | ISBN 9780199366095 (updf)
Subjects: LCSH: Nonprofit organizations—Evaluation. |
Organizational effectiveness--Evaluation—Methodology.
Classification: LCC HD62.6 .G84 2018 | DDC 658.4/08—dc23
LC record available at https://lccn.loc.gov/2017043942

9 8 7 6

Printed by Sheridan Books, Inc., United States of America

CONTENTS

AUTHOR'S NOTE

This book began with a question. It was a rainy day in Seattle in 2010, and we were presenting to a room full of nonprofit organizations. Dozens of small- and medium-sized Seattle-based organizations came to learn about measuring their impact. Donors often ask for evidence of impact, so the room was packed. Of course, many also wanted to measure impact because they were genuinely motivated to achieve their mission.

In the session, we introduced the basics of using randomized controlled trials (RCTs) to test the impact of social programs. RCTs are the method used in medical research to test drug and treatment efficacy. We use this method to measure impact in our own research because it is the best way, when feasible, of finding out how programs are affecting the lives of the poor. However, a lot rides on the words "when feasible." A big push in development economics in the 1990s has shown that "when feasible" is indeed fairly often. Our focus in this book, though, is not on when RCTs are feasible, but on what to do when they are not.

At the training session, clicking through a set of slides, we explained how impact evaluation via RCTs can help organizations get good answers to important questions. We discussed a series of technical issues, such as the importance of control groups, how to craft experimental designs, and what data to collect. Then we used case studies to show that RCTs do require certain conditions, such as a large enough sample size, in order to work.

As the session wore on, a sense of frustration seemed to be growing in the room. "I totally get it," said one attendee. "I get the setup you need to be able to randomize, and the sample size and everything, and yet I'm never going to be able to do an impact evaluation like that," she said.

She was right. And as more people in the audience spoke about their work, it was clear that most of them were not going to be able to conduct a reliable impact evaluation even though they all wanted one. Perhaps they could instead learn from other, larger organizations that can pave the way by creating knowledge. But will the lessons from these larger organizations hold for the smaller ones, working in different settings?

The audience members at that workshop wanted to use their own data and undertake their own impact measurement. Yet their organizations were either too small for an RCT—some were running programs in just one or two towns—or their work focused on advocacy or institutional reform, which typically cannot be evaluated with an RCT.

Then came the question that triggered a long conversation and, ultimately, this book: "So if I can't do an impact evaluation, what should I do?"

At the time, we did not have a set of slides for that. It was awkward. We gave some broad generalities and then a few examples. We had no manageable framework, usable by organizations, to think through the alternatives. We did notice that many of the questions the audience posed were not actually impact questions. Rather, they were management questions. Accountability. Quality control. Client satisfaction. These are important concepts, yet not always part of the "impact evaluation" movement.

As we talked after the event, we discussed how many organizations—large or small, based in Kenya or Seattle—also lacked a guiding framework for what to measure and how.

Soon after the conference, we spoke with someone who represented a donor that was dealing with this same question. The donor supported a number of small organizations in Uganda that were struggling to collect the right data on their programs. "How do you think we could raise the bar on [monitoring and evaluation] for our grantees?" he asked.

Over the next few years, we set out to investigate that question—to find out what organizations were doing right in monitoring and evaluation and what they could do better.

We found a system that is out of balance: the trend to measure impact has brought with it a proliferation of poor methods of doing so, resulting in organizations wasting huge amounts of money on bad "impact evaluations." Meanwhile, many organizations are neglecting the basics. They do not know if staff are showing up, if their services are being delivered, if beneficiaries are using services, or what they think about those services. In some cases, they do not even know whether their programs have realistic goals and make logical sense.

To correct this imbalance and strengthen programs, we propose a framework for building right-fit monitoring and evaluation systems. This framework does not just apply to organizations that are ill-suited or too small for impact evaluations; it applies to all organizations—including nonprofit organizations, governments, and social enterprises—aiming to do good around the world.

As we wrote this book, we each brought different, though complementary, perspectives to the subject. We have known each other since our graduate school days at Harvard and M.I.T., where we studied development economics. Since then, we have both landed at universities and conducted field research internationally, but our paths and research interests have diverged.

Mary Kay studies nonprofit performance and accountability systems and teaches public policy to master's students at the Evans School of Public Policy at the University of Washington. She focuses on the management and accountability issues facing US nonprofits and global nongovernmental organizations (NGOs). Many of her students hope, one day, to run a social-sector organization. While writing this book, she often saw things from the perspective of the people inside organizations trying to improve their programs. They struggle to identify and collect data that help them track their performance. They strive to develop decision-making systems that turn that data into programmatic improvements. They feel pressure to evaluate their impact but worry about the expense of doing so and whether it would yield any actionable information.

Dean conducts his research around the world, in Africa, Asia, and Latin America, as well as the United States. In 2002, upon finishing graduate school, he founded an international research and policy advocacy nonprofit, Innovations for Poverty Action (IPA). In 2015, he co-founded a charity rating and feedback nonprofit, ImpactMatters. Dean has focused his research on measuring the impact of programs. He tests development and behavioral theories that have implications for how to best implement programs or run businesses with social goals. Through his research and the work of the team at IPA, he has seen such impact evaluations identify successful programs to fight poverty and then seen the evidence influence policy for hundreds of millions of families. Hence IPA's motto: More Evidence, Less Poverty. But he also has seen organizations try to measure their impact before they knew if they were implementing their program as intended. And he has seen countless impact evaluations, good and bad, go unused because they were not designed to address an organization's key questions or did not come at the right time in the program cycle. The result is wasted money, misspent staff time, and lost opportunities to learn.

Both of us are passionate about making programs work better for the poor. Although we envision this book being used in classrooms, this is not a textbook *per se*. Whether you are a student, practitioner, or funder, we hope this book helps you use data to drive decisions that make the world a better place.

PART I

The CART Principles

Building Credible, Actionable, Responsible, and Transportable Evidence Systems

CHAPTER 1

Introduction

In 2011, a woman named Lucia moved to Kampala, Uganda, to work for a nonprofit aiming to help families with children improve their food security. On her first day on the job in the monitoring and evaluation group, she found an extensive system in place for tracking changes in nutrition and income for beneficiaries of the organization's food security program. She began working with her team to compile and analyze these data about the program's progress—data that surveyors had collected through multiple rounds of detailed interviews with people in far-flung villages. Every day, Lucia spent most of her time converting 303 indicators from two project sites and 25 partner organizations into a vast, organized system of spreadsheets.

As months passed and Lucia continued her work, however, she realized the organization was not using—or learning from—most of the data she and others laboriously collected and compiled. Instead, the data were sitting on hard drives and on shelves at headquarters gathering dust. Even when the information Lucia compiled got used, she worried program managers were drawing faulty conclusions by using monitoring data to assess the program's impact. For example, by comparing income data from parents before they enrolled in the program to their income after they "graduated" from it, staff claimed that the program had lifted thousands of children out of poverty. But they were unable to say whether the income change they saw was the result of the program's food assistance, its cash-for-work component, or on the more pessimistic side, merely the result of broader economic shifts that had nothing to do with the program.

The organization Lucia worked for was not fulfilling its responsibility to learn. It was monitoring and evaluating projects, but the program's leaders were not learning from these efforts. In the end, they had no idea which activities, if any, actually helped people they served. As one staff member lamented, "Currently the [monitoring and evaluation] system helps us write reports, but it does not actually teach us what's working best."

A few miles away, the Director of Programs at another nonprofit was dealing with an entirely different problem. The organization had been operating in Uganda for about eight years, working to help conflict-affected young men and women in Northern Uganda, but it had never assessed whether its programs were working as intended or achieving their goals. The organization raised funds largely from small donations from the public and the sale of merchandise; as a result, it had never been asked to demonstrate accountability to specific donors. But, over time, the organization had become better known and its model had started generating broader interest. In light of this increased attention, the Director of Programs felt that the organization had the responsibility to demonstrate—to its staff, donors new and old, and those looking to learn from its model—that the program was well run and was changing people's lives in the way it promised. This would mean gathering data on exactly how the program was being implemented and proving the impact it was having on people's lives.

But that would be no easy feat. Since the organization had never tracked or evaluated its programs, it had no data to share with donors or the public on its participants. Nor did it have much administrative or operational data that could help articulate its model and what exactly the staff did every day. To address these information gaps, the organization established a monitoring and evaluation team and began tracking program activities.

Around the same time, the organization also hired an external firm to conduct an impact evaluation of its work. Midway through the evaluation though, the Director of Programs made a frustrating discovery. The evaluation firm was taking a lot of short cuts, such as simply comparing participants' lives after the program to their lives before the program. Yet people's lives change, for better or worse, for many reasons. So how could the organization know if the changes observed were because of what they did, rather than other factors? Moreover, the firm had sent surveyors into the field who did not even speak the local language. How could they possibly gather good data in face-to-face interviews? It became rapidly clear that the "*impact* evaluation" would not actually provide any information about the program's impact and that any data collected would be of suspect quality. It was just a huge waste of money—not at all what the Director had wanted.

These accounts are based on interviews conducted in Kampala, Uganda. We are grateful to the organizations for sharing their stories with us for us to share publicly, and we have kept their names anonymous. The identity of these groups is not important for the point we are making, and the people we met are trying to help the poor and their data collection efforts are well intentioned.

These two organizations have different problems with their monitoring and evaluation systems, but both systems share one commonality: they do not provide the information that stakeholders really want. In the first case, Lucia's organization collects more monitoring data than it can analyze or use to improve operations. Beyond that, the organization uses these monitoring data to make claims of impact but, unfortunately, that is not a credible way of demonstrating the effect of the program. In short (and we will talk more about this later), their data fail to include a comparison group—a group that shows how participants would have fared without the program. Without that, it is quite challenging to know whether the program caused the observed changes to occur. The cause could have been good economic conditions, some other government or nongovernmental organizational (NGO) program, or the drive and ambition of the participants. In the second case, the organization has too few data on the implementation of its program to know how it is actually being run, how to manage and improve day-to-day operations. It also ended up measuring impact poorly, in this case with a poorly designed and managed evaluation.

Are these organizations unique? Not at all. Countless organizations around the world face similar problems every day. ("Organizations" is the term we use in this book to refer to nonprofits, government, and social enterprises; see the glossary for our definition of a social enterprise.) Motivated to prove that their programs work, many organizations have developed systems that are too big, leaving staff with more data than they can manage. And the data that are available often fail to provide the information needed to support operational decisions, program learning, and improvement. For other organizations, data collection efforts are too small, providing little to no information about program performance, let alone their impact on people's lives.

The struggle to find the right fit in monitoring and evaluation systems resembles the predicament Goldilocks faces in the fable "Goldilocks and the Three Bears." In the fable, a young girl named Goldilocks finds herself lost in the forest and takes refuge in an empty house. Inside, Goldilocks finds an array of options: comfy chairs, bowls of porridge, and beds of all sizes. She tries each, but finds that most do not suit her: the porridge is too hot or too cold, the bed too hard or soft—she struggles to find options that are "just right." (See the box at the end of the chapter for a longer version of the fable.) Like Goldilocks, organizations must navigate many choices and challenges to build monitoring and evaluation systems. How can organizations develop systems that work "just right?"

Answering that question is the goal of this book. We tackle the challenge using a new framework of four basic principles: *credibility, actionability, responsibility*, and *transportability*. We call these the *CART principles*. And because evaluation and monitoring are concepts often taught in the abstract, this book will present case studies of actual organizations and their struggles to develop the right monitoring and evaluation systems. In the process, we hope you come to agree with us that high-quality monitoring is necessary for sound implementation, learning, and improvement. It should be a bedrock of every social sector organization. And we hope to convince you that while impact evaluation is important for accountability and learning, it is not the right fit for every organization or every stage of a program's life. It should be undertaken only when certain conditions are met. Sometimes less is better.

THE EVIDENCE CHALLENGE

Let's remember how we arrived at this dilemma. Unlike for-profit companies with no stated social impact goal, nonprofits and social enterprises claim to make a positive impact on the world. And they raise money, either from donors or investors, based on this premise.

Often, organizations trying to produce social impact have marketed their work to donors through stories about specific individuals who benefitted from their programs. Stories about how a program has changed the life of a specific individual can be persuasive.[1] We have all seen ads highlighting how an organization's program can help a particular child attend school or help a particular young mother pull herself and her family out of poverty.

Even though these stories may be compelling, they do not tell us the impact of the program on people's lives—whether the program is *actually* working, whether the program *caused* those changes to happen. One person's success story does not mean the program caused that success. And one person's success story does not mean that everyone in the program succeeded, or even that, on average, the program succeeded. How did we arrive in a situation where stories are often seen as a substitute for impact?

New Pressures, New Trends

A confluence of factors has contributed to this push for impact.

Data today are radically cheaper to collect, send, and analyze. Twenty years ago, organizations could only dream of collecting data at the scale they can now. In the past, it was simply too expensive to gather information on programs. The Information Age, and mobile technology in particular, has changed that. Cellphones, GPS devices, satellite imagery, wi-fi, and many more technological innovations have made it less expensive to gather and transmit data, while a myriad of software innovations has made information easier to analyze and use. Previously, organizations might have said, "we'd like to get data on results, but it is too time-consuming and expensive." Today, organizations can collect data on almost anything they can imagine and do so with relatively little expense. Naturally, cheaper data then also makes donors more willing to demand it: "no more money without evidence of impact."

Meanwhile, we have seen calls for more accountability in the public sector, particularly the development aid sector. Calls for concrete development aid targets and more proof of aid's general effectiveness have been steadily increasing. In 2000, the United Nations adopted the Millennium Declaration, establishing international development goals to reach by 2015.[2] In the mid-2000s, 91 countries and 26 major development organizations came together to improve the quality of aid and increase its impact with the Paris Declaration on Aid Effectiveness.[3] One of the declarations' five main principles, "Results," asked that "developing countries and donors shift focus to development results and [make sure] results get measured."[4] Other international conferences in the 2000s solidified this agenda, giving birth to a culture of measuring outcomes.

This push to ensure accountability by measuring results is not limited to the development sector; organizations in the US face similar pressures. In recent years, the US government has introduced a number of initiatives that promote the use of evidence in policy-making.[5] One such program is the Social Impact Fund (SIF), which directs federal grant money to evidence-based organizations and requires all grantees to conduct a rigorous impact evaluation to quantify the results they produce. The SIF also implements a "Pay for Success" program that uses results-based contracting. In this model, the government only pays for services when a program has produced the promised results.[6] Similar trends exist elsewhere. In the UK, for example, the government has initiated more than 30 social impact bonds, which are a way of committing public and private expenditures that rely on similar "pay for results" contracts.[7]

At the same time, philanthropic culture has changed. According to a 2013 report based on a national survey of 310 major donors aged 21 to 40, young and wealthy philanthropists are different from their parents and grandparents: they want to make sure their dollars are having a measurable impact. "They see previous generations as more motivated by a desire for recognition or social requirements, while they see themselves as focused on impact, first and foremost," the report summarizes. "They want impact they can see. . . . They want to use any necessary strategies, assets, and tools—new or old—for greater impact."[8]

Technological advancement and the push for results increase the supply of information available to both organizations and donors. Organizations now have data and information that can be used to make decisions large and small, from how to improve a program model to whom to promote within their organization. They also have access to data and tools that, if used correctly, can rigorously measure their programs' impact. And donors now have a growing body of evidence on the impact of many kinds of programs. These abundant data give them the ability to direct resources to programs that work and to avoid ones that do not, injecting a results orientation into philanthropic giving.

But the push to estimate impact is fraught with challenges. Many organizations fall into one of three traps in their monitoring and evaluation efforts:

- *Too few data*: Some organizations do not collect enough appropriate data, which means they cannot fulfill what should be their top priority: using data to learn, innovate, and improve. The solution is often collecting more data on what an organization is actually doing and on whether people are actually using its services.
- *Too much data*: Other organizations collect more data than they actually have the resources to analyze, wasting time and effort that could have been spent more productively elsewhere.
- *Wrong data*: Many organizations track changes in outcomes over time, but not in a way that allows them to know if the organization *caused* the changes or if they just happened to occur alongside the program.

This distinction matters greatly for deciding whether to continue the program, redesign it, or scrap it in favor of something more effective.

Ultimately, poorly done monitoring and evaluation drains resources without giving us the information we think we need—be it useful information for managing programs or the evidence of impact that donors (and organizations themselves) desire. Misdirected data collection carries a steep cost. By monitoring activities that do not help staff learn how to improve programs, or conducting poorly designed evaluations that do not accurately estimate the impact of a project, organizations take resources away from program implementation.

In short, the push for more data on impact has often led organizations to develop "wrong-fit" systems, depleting resources but failing to actually measure impact or provide useful data for decision-making. It is time for a change.

Just in case one doubted how big a fan we are of measuring impact: Karlan's first book, *More Than Good Intentions*,[9] is entirely about measuring the impact of efforts to alleviate poverty in low- and middle-income countries, and he founded a nonprofit organization, Innovations for Poverty Action (IPA), which has conducted more than 500 randomized controlled trials of poverty programs since its inception in 2002.

A key punchline of this book: there is a time and place to measure impact. But in many situations, the best questions to address may be "Did we do what we said we would do?" (accountability) and "How can data help us learn and improve?" (performance management) instead of "Did we change the world in the way we set out to?" (impact).

OUR APPROACH: THE CART PRINCIPLES

How can organizations find "right-fit" monitoring and evaluation systems that support learning and improvement? As with Goldilocks' search for the best "fitting" porridge, chair, and bed, the key is to find the *right* data. More is not always better. Nor is less. And simply "in between" is not always the answer either (that is where we deviate a bit from the Goldilocks fairytale). What is the right balance?

The number of different approaches to data collection and management are enough to make anyone's head spin. Organizations need a framework to help them wade through the decisions they encounter—whether they are setting up a whole monitoring and evaluation system from scratch;

reforming an old, tired, and poorly fit system; or simply designing a small survey.

After working with many organizations to design their monitoring and evaluation systems, we identified four key principles of a right-fit system. We call them the "CART" principles:

- **C**redible—Collect high-quality data and analyze them accurately.
- **A**ctionable—Collect data you can commit to use.
- **R**esponsible—Ensure the benefits of data collection outweigh the costs.
- **T**ransportable—Collect data that generate knowledge for other programs.

Sounds simple, right? And in some ways it is. But building right-fit systems sometimes means turning some current practices on their head and learning when to say "yes" and when to say "no" to data. This book aims to take you on that journey.

THE ROAD AHEAD

Part I of this book focuses on how organizations can build a strong base for their programs using the CART principles and a well-constructed theory of change.

Chapter 2 discusses the differences between program monitoring and impact evaluation; demonstrates why all organizations should monitor themselves, even if they do not evaluate their impact; and introduces the heart of this book, the CART principles.

Chapter 3 introduces a process called "theory of change" and explains why it is a critical underpinning for designing a monitoring system or impact evaluation. We then get a bit less abstract and walk through the process of creating a theory of change using a hypothetical supplemental feeding program for malnourished children.

Chapter 4 presents the CART principles in detail, providing a foundation for right-fit, action-oriented measurement and impact evaluation.

Chapters 5 through 7 dive into monitoring and impact evaluation in greater detail. Chapter 5 covers the role that monitoring plays in strengthening organizations and programs: the types of monitoring data all organizations should collect, how the CART principles can help organizations build right-fit monitoring systems, and the management issues related to designing and using data to improve operations.

Chapter 6 explores common biases that get in the way of measuring impact and explains what it means to conduct *credible, actionable, responsible,* and *transportable* impact evaluation. Chapter 7 then dives into the details of the data collection process, exploring some of the mechanics of gathering high-quality, credible data.

Part II of the book presents six real-world case studies from a range of social sector organizations—large and small, well-established and new—that provide concrete examples of the Goldilocks approach to right-sized monitoring and evaluation:

> *Educate!*—Educate!, an NGO based in Uganda, aims to teach entrepreneurial skills to young people. As its program rapidly grew, Educate! saw the need to demonstrate how its program connected to its intended outcomes. Yet staff did not agree either on the problem they were addressing or on the type of change they expected to see from the program. This case study illustrates how to find a common vision and guiding framework using a theory of change.
>
> *BRAC*—A global development organization with operations in 11 countries, BRAC has been operating in Uganda since 2006. To improve its operations on the ground, BRAC wanted to find out if a key component of its theory of change—an incentive structure for field staff—was working. This case study breaks down the steps it took to find out, focusing on the process of collecting credible, actionable data and actually turning that data into action.
>
> *Salama Shield Foundation*—The Salama Shield Foundation, an organization focused on community capacity-building in Africa, had a microcredit program that boasted 100% repayment rates. To the staff, this reflected the success of the program. But staff had two main questions they hoped to answer through data collection: first, were repayment rates really 100%? And second, if so, what motivated people to pay on time? This case study explores how Salama Shield went about answering those questions and provides a lesson on collecting actionable data.
>
> *Invisible Children*—Invisible Children, a Uganda-based NGO best known for its media and advocacy efforts (in particular, the Kony 2012 campaign), also implemented a set of traditional antipoverty programs. Invisible Children did not have a monitoring and evaluation system in place for these programs and wanted a way to prove to institutional donors that its programs were being implemented according to plan and making an impact. This case

study illustrates the drawbacks of having too little data and offers a warning about "impact evaluations" that do not actually measure impact at all.

Deworm the World—Deworm the World, which develops and implements national school-based deworming programs, helps administer a program in Kenya that reaches 5 million students per year. This case study sheds light on how to monitor a program of such massive size and scale.

Un Kilo de Ayuda—Un Kilo de Ayuda, a Mexican NGO that is working to end child malnutrition, collected data tracking the progress of all 50,000 children in its program. A massive task! Although the system provided actionable monitoring data that fed back into the program, it was costly and time-consuming to enter it all, raising the question: How much data is too much? This case study explores how Un Kilo de Ayuda answered that question and examines the challenges involved in designing a credible impact evaluation for the program.

Part III of the book then approaches these issues from the donor perspective. Chapter 14 focuses on large, institutional and government or government-funded donors, and Chapter 15 focuses on the perspective of individual donors, i.e. those without staff employed to set philanthropic strategies and metrics.

Chapter 16 presents online tools that complement this book and that we will continue to develop. These are publicly available at no cost on the IPA website at https://www.poverty-action.org/goldilocks/toolkit. We also provide additional resources to help design and implement CART-adherent monitoring and evaluation systems. And we discuss some related areas that we are eager to tackle but that are outside the scope of this first book on the subject. We are keen to hear from readers about ways we can expand these tools.

IS THIS BOOK FOR ME?

The Goldilocks Challenge aims to help people across the social sector use better information to make better decisions. As you read this book, we hope you agree that we manage to hit the "right-fit" balance between engaging and actionable (although to get there, we do have to present some critical theoretical concepts). While many of our examples come from the field of international development, our framework and lessons can be broadly applied to all mission-based organizations.

If you are a "doer" in a nonprofit or a social enterprise, we hope the framework and principles this book offers can help you build an evidence strategy from scratch, revamp an existing strategy, or better understand what others are doing.

If you are a "giver," we hope this book can guide you to support and advance the work of the organizations you fund. Funders often lead the push for more evidence without full awareness of what that pressure means for the organizations they support. *The Goldilocks Challenge* will help funders better understand what data collection is appropriate for the organizations they fund. By asking for useful and appropriate data, funders can steer organizations to collect information that furthers learning and advances their mission. This book will also help funders relieve pressure to collect data that does not advance organizations' learning needs.

We also address the particular data needs of funders themselves— needs that require their own lens. For example, what should funders do if they want to compare grants within their portfolio, but different grantees have different right-fit data needs? Should they demand second-best data from an organization, taxing the organization's resources, in order to be able to compare one to another? For funders that want to pay for performance, what metrics should they use and how should they validate them?

Ultimately, we seek to make data collection more useful, approachable, and feasible. We cover both the science (theories and principles) and the art (applying those theories and principles) of monitoring and evaluation. We hope that, after reading this book, organizations can build stronger monitoring and evaluation systems and that donors can support organizations most committed to learning and improvement. While impact evaluations are wonderful, when feasible, there are many other types of evaluations that are important and often overlooked in the never-ending quest to measure impact. At minimum, we hope we can help organizations avoid wasteful data collection that uses money that could be more productively spent delivering services. More ambitiously, we aim to guide the reader through complementary data and analysis that can help improve operations, even if they do not provide answers regarding impact. Ultimately, by providing a framework for the messy field of monitoring and evaluation, we aim to help each organization find their ideal path.

Box 1.1 THE STORY OF GOLDILOCKS AND
THE THREE BEARS

Once upon a time there were three bears—a big father bear, a medium-sized mother bear, and a little baby bear. They lived in a charming cottage in the forest. One morning, mother bear made some porridge for breakfast, but it was too hot to eat. While it cooled, the three bears went for a walk in the woods.

Not far away lived a little girl named Goldilocks. That very same morning, she was wandering through the woods picking flowers. When she came upon the three bears' cottage, she knocked on the door and called "Anyone home?" Nobody answered, so she opened the door and went on in.

Goldilocks came to the table and saw the three chairs. She sat in the great big chair, but it was too hard. She tried the medium-sized chair, but it was too soft. Then she tried the little chair, which was just right, but it broke when she sat on it!

Then Goldilocks spied the porridge. "I sure am hungry," she said, and began tasting the porridge. The porridge in the big bowl was too hot. The porridge in the medium-sized bowl was too cold. The porridge in the little bowl was just right, so she ate it all up!

Then Goldilocks went upstairs and tried the beds. The big bed was too hard, and the medium-sized bed was too soft. But the little bed was just right, so Goldilocks lay down and fell fast asleep.

Just then, the bears came home from their walk, hungry and ready for their porridge. Father bear looked around and noticed that something was amiss. "Someone has been sitting in my chair!" said father bear. "Someone has been eating my porridge!" said mother bear. Little bear ran upstairs and cried, "someone has been lying in my bed, and she's still there!"

At that very moment Goldilocks awoke and saw the three bears peering at her. Terrified, she jumped out of bed, ran through the door, and escaped into the woods. She ran all the way home, and promised never to wander through the forest again.

CHAPTER 2

Introducing the CART Principles

The mounting pressure on nonprofit organizations to demonstrate their impact has led to a huge increase in data collection for many organizations. While this trend toward impact measurement is mostly positive, the push to demonstrate impact has also wasted resources, compromised monitoring efforts in favor of impact evaluation, and contributed to a rise in poor and even misleading methods of demonstrating impact. Other organizations never begin the journey to a right-fit system, finding the plethora of options overwhelming.

These missteps are rarely intentional. But building systems that support programmatic learning and also yield reliable information about impact is a huge challenge. Many organizations lack a set of guiding principles that can help them make hard decisions and assess tradeoffs.

The CART principles—Credible, Actionable, Responsible, and Transportable—attempt to provide just such guidance: how to collect useable data, use those data to make decisions, and make those data useful for learning and improvement. These principles also inform how to measure impact reliably and, crucially, on whether to focus resources on measuring impact at all. Overall, the CART principles enable organizations and staff at all levels to make informed decisions based on sound data.

Before we dive into the CART principles in detail, we need to describe some of the current chaos in the landscape of monitoring and evaluation in order to understand what has gone wrong. We begin with the theme that currently dominates the field of monitoring and evaluation: impact measurement.

IMPACT: AN OFTEN MISUNDERSTOOD CONCEPT

Many organizations collect data primarily to try to prove that their programs are making a difference—that they have impact. But what exactly is "impact?" The answer depends on whom you ask. Organizations and donors often use the word "impact" imprecisely. But loose definitions create a problem: without a clear conception of what impact is, organizations often end up collecting data that cannot demonstrate it. And since bad (and poorly analyzed) data lead to poor decisions, some organizations are spending a lot of time, energy, and money collecting "impact" information that is ultimately useless or even counterproductive.

There are three common mistakes organizations make in attempting to illustrate their impact:

1. Measuring impact by counting the number of goods distributed, services provided, or individuals served.
2. Assuming that individual anecdotes are representative of overall impact.
3. Believing that before-and-after comparisons demonstrate impact.

Let's begin with the first mistake.

Many organizations claim to demonstrate impact by citing impressively high numbers of how many goods and services they have provided or the number of people who received those services. One organization claims on its "Our Impact" webpage that "9.4 million of the world's poor have been helped by our microfinance institution partners, enabling them to begin their journey out of poverty." Another boasts, "288,303 sanitation facilities have been built with (our) guidance."

Providing figures on the number of individuals a program reaches or the number of structures it builds is certainly an important step on the path to measuring impact. However, delivering programs is not the same as improving people's lives. These figures should be listed under a label like "Our Reach" or "Our Scale" (yes, less exciting, but more accurate). The 9.4 million borrowers figure says little about whether microfinance actually improved the lives of people who received loans—if, for example, they actually became less poor as a result of the loan. In fact, we now have strong evidence that, on average, microcredit clients do not have increased household incomes or consumption. Research from seven randomized impact evaluations shows that microloans that target microentrepreneurs have some benefits but do not on average improve income and consumption, the typical measures of poverty. From four continents, the seven studies, several of which were conducted by researchers at Innovations for Poverty Action (IPA) and the M.I.T. Abdul Latif Jameel Poverty Action Lab (J-PAL), did find that microloans can increase small business ownership and investment. But the hoped for near term results of average increases in income and consumption did not materialize, never mind longer term investments in children's schooling or substantial gains in women's empowerment.[1]

Similarly, learning how many sanitation facilities an organization constructed or how many people accessed clean water from this program does not tell us if people's lives or health improved as a result. What if no one used the handwashing facilities? What if they kept using their old water sources instead? What if everyone used these resources, but they were not well maintained and still harbored disease? In all these cases, people may still get sick as often as before, meaning the organization's impact could be limited. Or its impact could be huge. We simply cannot tell merely from knowing how many are reached.

Another way organizations often illustrate impact is by telling an inspirational story from a single beneficiary of a program. For example, suppose an organization trains women to repair bicycles. One may be likely to find the following on their "Our Impact" page:

> Before she attended training, Sophia never left her home. Now she goes out to work every day, and in nearby villages people recognize her and ask for her help. She earns a steady income, and her work as a bicycle mechanic has helped to improve the standing of women in her community, too. "At first I doubted she could do it" said a male neighbor, "but she does the job as well as any man I've seen."

This anecdote implies that this woman's experience represents the experience of all program participants, but how can we be sure? Should we assume that the program produced a general improvement in income and empowerment for all the women trained in the program? We have no way of knowing that, nor can we be sure the program was actually responsible for the change in this particular woman's life. Like counting beneficiaries served, individual stories are also flawed portrayals of impact. They may appeal to people emotionally. But when a page titled "Our Impact" cites such stories as its main (or only) evidence, we have a problem.

The third mistake many organizations make is to try to demonstrate impact by collecting information about beneficiaries' lives before and after the implementation of a program. They then attribute any changes in participants' lives over that time period to the program. For example, take a look at the chart in Figure 2.1. It intends to illustrate how one organization's

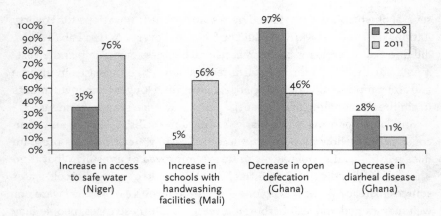

Figure 2.1 Impact of WASH interventions in program countries.

water, sanitation, and hygiene (WASH) programs are increasing access to clean water and hygiene facilities and decreasing water-borne diseases in targeted areas.

At first glance, this approach seems more promising than the others. After all, the figures in the chart reflect data collected on what happened to beneficiaries over the course of the program, not just how many people the program reached. But simply measuring changes in the lives of program beneficiaries brings its own problems. Why? Because this organization's WASH programs are only one possible explanation for the diarrheal disease decreases seen in Ghana, improved access to clean water in Niger, and improved handwashing access in schools in Mali. If that sounds overly skeptical, consider some of the trends and activities that occurred in these three countries during the same time period.

In Mali, in 2009, the Ministry of Health and UNICEF conducted nationwide public awareness campaigns on handwashing.[2] During a publicized event on handwashing held in Bamako, the president of Mali even washed his hands in front of a crowd of thousands of spectators, with 10,000 children following suit. In Niger, major development organizations such as SNV Netherlands conducted WASH programs on a massive scale at this same time the organization we are discussing was conducting its own campaigns. Meanwhile, during this same time period, Ghana experienced record economic growth—some of the fastest in the world—and a significant reduction in poverty,[3] which could have led to better food, nutrition, and infrastructure that in turn improved public health.

We cannot know which of these events, if any, was responsible for the changes shown in Figure 2.1, and that is the key point. In order to actually measure if any particular WASH initiative worked, comparing participants before and after the intervention is not enough. We need to compare the beneficiaries of that WASH intervention to another similar group *not* receiving the intervention at the same time.

And that brings us to the real definition of impact.

Impact is more than a buzzword. Impact implies causality; it tells us how an organization has changed the world around it. Inevitably—and here is the important part—that means knowing what would have occurred in the absence of the program (see Box 2.1).

When it comes to measuring impact, it is absolutely necessary to have some way of assessing what would have occurred if the program had not existed. We call this alternate reality the "counterfactual" (Box 2.2).

In other words, to measure impact, it is necessary to find a way to credibly estimate the counterfactual. Does that sound impossible? It is not.

First, let's go back to the before-and-after WASH chart in Figure 2.1. The chart appears to make a counterfactual argument, but we argue that it is doing so inappropriately. By claiming that these charts show impact, organizations effectively treat the "before" as the counterfactual and assume that nothing else could possibly have changed for these people. If it is inconceivable that anything else could have led to such a change in sanitation, then indeed the "before" data would be a valid counterfactual. Unfortunately, in the real world, that assumption almost always fails.

What could be done instead? How can organizations measure impact credibly? To begin to answer that question, consider Figure 2.1

Box 2.1

Impact: The change in outcomes for those affected by a program compared to the alternative outcomes had the program not existed.[5]

Box 2.2

Counterfactual: How individuals or communities would have fared had a program or policy not occurred (or occurred differently).

again. Imagine that the organization wanted to learn if building toilets reduced diarrheal disease. It could take an area where the program was still expanding and randomly assign a sufficiently large number of villages to either receive toilets or not. Then, over time, it could compare changes in diarrheal disease in "toilet" and "non-toilet" villages. Since the decision about which villages would receive toilets was made randomly, the main difference between the villages would just be the toilet project. As a result, the organization could then directly attribute changes to their program. Although this example is extremely simplified (and glosses over key details required for the evaluation to work), it demonstrates how to create a counterfactual to credibly estimate impact. Using randomization to create a counterfactual is often referred to as a randomized control trial (RCT), one method of conducting an impact evaluation.

Designing and conducting an evaluation that measures not only what occurred but also what *would have occurred* without the program may sound like an arduous task. This raises two questions: Is a counterfactual really necessary to measure impact, and is it possible to carry out a worthwhile impact evaluation that does not adhere to the same standards of rigor advised here? The answers are "yes" and "often not", respectively. In Chapter 5, we go through some nonexperimental methods that can generate credible estimates of impact under certain conditions, but, as we explain, these methods are riskier than RCTs, typically require more technical expertise and more difficult or impossible to test assumptions.

Why does this matter? One reason is that poor estimates of impact can cause large-scale resource misallocation, underfunding or eliminating effective programs or expanding or continuing ineffective ones. Take the recent findings about the limited impact of microcredit we mentioned earlier. Before these credible estimates of impact were produced, millions, if not billions, of donor dollars flowed to microcredit programs; these donor dollars might have been better used elsewhere.

Our conclusion may seem unconventional (or even provocative): We believe that many organizations are collecting too much data and conducting too many (bad) analyses of impact. Many organizations would be better off simply collecting data on their activities, learning from the data, and then using the money saved to deliver more of their (improved) program.

In Chapter 6, we will explore this topic in more depth, examining the common biases that get in the way of accurately measuring impact,

Finding the right fit in impact measurement sometimes means stepping back from a full-scale impact evaluation. Consider the case of UKA, an organization that tackles the challenge of improving childhood nutrition in rural areas of Mexico. The organization has a well-developed monitoring system that program staff use to guide their activities and track progress toward nutritional goals. But UKA has struggled to find ways to credibly test its impact. The organization originally used such data to demonstrate impact, but evaluation staff noted the shortcomings of their approach to measure impact credibly. So UKA partnered with IPA to examine how it could demonstrate impact.

Unfortunately, because of the size and complexity of UKA programming, UKA and IPA were unable to design an impact evaluation that could credibly assess the program's impact or determine which components were most effective. Rather than move forward with a faulty impact evaluation, UKA looked into other options. UKA was piloting a handwashing intervention to add onto its existing nutrition program. Working closely with researchers, the organization designed an operational evaluation that would test the effectiveness of different components of the intervention and determine which, if any, were most effective at encouraging families to adopt good handwashing practices. This partial impact evaluation focused on how the organization could do a better job (rather than measure their overall impact), but it still yielded concrete information about program effectiveness that UKA was able to apply across the organization.

providing details on how to conduct an impact evaluation with a counterfactual, and exploring what it means to conduct a *credible, actionable, responsible,* and *transportable* evaluation. In the meantime, you may be asking yourself: If I should not do an impact evaluation, what should I do? The answer is straightforward: monitor, learn, and improve! See Box 2.3 for an example from our cases.

THE CRITICAL (AND NEGLECTED) ROLE OF MONITORING

Regardless of whether or not organizations are going to conduct a rigorous impact evaluation, they should first strive to do good monitoring.

High-quality, actionable data about program implementation, which we call "activity monitoring," is a critical and often overlooked component of monitoring and evaluation systems. At its root, monitoring is simply good management. Organizations should gather data to understand how a program is being implemented and that can inform decisions about what changes, if any, to make in design or implementation. Monitoring data can further internal learning, demonstrate transparency and accountability, and complement impact evaluations. Yet many organizations underinvest in this capacity (Box 2.4).

Why collect monitoring data? There are two broad reasons: external accountability and internal management. Monitoring data facilitate accountability by allowing organizations to report back to their stakeholders that they did what they said they would do. Monitoring data improve management by providing staff of organizations the information necessary to quickly and effectively strengthen programs.

Program monitoring receives both too much and too little attention. It receives too much attention when monitoring data are collected to make claims of impact. Such cases are a waste of resources—superfluous data that do not provide a good counterfactual-based argument for impact. And monitoring receives too little attention when data aren't collected that could provide important insight into how to manage and improve

---

Box 2.4 FROM THE CASES: BRAC AND MONITORING FOR PERFORMANCE

BRAC is a large nonprofit that operates in 11 countries and serves nearly 110 million people around the world. In Uganda, BRAC deployed its monitoring team to find out whether its Livestock and Poultry Program "microfranchises"—where community members become entrepreneurial extension agents (individuals responsible for sharing information and training others in entrepreneurship)—were reporting their activities accurately and whether BRAC's theory of change accurately represented their activities. This is useful for two reasons. First, for quality control and program improvement by management: collecting data on activities means managers can hone in on problem areas where microfranchises are not performing as expected. Second, for validation of program design: if the program is not working as intended, there is no reason to expect intended impacts to occur. Monitoring data revealed that the microfranchises were not as active as BRAC expected, enabling program management to propose changes in vaccination incentives to help improve microfranchise performance.

program implementation. Even when collected, monitoring data receive too little attention if they are ignored and are disconnected from organizational decision-making. In both cases, resources are wasted.

Good monitoring is also foundational for conducting rigorous impact evaluations, as the following example illustrates.

Consider the case of an Indian organization that provided clean cookstoves to households to help reduce fuelwood use and improve indoor air quality. Eager to know whether the program was making an impact, the organization worked with researchers to conduct an impact evaluation. A three-year evaluation yielded disappointing results. The researchers found that, in practice, providing stoves to households did not actually reduce household fuelwood use, mitigate indoor air pollution, or improve health.[4] They discovered that most households hardly used the new stoves, and those that did often continued to cook over open fires as well, so they did not reap the full benefits of the cleaner stoves.

While this evaluation offers many lessons, the point we want to highlight is the power and importance of monitoring data. Without usage data, we would not know whether the technology was flawed (perhaps the cookstoves do not actually reduce pollution or fuelwood use) or simply not being used. Such distinctions make a huge difference when thinking through what to do differently.

"I get that monitoring is important," you might be saying, "but what should I monitor? And what exactly is the difference between monitoring and evaluation?" We go into these questions in detail in Chapter 5, but the basic answer is that monitoring tracks whether a program is being implemented as intended and whether participants are using the program as anticipated, whereas impact evaluation identifies what change resulted from the program.

Monitoring tracks implementation. Is the program delivering goods or services as intended, to the intended people? Are individuals using the program as expected? If so, how? And if not, why not? Do budgets accurately reflect actual program costs? What do program beneficiaries think about the program, and what feedback do they have? With the exception of use and feedback data, these variables are all under direct control of the program. Impact evaluations, on the other hand, require the evaluation to make a comparison between post-program outcomes and the alternative outcomes had the program not existed. And impact evaluations often require waiting a long time, if achieving the desired impact is a long-term story. Analysis using monitoring data, on the other hand, can be done during implementation and the results put to use immediately to improve programs.

Yet, in spite of their usefulness, many organizations neglect to collect informative monitoring data. Some organizations collect mountains of data, but do not use them. Others collect too little data and cannot report on basic program implementation. The upshot: too few organizations know whether they are doing what they promised. Many also cannot clearly connect the delivery of goods and services to their intended results.

By inadequately monitoring program implementation, programs risk missing opportunities for internal and external learning. Internally, monitoring data can answer questions about program progress. Does the program allocate resources and implement activities as promised? What is the quality of their execution? For example, if it is a training program, how effective are the trainers? Do they engage with participants in a fruitful manner, to help participants learn the material well? Finding a way to answer these questions at a reasonable cost is critical to optimizing program delivery. With such a system in place, organizations can satisfy external demands for transparency and accountability. And when organizations share their program design and measurement results with others, they create opportunities for other organizations to learn and improve as well.

Monitoring data are also crucial to guide and inform impact evaluations. Monitoring data ought to be collected *before* an organization begins thinking about conducting an impact evaluation. Before incurring the expense of an impact evaluation, how about first making sure the program is doing the activities it set out to do? Monitoring data also ought to be collected *during* an impact evaluation: if the impact evaluation reveals no impact, we will want to know whether the program implementation was off or if the program idea itself was off. Monitoring data help an impact evaluation answer the "why" question: Why did the program generate impact (or not)?

We hope we have begun to make the case that monitoring, when done well, provides important insight to organizations and donors into how to manage and improve programs—information worth far more than the results of a poorly run impact evaluation.

At this point, you might be thinking, "Great, I get it now. But if I have been collecting data the wrong way, how can I shift to a right-fit system? How do I know what 'right' looks like?" Glad you asked. There are two main components to a right-fit system.

The first is a solid model of how a program works. Remember the Ugandan education nonprofit we described in Chapter 1? The organization had never developed a clear model for the problem they were trying to solve and how their program could make a dent in that problem. As a result, they had no framework for deciding what data they needed or how to evaluate their programs. Developing such a model—a theory of change—is the subject of the next chapter.

The second component of a right-fit system is adherence to the CART principles: *credible, actionable, responsible,* and *transportable* data. Consider the Ugandan food security organization we met in Chapter 1. It had collected so much data that staff could not begin to use them. The CART principles can help organizations like this one evaluate tradeoffs and decide which data are worth collecting. The four CART principles are designed to help any organization make better decisions about what data to collect, when to collect them, and how to use them. We discuss the principles briefly here and return to explore them in more detail in Chapter 4.

THE CART PRINCIPLES

Most organizations want to demonstrate accountability to donors and provide decision-makers with timely and actionable data. But without a framework for approaching this challenge, it is hard to know where to start or what data are most critical. Therefore, we developed a set of principles that all organizations can use to build strong data collection systems. We call these principles CART: *credible, actionable, responsible*, and *transportable* data collection. They are essential for both activity monitoring and impact evaluation. Let's look at each of the principles in turn.

CREDIBLE

Collect high-quality data and analyze them accurately.

The *credible* principle has three parts: data must be valid measures, data collection must be reliable, and analysis must be conducted appropriately.

Valid data accurately capture the core concept one is seeking to measure. While this may sound obvious, it turns out that collecting valid data can be tricky. Seemingly straightforward concepts like "schooling" or "medical care" may be measured in quite different ways in different settings. Developing a good measure of a concept can be challenging, especially when working across cultures or contexts.

Next, data should be reliable. Reliability means consistency; the data collection procedure should be consistent. An unreliable scale produces a different weight every time one steps on it; a reliable one does not. An unreliable surveyor training leads to each interviewer asking a particular question differently; a reliable surveyor training minimizes such variation.

The final component of the *credible* principle is appropriate analysis. Credible data analysis requires understanding when to measure impact—and, just as importantly, when *not* to measure it. We argued earlier that using even high-quality data to measure impact without a counterfactual can produce incorrect estimates of impact. So, in our earlier WASH example, comparison of before and after rates of handwashing was not credible impact analysis.

ACTIONABLE

Collect data you can commit to use.

Under what conditions would this sign change behavior?

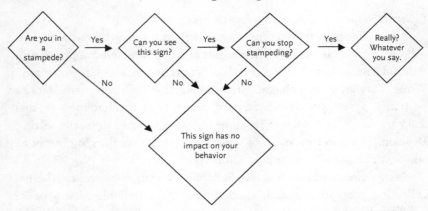

Credit: Dean Karlan, Xi'an China, at the exit from the Terracotta Soldiers

Today, organizations have access to more data than ever before. Electronic data collection, efficient storage systems, and other new technologies allow them to collect increasing amounts of data at low cost. In addition, the pressure to appear "data-driven" often leads donors and program staff to collect data about a wide range of issues with the hope that it will somehow be useful. In theory, more information should help organizations make better-informed decisions. But, in reality, gathering more data often has the opposite effect. By collecting more data than they can possibly use, or at the wrong time, organizations struggle to figure out which information will help them decide on a course of action (see Box 2.5).

A critical question to ask oneself: is there a world in which the data will change behavior? If the answer is no, then the data should not be collected. Data become like the "Do not stampede" sign and accompany decision tree: all endpoints are the same, and no outcome changes because of the data (or sign).

The *actionable* principle aims to solve this problem by calling on organizations to only collect data they will use. Organizations should ask three questions of each and every piece of data that they want to collect. The first question: "Is there a specific action that we will take based on the

---

Box 2.5 "WE'VE BEEN JAMMED"

A famous experiment conducted by Sheena S. Iyengar and Mark R. Lepper explores whether more choice is better and illustrates another benefit of right-fit data.[6] The researchers set up a display of jams in a grocery store and offered shoppers a coupon that would give them a discount on a jam purchase. Every hour, they varied the jam display to offer a selection of either 6 flavors or 24 flavors.

Although about 40% more people *visited* the stand when it had 24 flavors, only 6 people who visited the stand purchased jam. When presented with only 6 jams, however, 35 people purchased jam. In short, while choice is attractive, it can make decisions more difficult.

What does this have to do with monitoring and evaluation? Well, data are like jams—too much is overwhelming and can impede decision-making. So, when thinking about how to find the right fit in data collection, remember that more is not always better.

findings?" Second: "Do we have the resources necessary to implement that action?" And third: "Do we have the commitment required to take that action?"

RESPONSIBLE

Ensure that the benefits of data collection outweigh the costs.

Most organizations do not have a blank check to implement their ideal system of data collection and many face strong pressures to keep monitoring and evaluation costs low. Donors and charity watchdogs scrutinize organizations, searching for those with the largest impact and lowest overhead. Since monitoring costs are typically counted as overhead, many monitoring and evaluation departments feel pressure to collect data at the lowest possible cost. The unfortunate result of this pressure is that data collection costs come to be viewed as administrative excess rather than an integral part of program operations. While it is a mistake to view data collection as inessential to programming, data collection also has real costs in terms of staff time, resources, and time it asks of respondents.

The *responsible* principle requires that organizations weigh the costs and benefits of data collection activities to find the right fit for themselves. Cost encompasses several components. First, employing a term from economics, costs include the *opportunity cost* of collecting data. That is, any money and time that organizations spend collecting data could instead be used elsewhere in the organization. One thousand dollars spent on monitoring could instead have been $1,000 of program implementation, staff training, or office equipment. The foregone "opportunity" is a real cost, and taking it into consideration is a key part of responsibility. Of course, costs also include the direct costs of data collection, including money, staff time, and other resources. Finally, an often overlooked aspect of costs is the costs to those providing data to organizations, for example participants in a program spending time with surveyors or providing private information about their finances. Responsible data collection also requires minimizing risks to constituents through transparent processes, protection of individuals' sensitive information, and proper protocols for research with human subjects.

While collecting data has real costs, we pay a large social cost by collecting too little data. Think about it: Is it responsible to implement a program and not collect data about how it went? As we explored earlier, a lack of data about program implementation could hide flaws that are weakening a program. And without the ability to identify a problem in the first place, it cannot be fixed. Too little data can also lead to inefficient programs persisting and thus wasted money. And too little data also means that donors do not know whether their money is being used effectively. That money could be spent on programs with a greater commitment to learning and improvement or on those with demonstrated impact.

There is no one-size-fits-all approach to getting this tradeoff right. What is key is that organizations start assessing the tradeoff.

TRANSPORTABLE

Collect data that generate knowledge for other programs.

The essence of the *transportable* principle is that the valuable lessons generated from monitoring and evaluation help others build more effective programs. To be transportable, monitoring and evaluation data should be placed in a generalizable context or theory. Such theories need not always be complex, but they should be detailed enough to guide data collection and identify the conditions under which the results are likely to hold.

Transportability also requires transparency—organizations must be willing to share their findings. Monitoring and evaluation based on a clear theory and made available to others support another key element of transportability: replication. Clear theory and monitoring data provide critical information about what should be replicated. Undertaking a program in another context provides powerful policy information about when and where a given intervention will work.

By applying the CART principles to monitoring and impact evaluation, organizations will be able to build "right-fit" data collection systems. These systems will deliver relevant, high-quality information to help build strong and resilient programs.

In the next chapter, we outline the basic process of laying out a program design through a tool called "theory of change," which helps organizations articulate the key elements of their programs and how they lead to the desired impact. We will show how a clear theory of change anchors the collection of actionable data that supports both learning and accountability. A clear theory of change guides organizations to responsible decisions on what data to collect. *Box 2.3*

Impact evaluation: An analysis that estimates the impact of a program using a method that builds a credible counterfactual.

CHAPTER 3

The Theory of Change

Before beginning to monitor or evaluate impact, organizations must first make sure their programs are sitting on solid ground. A *theory of change* explains the "why" of a program by telling a sequential story: what goes in, what gets done, what comes out, and how the world thus (hopefully) changes for the better. Clearly articulating this theory helps organizations design sound programs and lays the foundation for right-fit data collection.

A strong theory lays the groundwork for the CART principles (*credible, actionable, responsible, transportable* data). As a simple example, we use a hypothetical nutrition program to walk through the process of developing a theory of change.

Our goal in this chapter is not to provide a complete manual on building a theory of change—many resources exist for that—but rather to illustrate how a clear theory, together with the CART principles, provides the foundation for a strong, right-fit system of data collection.

WHAT IS IN A THEORY OF CHANGE?

A theory of change is a map of a program or intervention and the changes it seeks to create. It connects the inputs and activities of the program with its intended outputs and shows how those outputs should change outcomes and thus produce the intended impacts. A theory of change represents the vision of how a program will create social change. Mapping the connections between program elements visually can make the logical connections—or "theory"—apparent (although using mere words can work, too). This conceptual map helps organizations determine if their program addresses problems in a logical and appropriate way, what assumptions the program is making, and what results it hopes to achieve (see Figure 3.2 for an example). Developing a theory of change also provides a way for organizations to create internal agreement on what they are doing and why (see Box 3.1).

A theory of change underpins right-fit data collection by identifying a program's measurable operating steps and thereby defining what organizations should monitor and measure. A theory of change also helps identify the components of the program that a monitoring system should track (outputs) versus those that should only be measured and analyzed with a counterfactual (outcomes). Without a counterfactual, organizations are often better off not measuring outcomes at all (and instead focusing on outputs).

Organizations typically develop a theory of change in one of two ways. For new programs, an organization begins by identifying the problem it wants to solve or the need it intends to address. Once the problem is well-defined, the organization works backward (often called *backward mapping*) to lay out the actions needed to produce those results. At this point, the organization defines the specific activities it will undertake, the goods and services it will deliver as a result, and the intended social changes it will create. At every step of the way, the assumptions underlying each step are clearly laid out and examined. This is the "theory" part of the theory of change—an organization's set of hypotheses about how specific actions will result in particular changes in the world.

For organizations that already have a program in place, developing a theory of change is more like self-reflection. Reflecting and clarifying their theory of change can help organizations evaluate their assumptions and ask whether sufficient evidence exists to support their current strategy. Such moments can be reassuring, but they can also help to identify crucial gaps in current operations. Either way, the process of developing a theory of change will help strengthen programs.

No matter when an organization starts developing a theory of change, the theory needs to articulate the assumptions that must hold for the program to work. These include the assumptions about the need for the program, assumptions about how the program will work, and assumptions about whether program activities are likely to produce the intended results. In addition, the organization needs to identify conditions in the larger world that—if altered—would change the program's chances for success. These risks could include things like government policy, weather, and food prices.

In an ideal world, organizations would start the theory of change by identifying the challenge they seek to address. Then they would map backward to identify strategies to address that challenge, consult research about the effectiveness of those strategies, and then build out a theory of change before implementing their program. However, in the real world, programs are often developed under tight deadlines or with constraints on their structure. Sometimes donors require organizations to include certain activities in a project. Under such constraints, organizations cannot begin with a problem and map back to activities. We know this is a reality. Thus, while developing a theory of change earlier in a program's life is better, a theory is always useful. A theory of change provides the template for testing assumptions, evaluating data, and improving program performance.

NUTRITION FOR ALL'S THEORY OF CHANGE

To show how a theory of change forms the backbone of right-fit data collection, we will use the case of Nutrition for All (NFA), a hypothetical development organization. NFA provides food supplement packages to families with children identified as "moderately malnourished" by a government community health worker (CHW). CHWs use a weight-for-age scale to assess the nutritional status of the children, which allows them to identify varying levels of malnutrition. Once CHWs identify moderately malnourished children, an NFA field worker visits the family, explains the program, and encourages them to join. Participating families receive a monthly supplement package of fortified blended foods and micronutrient powder. Families also receive instruction on using the supplements in a follow-up visit from the NFA field worker. Field workers then conduct monthly field visits for a year in which they track the nutritional status of children, survey families on their use of the supplements, and provide additional training on childhood nutrition.

NFA's program is relatively simple, but developing a concrete theory of change can still help the organization think systematically about right-fit data collection.

STEP 1. DEFINE THE PROBLEM AND INTENDED RESULTS

The first step in developing a theory of change is to clearly define the problem the organization aims to address and the results it hopes to achieve. This sounds obvious, but often organizations move directly into implementation without full consideration of the problem they seek to address. By specifically articulating its target problem and intended results, an organization can build on available evidence, explore the program's underlying assumptions, and create a program that is more likely to succeed.

Organizations can conduct on-the-ground research in order to define a problem and identify a solution. They may also examine the work other organizations have done in the same field or location. What elements of program design are most promising? What high quality evidence exists on the issue? What role does context play in program effectiveness? In the case of NFA, the extensive literature on treating malnutrition could provide valuable information on program design. For a young organization, examining the context of the problem, consulting with those who have implemented similar programs, and reviewing the literature can help test how sound a program's logic really is.

NFA was created by two doctors to address the problem of childhood malnutrition. The doctors worked in a regional hospital that saw the worst cases of malnutrition from around the region. They were troubled by the number of severely undernourished children they saw. Malnutrition can lead to child mortality, but even if it does not actually kill the child, it harms long-term cognitive and health development. These developmental challenges can lower educational achievement and can reduce adult earnings and quality of life.

The underlying problem was simple, they thought: parents were not giving their children a sufficient amount of high-quality calories. At its root, they believed, was a combination of poverty—simply not enough money available to provide enough calories—and a lack of knowledge about the nutrients children need to thrive.

The doctors founded NFA to address the causes of childhood malnutrition at home, intending to fix the problem before children needed specialized medical care. They conducted an evidence review to identify proven strategies for reducing malnutrition, determining that nutritional supplementation was the most effective intervention and that CHWs offered the most effective way to deliver it. Armed with this theory and evidence to support it, they launched the project in 10 villages with high rates of childhood malnutrition in partnership with the regional health authority.

STEP 2. DEFINE PROGRAM ACTIVITIES

After identifying what problem to address and what change is needed, the second step in crafting a theory of change is to define program activities—how the program intends to create change. You will notice that many logical frameworks start with inputs—the raw materials that are needed to run the program—first or along with activities. Inputs are undoubtedly important, but implicitly part of what we mean by "activities." Like many service-delivery programs, NFA's activities are a series of sequential steps, all of which must be successfully carried out in order to produce the intended results (see Box 3.2).

NFA delivers food supplements and trainings to families with malnourished children. The program's key activities include training government CHWs, deploying CHWs to conduct regular household visits, and identifying which children need supplements. Once those children are identified, NFA receives a list of the children from CHWs. It then deploys its own field workers to recruit families into the program and train them how to use the nutritional supplements. Field workers deliver nutritional supplements to families on a monthly basis, and, on each visit, they track children's nutritional status and gather data on family use of the supplements.

STEP 3. IDENTIFY THE PROGRAM OUTPUTS

Each program activity will have at least one output associated with it. Outputs are the products or services produced by program activities;

Box 3.2

Activities: The essential program elements involved in providing a product or service.

> *Outputs*: The products or services generated by program activities; deliverables.

identifying and measuring them is a key function of an organization's data system. Outputs are the direct deliverables of a program. Typically, activities undertaken and outputs produced are immediately controlled by the organization and reflect the amount and quality of program implementation (see Box 3.3).

Although outputs are vitally important to the theory of change, many organizations and donors fail to give them the respect they deserve. Part of the oversight stems from the fact that outputs often sound like a rephrasing of activities: conducting training is an activity, the number of trainings conducted is the output. As a result, organizations face pressure to skip the measurement of outputs and instead measure outcomes. But consider NFA's case. One of the key outputs of NFA's program is that families possess food supplements, a direct result of program activities. So collecting data on whether and when families received the supplements is important operational information. What if the organization discovered a gap in the delivery of the supplements? NFA could use that information to improve the program. Clearly defining activities and outputs is an essential element of actionable data collection as it gives managers clear guidance on which program components are working well and which could be improved. Carol Weiss, a renowned expert on evaluation, organizational decision-making, and research methods, called this the difference between implementation failure and idea failure. In monitoring, organizations are testing for implementation failure, whereas an impact evaluation tests an idea (so a failure to see results indicates an idea failure).[1] If families are not receiving the supplements (or, for example, selling them for needed cash when they receive them), there is no point in looking for changes in nutritional status.

The key activities of NFA's program and the associated outputs appear in Figure 3.1.

Throughout this book, we argue that data on outputs provide critical program information that goes beyond simple accounting. We focus on this argument in Chapter 5. The pressure to measure "impact" and "results" often leads organizations to undervalue the role of tracking basic activities and outputs. Yet collecting data about these elements of the theory of change

ACTIVITIES		OUTPUTS
CHWs trained to identify malnourishment using weight-for-age assessment	à	Trainings conducted CHWs trained
CHWs conduct household visits	à	Households visited
CHWs assess children for malnourishment	à	Malnourished children identified
Field workers recruit families with malnourished children to join the program	à	Families recruited Families enroll in program
Field workers train families in use of nutrition supplements	à	Trainings conducted Families attend trainings Families know how to use supplements
Nutrition supplements provided to families	à	Families receive supplements Families serve malnourished children supplements
Field workers conduct follow up visits	à	Families receive additional advice on childhood nutrition

Figure 3.1 Nutrition for All's activities and outputs.

can highlight inconsistencies in implementation and lead to insights on how to improve a program. This actionable information is much more valuable than poor quality impact evaluations that lack credible analysis.

STEP 4. DEFINE THE PROGRAM OUTCOMES THAT DETERMINE IMPACT

Through its program outputs, an organization seeks to achieve its intended outcomes—the reasons it provides the program in the first place. Outcomes are a bit more complicated to identify and measure than outputs, in part because they bring us firmly to the "theory" part of the theory of change (see Box 3.4).

Outputs are under the control of an organization to some degree— they are certainly related to the effectiveness of program implementation. But program outputs intend to set in motion a series of changes that rely partly on the quality of program implementation and partly on whether the underlying assumptions of the program hold; outcomes also depend on whether there are unanticipated changes in the program environment.

An important part of any theory of change is to map out this series of hypothesized outcomes—including those outcomes the program intends to create as well as possible unintended consequences. This process is sometimes referred to as "outcome mapping" or "pathway mapping." We return to this concept later in the chapter.

A clear distinction between outputs and outcomes is essential for credible data collection, even if the line between the two can be blurry. (Remember, outputs are the main program deliverables, while outcomes are the results of those outputs.) An organization has control over its outputs, but, ultimately, the outcomes are out of its control. Perhaps the crispest question to ask is whether one needs a counterfactual in order to sensibly use the data. An output should not need a counterfactual, whereas an outcome likely does.

Think back to the example presented in the preceding chapter of the Indian organization that distributed clean cookstoves. It had direct influence over its outputs—the number of cookstoves delivered to households. But the outcomes—the extent of change in health and fuel use in targeted households—were beyond its control. Measuring outcomes like fuel use and health status requires a credible assessment of these outcomes through a counterfactual because many factors aside from program implementation affect those results.

Distinguishing outputs from outcomes is not always easy. Some outputs are partially outside the control of a program. In the cookstove example , once households receive the cookstoves, they need to use them for cooking in order to experience health benefits. Cookstove usage is outside the direct control of the program but still needs to be measured in program monitoring. If cookstoves are not being used, then the program should not expect to see reduced fuel use and improvements in health.

In Figure 3.1, some of NFA's outputs are a bit outside the program's control. Families can be recruited for the program, but may decide not to join. Trainings may be conducted, but families may not understand the information on how to use the supplements. Nonetheless, collecting information on these components of the program will be critical to understanding whether the program is working as intended. Similarly, NFA needs to know whether families are serving the supplements to malnourished children even though this is also not fully under their control. The key is to use these data for program improvement, not as a measure of impact, as we take up in the next chapter.

Let's consider the relationship between outputs and outcomes in NFA's theory of change. NFA seeks to create three key outcomes for program participants, all of which rest on successful implementation of program activities and delivery of outputs. Figure 3.2 shows the intended outcomes of the program.

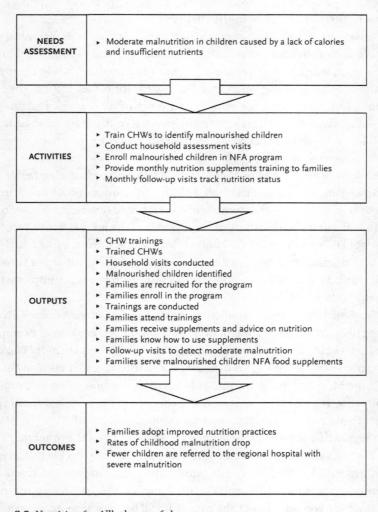

Figure 3.2 Nutrition for All's theory of change.

Once families enroll, receive supplements, and get nutrition advice, NFA expects that families will adopt better nutrition practices, such as buying and cooking vegetables, but the organization cannot directly control this outcome. Other factors like weather might affect the availability and price of vegetables and change consumption. And even if nutrition practices are adopted and supplements are given to children, economic shocks could lower household income and food consumption, meaning that rates of malnutrition do not drop.

Imagine for a moment that NFA measured malnutrition in participating children after delivering the program and found that malnutrition was 25% lower than before the program started. Would this be a success? Now imagine malnutrition was 25% higher. Would we call that a failure? Without knowing what the malnutrition rate would have been without the program, neither of those questions is credibly unanswerable.

The only way to understand what role NFA had in affecting these outcomes is through a counterfactual analysis. Some counterfactual analyses are quite strong; others are weaker. But to argue that a program *caused* an impact, implicitly one must be estimating the difference between the outcome observed and the outcome that would have been observed had the program not done what it did (i.e., the counterfactual). We will talk more about this in Chapter 6, when we dig in on impact evaluations.

If confused about whether to consider something an output or an outcome, ask the following question: does collecting the data without a counterfactual provide meaningful program information? In the NFA example, consider the output "families serve malnourished children NFA food supplements." While this output is somewhat outside NFA's control, it provides a meaningful measure of whether NFA's program implementation was successful. If NFA food supplements are not being used, there is no point looking at further outcomes. Instead, NFA is better off considering implementation improvements. If NFA wanted to collect data on "families serve malnourished children *any* food supplement", then a counterfactual is necessary to decide whether the proportion of families using supplements is an indication of success. A necessary but not sufficient metric for success is whether the children are eating the NFA supplements. While this does not prove impact, if children are *not* eating the supplements it tells the management that something is wrong with the operations. And that is useful.

STEP 5. IDENTIFY ASSUMPTIONS

Any good theory rests on assumptions, both implicit and explicit, that embody our ideas about how the world works. A theory of change is no different. In every link between activity, output, and outcome, many different assumptions are made that must hold for the program to work as expected. An important part of developing a theory of change is to identify these implicit and explicit assumptions and include them in the theory of change so that data can be collected to verify that the program's key assumptions hold (see Box 3.5).

Assumptions are the links between the elements in a program theory. They fall into two categories: assumptions about the connections between activities and outputs, and assumptions about the connections between outputs and intended impact.

The connections between activities and outputs assume that a program will be implemented as planned and that each activity will produce the desired output. These connections also assume that demand for the program exists. While such assumptions may seem straightforward, program implementation can suffer if they are wrong. Making these assumptions explicit and identifying the most critical among them helps to figure out what we need to test and monitor to ensure the program works as planned. Organizations can test their assumptions in many ways. For example, they can consult a topic's literature, hold focus groups with intended beneficiaries, or track usage data and investigate anomalies. Identifying and monitoring assumptions is key to ensuring a program is working as intended and allows organizations to change course if needed.

Figure 3.3 examines some of the assumptions NFA makes about a single activity: household visits to enroll malnourished children in NFA's supplemental feeding program.

As this example shows, NFA makes multiple assumptions about how a single activity will produce a single (particularly important) output! Only one of these—CHWs visiting all the households they are assigned to visit—is fully under control of the program. NFA can also try to address

---

Box 3.5

Assumptions: The conditions that have to hold for a certain part of a program or policy to work as expected.

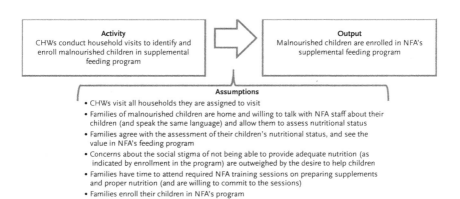

Activity
CHWs conduct household visits to identify and
enroll malnourished children in supplemental
feeding program

Output
Malnourished children are enrolled in NFA's
supplemental feeding program

Assumptions
- CHWs visit all households they are assigned to visit
- Families of malnourished children are home and willing to talk with NFA staff about their children (and speak the same language) and allow them to assess nutritional status
- Families agree with the assessment of their children's nutritional status, and see the value in NFA's feeding program
- Concerns about the social stigma of not being able to provide adequate nutrition (as indicated by enrollment in the program) are outweighed by the desire to help children
- Families have time to attend required NFA training sessions on preparing supplements and proper nutrition (and are willing to commit to the sessions)
- Families enroll their children in NFA's program

Figure 3.3 Assumptions linking activities and outputs in Nutrition for All's theory of change.

some of the others. For instance, they can time visits to correspond with when families are likely to be around and make sure that field staff speak the same language as the families. Such important operational decisions may emerge from identifying assumptions.

But some assumptions concern the social context in which the program operates and the demand for NFA's services. For example, is there social stigma attached to not being able to adequately nourish a child, and, if so, will this deter enrollment? Are families too busy to attend the training sessions NFA requires? And finally, given all of these assumptions, will families actually enroll their children in NFA's supplemental feeding program? The answers to the questions may determine whether families enroll in NFA's program or not. But now that NFA is aware of these assumptions, what should it do? In Chapter 5, we discuss how to develop a right-fit monitoring and evaluation system that uses these assumptions and the CART principles to make decisions about what data to collect.

Once we move beyond the realm of outputs to program outcomes, organizations are making an even larger number of predictions about how people will respond to their programs. Predictions about how outputs will lead to desired outcomes and impacts are where the theory of change becomes truly theoretical. We illustrate one such prediction in Figure 3.4: the prediction that, once provided with training and supplements, families will give the supplements to their children and stop poor nutrition practices (see Figure 3.4).

This link between outputs and outcomes is a key link in the theory of change: NFA believes that if malnourished children receive NFA supplements and eat more nutritious foods, rates of malnutrition should

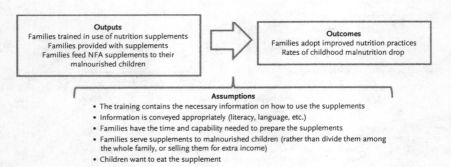

Figure 3.4 Assumptions linking outputs and outcomes in Nutrition for All's theory of change.

fall. (Remember that NFA supplements are not the only reason that rates of malnutrition could fall. To know whether NFA's program caused change in malnutrition rates, ones needs to measure a counterfactual.)

The relationship between outputs and outcomes relies on a number of predictions about how families and children will respond to training and supplements. One important prediction is that training will result in knowledge transfer and behavior change. But a number of things could mean this prediction does not come true. Information could be presented unclearly. Illiterate families could be unable to read instructions. Families could be unwilling or unable to take required actions. If for any reason NFA's training sessions do not transfer knowledge or change behaviors, then the program will not attain its desired outcome.

Another major prediction underlying this connection is that families will follow NFA instructions to serve supplements only to their malnourished children. But they may prefer to divide the supplements among all their children, not just the malnourished, which would diminish their efficacy for the neediest children. Or they may sell them for extra income, or do something other than feed them to their needy child. If families do not provide supplements as instructed, the crucial outcome of reduced rates of malnutrition may not happen. A theory of change helps shed light on the critical assumptions and predictions that must hold for key outcomes to occur and suggests important areas for data collection.

STEP 6. CONSIDER NON-PROGRAM FACTORS THAT ALSO CAUSE CHANGES

The next important step is to ask what besides the program could cause the intended outcome to change. If malnutrition rates change, what else (apart from NFA activities and outputs) could have caused that change?

Listing the most important alternative causes helps organizations better understand the counterfactual. Knowing alternative causes helps clarify whether one will be able to attribute a change in the outcome to the program or policy. This is part of the credible principle. Some alternative causes are obvious: other programs in the area begin working on malnutrition, good (or bad) rainfall could affect food availability, breakouts of disease could affect health status. Other alternative causes may require more reflection.

One theme of this book is asking organizations to consider: If there is no way to isolate those other factors, is it worth it to collect outcome data? To answer that question, it is critical to think through the likely presence and importance of these other factors.

This step is often *not* included as a component in what other books or guidelines put forward for a theory of change. We include it for a simple reason: thinking through this draws attention to the issue of attribution and facilitates crisp thinking on this critical point.

STEP 7. IDENTIFY RISKS AND UNINTENDED CONSEQUENCES

We demonstrated earlier how assumptions and predictions connect the elements of a theory of change together. One other big assumption that many organizations make: the rest of the world will stay the same. The world around the program is unlikely to remain static, and changes in external conditions pose unavoidable risks to any program.

NFA faces a wide range of risks. Because the program relies on government-employed CHWs to identify malnourished children, if the government withdraws its cooperation, the program's ability to identify malnourished children will be threatened. Implementation depends on a steady supply of nutritional supplements; interruption in the supply chain for any reason (such as washed-out roads in the rainy season or a disruption in production) could leave the program without its key input. Violence could break out in the program's target area and restrict field worker movements.

Some risks are more probable than others; some would be more devastating than others if they became reality. It is often worthwhile to identify—ahead of time—the most likely and most potentially damaging risks and develop a risk reduction or mitigation plan.

OVERCONFIDENCE AND UNINTENDED CONSEQUENCES

Two mental challenges confront us in exercises like creating a theory of change. First, thinking about the assumptions we make and the risks to a program can be difficult because our biases tend to make us overconfident. Countless studies have shown that we tend to overestimate the prospects for success while simultaneously discounting the likelihood of failure.[2] Starting a new project is no different. Why start a program if an organization is not optimistic that it will make a difference? While this enthusiasm is good, it can get in the way of effective program design if risks are continually ignored or discounted.

One way to combat overconfidence and realistically assess risk is to start not by envisioning success, but by imagining program failure and then thinking through how that failure would happen. This is the flip side of creating a theory of change: one creates a theory of failure as a check on the program's logic. One way to visualize this is through a *fault tree*, a hierarchical diagram that outlines every specific path that can carry a program toward a given failure. Or, by using *scenario thinking*, staff can propose a potential failure, then articulate the possible reasons it would happen.

Research has shown that by simply thinking through alternate explanations, people address a question more rationally and consider both the upsides and downsides of a given choice. For example, Shell Oil once asked its staff to estimate the amount of oil they believed certain oil platforms would produce with a 90% confidence interval. They then told staff to think through two scenarios—successful and failed well construction—and after that revise their production estimate. The range of the estimates increased by 30%, a decrease in confidence that helped the company better assess the relative merits of different projects.[3] Similar scenario thinking could prevent poorly conceived projects from being implemented and help develop more resilient programs that take account of risk factors.

Second, the focus on expected or intended outcomes can make it hard to generate ideas about unexpected or unintended consequences—both positive and negative. When organizations analyze their assumptions, it is important to consider not just the circumstances that would render programs ineffective, but also those that would produce unexpected counterproductive effects. NFA, for example, should consider the possibility that its nutritional supplements unexpectedly disrupt household dynamics. Is there reason to believe that disagreement over how to use the supplements might provoke conflict or that this new food source could trigger resentment from the family members who are typically considered the household's breadwinners? Talking with intended beneficiaries about a program is an important but often neglected element of testing assumptions. Field staff also have important information about how things work "on the ground."

Unintended consequences are not limited to a program's immediate beneficiaries, either. The concept of *externalities* from economics is helpful here. An externality is a transaction's positive or negative impact on people who are not involved in that transaction. For instance, a coal power plant produces a net negative externality if it harms the environment through its pollution or carbon footprint. And using an insecticide-treated bed net produces a positive externality, as it protects the person who sleeps underneath it, but it also kills mosquitos and thus protects neighbors, too.

Could NFA's provision of food supplements result in positive or negative externalities? If the program succeeded in reducing hospital admissions for malnutrition, then perhaps it could reduce the operating cost of public hospitals. This might then allow local governments to lower taxes for all households, not just those receiving the supplements. Or perhaps families receiving the supplements decide that they can now get away with purchasing fewer vegetables at local markets, reducing local farmers' incomes and damaging the economy.

Since this can be a difficult conceptual exercise, it is important to dedicate some time and energy to specifically brainstorm unintended effects that a program may cause. Thinking through possible unintended consequences up front can help program staff plan to measure them. By examining key assumptions and considering how outputs might lead to counterintuitive outcomes, programs can identify likely unintended consequences ahead of time. And by tracking those critical assumptions, programs will know whether they should prepare to evaluate unintended outcomes.

PUTTING IT ALL TOGETHER: MAPPING THE PATHWAYS

Once all the elements are in place, the next step is to visually map how the activities, outputs, and outcomes connect to each other. Many activities will map to multiple outputs, and some outputs will map to multiple outcomes. Multiple connecting arrows indicate a particularly important component of the theory that must hold for the program to work. These points should likely become focus areas for data collection.

Although mapping every possible connection between activities, outputs, and outcomes is important for internal data collection, the complexity of some programs leads to an extremely elaborate diagram. When this is the case, many organizations find it helpful to develop a simplified theory of change that clearly represents the most important elements of the program to stakeholders and to reserve more complicated schematics for internal use.[4]

For an example of how this can look on paper, see the simplified mapping of NFA's activities, outputs, and impact in Figure 3.5.

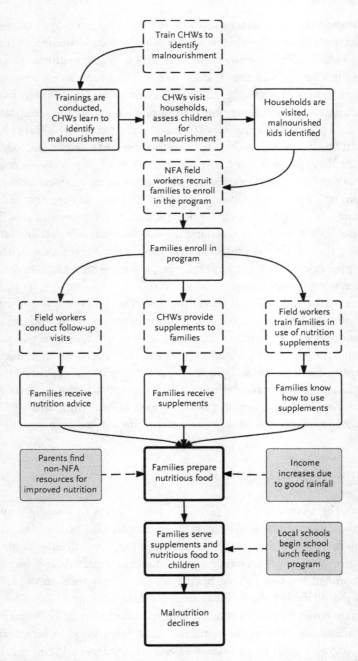

Figure 3.5 Nutrition for All outcome mapping. Dashed outlines represent activities, thin solid outlines are outputs, and bold solid outlines are outcomes/impact. Shaded boxes refer to external factors that could influence outcomes, thus making the counterfactual more challenging to identify

Looking at this map for NFA, several important areas become apparent. First, a critical step in the program is the CHW household visits that identify families with malnourished children. Family enrollment in the program is another critical output. Following the program logic shows that family identification and enrollment are necessary steps for all other outputs and outcomes. Similarly, for children to consume nutritious food (a necessary output for the desired outcome), families must receive supplements, know how to use them, and receive nutrition advice. Data collection should focus on these key areas. This program theory also demonstrates how important monitoring information can be. Imagine NFA spends a lot of money and effort to find out that malnutrition among program participants does not decline. Without monitoring data on receipt and use of supplements, they cannot be sure whether the supplements work as expected or whether the supplements were even used. More importantly, monitoring data on enrollment could support critical program improvements, such as improved training of the CHWs on how to target the right families for the program. Once NFA is sure that children are receiving the supplements, they can consider the need for an impact evaluation.

IT IS NEVER TOO LATE FOR A THEORY

Organizations often develop a formal theory of change long after a program has already started. Even at this late stage, the process of articulating a theory of change brings a number of benefits. It creates a clear understanding of the program and provides a conceptual map of a program that helps others understand it. This framework also gives organizations a better idea of how they can measure progress. However, the process can also be uncomfortable, exposing disagreement within the organization about how the program works or the problem it aims to address. Or it can reveal that the theory itself is not well formulated or makes problematic assumptions. Many programs, like many human actions, are undertaken based on implicit theories that can look a little fuzzy when exposed to the light of day.

To genuinely support learning and improvement, developing a theory of change should not be a compliance exercise undertaken to rationalize past programmatic decisions, but rather an opportunity to question, debate, and learn. Developing and validating a theory of change works best with broad organizational buy-in. The perspectives both of leadership and of staff working on the ground are needed to develop a theory of change that accurately captures the program's activities, logic, and aspirations. Otherwise, the exercise risks merely validating existing assumptions or satisfying the demands of donors or other external stakeholders such as boards or host governments. This also means that to properly develop a theory of change, program leadership needs to remain open to negative feedback. Program staff who raise concerns about program assumptions should be listened to and not punished. For a theory of change to be a living document, internal and external stakeholders need to remain open to learning and improvement.

Taking a learning stance toward program development can be challenging. In developing a theory of change, an organization may discover that certain activities are poorly suited to addressing the intended challenge or even actually address a different challenge. Cutting or drastically modifying the program may not be possible—imagine an organization telling a donor that it is ending a project they funded because, upon further reflection, it was not such a great idea! Nonetheless, when organizations take a step back to rearticulate their theory of change, they get information they need to build stronger programs. Developing a theory of change can help organizations identify unnecessary activities and make more space for the important ones. This is the case with the Invisible Children program highlighted in Box 4.2 in the next chapter. By using a theory of change to identify unnecessary data and adjust programs, organizations can save critical resources.

The theory of change is the foundation of a right-fit data system for both monitoring and evaluation. It helps organizations identify which activities and outputs to monitor and when to consider measuring outcomes and impact with a counterfactual. But a theory of change alone is not enough. Organizations also need a framework to guide them through tough decisions about what data to collect and when to collect it—and, just as importantly—what data *not* to collect. The CART principles provide this framework.

CHAPTER 4

The CART Principles in More Detail

In Chapter 2, we introduced the CART principles (Credible, Actionable, Responsible, and Transportable), a set of standards that help all organizations build strong activity monitoring and impact evaluation systems. We now discuss the CART principles in more detail and show how they can help organizations make difficult tradeoffs about the data they should collect. Throughout this chapter, we continue to use the example of the hypothetical organization Nutrition for All (NFA) to see how a theory of change combines with the CART framework to guide data collection.

THE CART PRINCIPLES FOR DATA COLLECTION, ANALYSIS, AND USE

Most organizations want to build right-fit data collection systems that demonstrate accountability to donors and provide decision-makers with timely and actionable operational data. But without a framework for approaching this challenge, it is hard to know where to start and what data are most critical for an organization. The CART principles remind organizations to follow four simple guidelines before investing in data collection:

- *Credible*: Collect high-quality data and analyze them accurately.
- *Actionable*: Collect data you can commit to use.
- *Responsible*: Ensure that the benefits of data collection outweigh the costs.
- *Transportable*: Collect data that generate knowledge for other programs.

Collect high-quality data and analyze them accurately.

Credible data
Credit: mooselakecartoons.com

The *credible* principle has two parts: the quality of data collection and how data are used—in other words, data analysis.

First, strive to collect high quality data. What does high quality mean in practice? High quality data have several characteristics. For each component of a theory of change to be measured, the underlying concept needs to be clearly defined. Then, the indicators that measure the concept must be a good measure of the concept (valid) and measured in a consistent way (reliable).

To be valid, data should capture the essence of what one is seeking to measure. This may sound simple, but developing a good measure of a concept can be tricky. The first step is to clearly define the concept. To learn someone's age, asking them how old they are is usually fairly straightforward (although in some contexts people may not readily know their age). But many concepts are far less clear. If an organization seeks to learn about health-seeking behavior, for example, and asks "How many times have you visited the doctor in the past month?" people may interpret the term "doctor" quite differently. Some people may count visits with nurses or technicians, others may not. Do acupuncturists count? Or traditional healers? So, valid data consist of clearly defined concepts and good measures of those concepts.

Data should also be reliable. Reliability means that the same data collection procedure will produce the same data repeatedly. One simple way of thinking about reliability is to consider the use of physical instruments in data collection. Suppose a study uses scales to measure the weight of respondents. If the scales are calibrated differently each day, they will not produce a reliable estimate of weight. If the scale sits on uneven ground, each weighing, even one separated by a mere few seconds, can vary. For survey questions, reliability implies that a survey question will be interpreted and answered in the same way by different respondents. Reliable data collection in a large survey requires each interviewer to ask the question in exactly the same way and at exactly the same point in the survey. This requires proper staff management and training (such as how to fill in surveys or forms, ask questions, and so on), quality checks, and other policies that ensure that data are collected consistently across surveyors. Chapter 7 focuses on how to collect high-quality data.

The second part of the credible principle argues that data must be appropriately used and analyzed. Credible data analysis involves understanding when to measure impact—and just as importantly—when *not* to measure it. A solid theory of change is the foundation for credible data. The theory of change helps clarify whether the outcome data—even if high quality— can help estimate impact. Remember in particular Step 6 of the theory of change: consider non-program factors that also cause the outcome to change. Without a good counterfactual, the analysis of outcome data can produce biased estimates of impact. Our example of the water and sanitation intervention in Chapter 2 showed that just comparing data on outcomes before and after an intervention can lead to flawed conclusions about impact. The theory of change contributes to credible analysis by helping to differentiate deliverables (outputs) from changes in outcomes attributable to the program (impacts). Outputs are measured through activity monitoring, or collecting data on what an organization is doing and delivering. Measuring impact requires evaluation using a counterfactual, that is, a way to measure what would have happened in the absence of the program.

ACTIONABLE

Collect data you can commit to use.

Credit: www.CartoonStock.com

The credible principle helps organizations identify data that can be collected with validity and reliability. But even with these criteria in place, organizations may find the options for data collection overwhelming. The *actionable* principle helps address this problem by calling on organizations to only collect data they can and will use.

To assess actionability, organizations should ask three questions before collecting any piece of data. First: "Is there a specific action that we will take based on the findings?" (the "use" in "collect data you can commit to use"). Second: "Do we have the resources necessary to implement that action?" (the "can" in "collect data you can commit to use"). And, third: "Do we have the commitment required to take that action?" (the "commit" in the "collect data you can commit to use").

The answer to all three questions should be "yes" in order to justify collecting that data.

Creating an actionable system for data requires organizations to do three things: define and narrow the set of data to collect, define the action to take based on the data, and develop a system that delivers high quality data in timely fashion.

Narrowing the Set of Data

A theory of change facilitates actionability by helping organizations focus data collection on the most essential elements of their programs. In many programs, the list of activities and outputs that make up the program theory is quite long, leading to a long list of data to collect. Should organizations measure everything they do? Probably not. Organizations should focus on data that will actually be put to use. If data address key questions about the program and provide information about key assumptions and unknowns, the organization is much more likely to be able to use this information to learn and improve. A theory of change helps streamline data systems by highlighting essential program elements, identifying a program's assumptions, and locating opportunities for learning.

Mapping essential elements of the program

Program areas that a theory relies heavily on—such as those where multiple outputs feed into a single outcome—should be a priority for monitoring. Consider our NFA example. One of the most critical components of NFA's theory of change is that undernourished children actually consume more nutritious food as a result of the program. A number of things *must* take place for this desired change to occur: (1) undernourished children must be identified and enrolled, (2) their families must receive training on basic nutrition and how to prepare the supplements, (3) supplements must be delivered to families regularly, (4) families must feed these supplements to malnourished children, and (5) outside factors (such as a good economic conditions) must not be the primary factor driving an improvement in the consumption of nutritious food for the children. If any one of the first three components fails, then undernourished children will not eat the supplements necessary to reduce malnutrition (the fourth step). If the fifth occurs, then the outcome (health of the children) may improve but may not be due to the program; it may be due instead to good economic conditions. Without a counterfactual, it is impossible to know how children would have fared in the absence of the good economic times. Tracking the first four outputs is an important check on the key assumptions of the program. Evaluating the fifth factor requires estimating a counterfactual, which we will discuss in Chapter 6.

Identify critical assumptions in the theory of change

All theories of change rest on a set of assumptions, but some assumptions are more critical than others. Like all programs, NFA will only be successful if certain assumptions are accurate. One critical assumption is that parents will see the benefits of the program and enroll their children. If this assumption does not hold, NFA will have to find a way to stimulate demand and encourage enrollment or else reevaluate its theory of change. Tracking the enrollment rate of eligible children will be crucial for NFA to know if the program is meeting its targets or if it needs to change its enrollment strategy. NFA should make tracking this assumption a priority for data collection, define actions to take if does not hold, and review the data regularly.

Locate critical information vacuums

When few data are available on program implementation, managers are often forced to assume that programs are being implemented as expected, and often the focus turns to collecting data on outputs and outcomes. Without implementation data, however, managers are unable to assess whether disappointing output data are the result of poor implementation or inappropriate or mistaken assumptions (the "theory" in the theory of change). When measuring outcomes, an impact evaluation will be much more transportable if one has data on the quality of implementation.

A system that narrows down the data to be collected using a theory of change and these three steps supports program learning and improvement. Opportunities for improving programs can be identified by first locating critical program elements and determining assumptions and whether the program can take action to strengthen those areas. For NFA, we noted that a critical program element is that families feed their children nutritious food—both the supplements NFA provides, as well as other daily meals. As we mentioned, for this to occur, families must understand the nutrition advice they receive, families must understand how to use the supplements, and families must give their children the supplements. The first and second conditions present opportunities for potential improvement, either in program content, delivery, or follow-up. To track that this critical knowledge is being successfully conveyed, NFA should monitor what families learn, investigate low retention, and act to remedy the content, delivery, or follow-up to families.

A theory of change also helps make data *actionable* by guiding organizations on what data to collect and what *not* to collect. (*Hint*: Only collect data that directly relates to the theory of change.) Without a system for identifying this critical information, organizations often end up collecting data "just in case" or because it would be "nice to know." The result can be an overwhelming amount of data that is rarely put to use. The theory of change guides actionable data collection by focusing organizational attention on the essential information. By limiting the amount of data collected and analyzed, organizations are much more likely to be able to take action on that data.

Defining a Response to Data

Organizations should specify the action that data will inform. We recognize that organizations cannot foresee all future decisions and that projects evolve over time. Nonetheless, thinking through in advance how the data will be used helps an organization separate necessary and superfluous data. The lesson? Data that are merely "interesting" do not make the cut. Everything should have a foreseeable purpose.

The programmatic response to data will depend on the indicator. For some pieces of information, the response is relatively straightforward. Take, for example, an organization tracking implementation of water filtration systems and handwashing stations in schools. One key question is: Are the water filtration systems operational? The response is either yes or no, and organizations should be able to specify their response to either result ahead of time. If yes, this organization could decide to check on the system in another two months. If the system is not working, action would require sending someone to fix it within the week and then following up the next week to be sure that the issue was resolved.

For other indicators, the response could be more nuanced. For example, consider a microcredit organization that collects data on the percentage of its clients who take out a new loan each quarter. One response could be to scrap the loan program entirely if loan take-up is below 5%. Another response could be to redesign the product if take-up is below 30%. And, finally, the organization could decide to collect feedback from its clients to tweak the program if take-up is below 60%. The exact thresholds will, of course, vary by program; the key point is to think through the potential responses to data in advance to ensure the data are actionable.

Even information that does not seem actionable, like demographic data on the age and gender of people in a program, can support action if gathered with a specific use in mind. If the theory of change operates under the assumption that an organization will help female heads of household gain access to credit, it should definitely make sure that the program actually reaches female heads of households! If monitoring data reveal that the organization misses that mark, it can consider how it is recruiting clients or institute more aggressive screening procedures to make sure that the program reaches female household heads. But the organization has to be willing and able to take action based on this information.

The main point of the *actionable* principle is not that organizations always decide up front *where* to draw the lines that will spur action, but rather that they must clearly define the actions data will support before they collect it. And sometimes the results may say "carry on," if all is being done as planned. In the preceding microcredit example, if the organization finds it is reaching female heads of household at the desired rate, no action is necessary. *Actionability* necessitates a commitment to taking action *if* the data suggest it necessary to do so.

Of course, implementing the *actionable* principle is easier said than done for several reasons. The first is technical: it can be hard to foresee how programs and environments will change, even in the short run. Many organizations work in rapidly changing environments that make it hard to plan activities for the next week, much less commit to action six months or a year in the future. But using the *actionable* principle as a filter for data collection decisions should greatly reduce the amount of data that gets collected while increasing its usefulness.

The second reason is more political: a commitment to taking action can be controversial. Staff or funders may be particularly attached to a program, even in the face of evidence that it is not working. Many organizational leaders struggle to commit to evidence-based management, preferring to rely on previous experience or expert opinion. To address these challenges, organizations should ask before seeing the data: What evidence would it take to convince us that this program is (or isn't) working? Being clear up front on the criteria for action can help generate the necessary will to take action by creating a kind of precommitment. To be clear, we aren't arguing that all decisions should be formulaic or that environment or other contextual factors shouldn't be taken into account. But the more that staff and leadership commit in advance to actions to be taken and the criteria for taking them, the harder it is to back-pedal when disappointing information comes along.

To integrate data into program decisions, the organization as a whole needs to commit to act on results, even if they are disappointing. If managers are not willing to do that, they should be honest about their intended actions. Sometimes staff or management believe so strongly in a program element that they will not change it no matter what the data reveal. If this is known beforehand, then investing in data collection on that topic may not make sense.

The *actionable* principle above all helps organizations decide what data are most critical to collect for both monitoring and evaluation. The principle can also help organizations decide whether it is worthwhile to conduct an impact evaluation at all. The rule is the same here: organizations should spend time and money conducting an impact evaluation only if they are committed to using the results. Therefore, an actionable evaluation must be designed to generate evidence that can improve a program, and it must include an honest commitment to use that evidence, regardless of the results.

Developing a System to Support Use

For data to be truly actionable, organizations need to develop systems that allow staff to actually use the data they generate. Even the most actionable data will not get used if staff do not know how to quickly access them, don't have the authority to change programs, or lack the resources to take action. We return to this issue in detail at the end of Chapter 5.

RESPONSIBLE

Ensure the benefits of data collection outweigh the costs.

"Big surprise. That Cost/Benefit analysis cost us more than any benefit we've ever gotten from it."

Credit: www.CartoonStock.com

Building an actionable monitoring and evaluation system means prioritizing the information that has the greatest power to improve a program at the least cost. Applying the *credible* principle helps eliminate indicators that cannot be measured with high quality or analyzed accurately. The *actionable* principle asks organizations to commit to using the data collected, further narrowing the set of possible indicators, and allowing organizations to produce data quickly enough to make program decisions. Next, though, management must weigh the costs of data collection against the potential benefits of the information provided. The list of credible and actionable data that an organization could collect may not fit well within existing resources. At this point, organizations may have to make some difficult decisions. This is where the *responsible* principle can help.

The first step in building a responsible system is to consider the costs of data collection.

Direct costs are the most obvious. Data collection is expensive. Designing forms and collecting data take time, and staff must be paid. Staff often need to get out into the field to collect data, which can be costly. Paper forms require printing. Electronic data do not require printing but still require some technology. Analyzing data also takes time, maybe even training. These real costs need to be assessed against the value of information the data will provide.

However, the cost of data collection goes beyond these direct costs; one must also consider the opportunity costs. *Opportunity costs* refer to what could have been done with the time and money organizations spend collecting, analyzing, and pondering data. For an example of opportunity costs, imagine a survey of 50 questions that staff barely have time to enter into a database. If that survey were cut down to 20 key, actionable questions, a field officer could spend more time implementing the program or analyzing data. With the extra time and the actionable information from the form, staff will be better positioned to actually make changes based on the data. As this example illustrates, the *responsible* principle requires asking if the potential benefits of more data collection are worth serving fewer people or spending less time on data analysis.

Data collection costs affect program participants as well as the implementing organization. Survey respondents have to stop what they are doing to respond, which has real opportunity costs in the form of foregone labor or leisure. Does the information to be gained justify the time a beneficiary must spend to provide it or the cost of compensating the beneficiary for his or her time? Will the organization actually use the data? Reams of data collected from program participants that end up sitting on shelves (or hard drives) is not a responsible use of participants' time.

All this suggests that organizations should strive to minimize the data they collect. But collecting too little data has social costs as well. Without data on the quality of program implementation, organizations miss important opportunities to learn, refine, and improve programs. Organizations may move too quickly toward impact evaluation, even in cases where program design needs work. The net result is ongoing programs that are operating below their potential, implying a waste of resources. How can an organization balance these tradeoffs?

It is tough to come up with a single rule that can correctly assess the tradeoff between the opportunity cost of collecting data and the potential social cost of not doing so. We get asked all the time if there is a particular amount of money that should be dedicated to monitoring and evaluation. There is no one right answer to this question. Although many organizations benchmark a fixed portion of the overall budget for data collection and analysis, needs often change over time, making such inflexible allocations a wrong fit. An organization just starting a new program may not spend a lot on monitoring and evaluation, instead focusing its resources on operations. As the program develops, though, it may be worthwhile to spend more on monitoring. That way the organization can learn about how implementation is going and figure out how to deliver the program more efficiently.

The *responsible* principle also tells organizations that the purpose of an impact evaluation should not be to look backward and ask how one did, but to look forward and ask what to do next. (And, as we will discuss next, if the lessons are *transportable,* to help guide others.) Funding an impact evaluation for a program that will not run in the future is not a good use of resources. Thus the appropriate evaluation budget should be thought of as a research and development expense for future work, and the *responsible* question should be "how much is it worth to generate knowledge to make the future budgets more efficiently spent?"

Minimizing Data Collection Costs

Once an organization has a list of the data it would like to collect, minimizing the costs of collecting these data is an important way to implement the responsible principle. Organizations should always ask: Is there a cheaper or more efficient method of data collection that does not compromise quality? Responsible data collection may mean conducting a survey at a local school instead of at students' homes to reduce travel costs, for example.

In addition, technology can make data collection cheaper. For example, an organization looking to verify program activities can call program participants and ask them whether someone from the program visited the area and did what they were supposed to. Collecting data in this way offers a large cost savings when compared to sending someone out to physically verify that information. And that is not the only advantage. Since staff will try to better implement the program when being audited (known as the *Hawthorne effect*), verifying program implementation remotely may give more accurate information as well.

Technology can also make it easier to gather feedback from program participants. Programs such as Feedback Labs allow participants to SMS message questions, comments, and concerns to a central server so that organizations can get and respond to this information in real time.[1] Satellite imaging and other data sources offer the possibility of remote verification of activities. These are just two examples of how to make monitoring cheaper. In an online Goldilocks Toolkit on the Innovations for Poverty Action (IPA) website, we discuss the power and potential of technology for monitoring and evaluation in more detail.

Using existing data is another clear way to make data collection more responsible. Many banks, hospitals, or other partners of organizations already collect administrative data that can be used to track program implementation. Since these organizations have to collect this information as a part of regular operations, it may be possible for organizations to get this information for free, making it a far more cost-effective choice than collecting the data through interviews. We talk more about administrative data in Chapter 6.

The responsible principle asks organizations to assess whether the total amount of spending on data collection is appropriate, given the information it will provide, when compared to the amount spent on other areas of the organization (such as administrative and programmatic costs) and considering the time of respondents and others involved. There is no magic formula for this, of course. It requires judgment. But often we observe the question is not even posed, and that likely leads to overexpenditure on data.

Responsible Program Design and Data Collection

Responsible program design requires addressing critical assumptions and risks. Responsible data collection requires balancing the desire for more data with the resources and capacity available to collect it, recognizing that all data have opportunity costs.

By grounding the design of its program in a sound theory of change that thoroughly assesses assumptions and risks, an organization can take the first step in responsible program design. The theory of change helps identify critical program components and key assumptions to prioritize in data collection. If resources and capacity allow, organizations can consider other metrics beyond these critical components to measure the quality and efficiency of program delivery.

As a consequence of identifying credible and actionable data, a clear theory of change also leads to *responsible* data collection by helping organizations avoid unnecessary and costly inquiries. Furthermore, a well-thought-through theory of change highlights evidence gaps: areas where intuition may be strong but evidence is light. Gathering data to test those key gaps would be a responsible way to make sure future resources are spent well (see Box 4.1).

TRANSPORTABLE

Collect data that generate knowledge for other programs.

CECIL COULD NOT FATHOM WHY THEY DECIDED *THEIR* DIETARY HABITS BY WATCHING *HIM* EATING DRY PELLETS.

Credit: © Hilda Bastian

The *transportable* principle urges organizations to communicate lessons from monitoring and evaluation in order to help others design more effective programs. This principle is particularly important for impact evaluations, which can generate useful evidence for organizations trying to design new programs or fund ones that work. But translating findings also requires an underlying theory that helps explain them. Such theories help organizations understand when findings will translate to new contexts. Developing a clear theory of change is an important part of making monitoring and evaluation transportable.

One clear example is vaccine distribution. We know that vaccines prevent disease[2]; the real challenge is getting them to people who need them. If, after trying a few different methods of vaccine distribution, an organization's monitoring efforts identify one delivery process that is more effective, why not share these insights with other organizations so they can also efficiently deliver vaccines to people who need them? Concerns about competitive advantage and protecting incentives to innovate are paramount in the private sector, but we argue that they have no place in the social sector if organizations are serious about their intent to improve lives.

Sharing failures is just as important, even though being candid about failures is much harder than crowing about success. If an organization tried to find clean water solutions for a town in rural Malawi but found that its particular solution was not a good fit (for example, it was hard to implement, broke often, or required extensive buy-in that was hard to get), making this information widely available allows other organizations to learn from and avoid these problems in the future. The information about failure can help others avoid the same mistakes.

A strong theory of change is critical to the transportable principle. For example, to explore the relationship between price and demand for health products, economists[3] tested how much people in Kenya were willing to pay for insecticidal bednets that protect against malaria and other mosquito-borne diseases. The *law of demand* in economics suggests that, all else equal, as the price of these bednets increases, people will be less willing to buy and therefore use them. Naturally, all else is not equal. An alternative hypothesis, termed the *sunk cost fallacy*, suggests that people are more likely to use something they purchased rather than got for free. The potential regret of having wasted money may inspire people to use the bednet, whereas if they got it for free they may not feel bad about leaving it unused in the closet. By designing an experiment around these questions and collecting appropriate data, the study builds a strong case that giving away bednets better reduces malaria than selling them.[4,5] This study created valuable transportable knowledge. For malaria bednets in Kenya, the law of demand has better explanatory power than the sunk cost fallacy.

Having a clear theory makes lessons transportable. In this case, the basic theory is the law of demand, something we all use instinctively every time we go shopping. When the price of a good goes down, we are more likely to buy it or buy more of it. But appropriate theory is rarely that simple. Context almost always also influences predictions. Would these results hold in a setting with different prior information and knowledge about bednets? Would these results hold with a different business environment for selling bednets? Would they hold with a different distribution channel? Would these results hold for other health products, such as water-cleaning tablets, deworming pills, or antidiarrheal medicine? It is not possible to answer all of these questions. And no single study will ever "hold" for the rest of the world. The key is to think through which conditions are critical. If different conditions cast doubt on the validity of one evaluation's results in another setting, that second setting is a prime candidate for another impact evaluation, to check the limits of the original results. Such replication is a second, complementary method of addressing transportability. There is no better way to find out if something will work somewhere else than to try it there.

We have seen the power of replication firsthand with a set of seven randomized trials of a social safety net program for the ultra-poor. The program employs an integrated approach to alleviating poverty among the ultra-poor by providing productive asset grants (typically around four animals), livelihood training, and household visits to give information, support families, and provide "life coaching." The program also includes health services, access to savings, and food or cash for consumption needs at the beginning of the program. The program's theory of change proposes that each component is necessary to address the multiple constraints facing the ultra-poor. Results from the seven sites were published in two papers, one paper by one set of researchers for a Bangladesh site[6] and the other six by another set of researchers from IPA and Jamal Latif Poverty Action Lab (J-PAL) for Ethiopia, Ghana, Honduras, India, Pakistan, and Peru.[7,8] The intervention worked surprisingly similarly in the seven sites, with the exception of Honduras.

Although the *transportable* principle applies most directly to impact evaluation, it can also guide monitoring decisions. When organizations are clear about their theory of change and implementation strategy, it helps others who are doing similar work—either internally or at other organizations. For example, when organizations share lessons about how to increase the usage rate of effective products or how to most credibly collect data on a particular topic, it builds our collective knowledge base. The *transportable* principle dictates that every organization ought to provide clear information on its programs.

Transportable Programs

Just as the theory of change can help programs improve, it is also critical for replication—both for the program itself and for others. Developing a theory of change is a key component of transportability, as is updating it to reflect lessons from monitoring data. By formulating a theory of change, organizations take the first step toward ensuring the transportability of their data. As we will see in the next chapter, targeting and monitoring data identified through the theory of change help organizations understand usage patterns and expand the program to new areas. And when

---

Box 4.2 FROM THE CASES: STEMMING "ACTIVITY CREEP" WITH A THEORY OF CHANGE: INVISIBLE CHILDREN

Over time, development programs often evolve and adapt to changing contexts and changing needs of the populations they are serving. While these shifts are normal, it sometimes leads to a sprawling program design; activities are added to a program simply because they seem worthwhile or because there is funding for them, not because they contribute to the overall goal. A strong theory of change can stop or slow this "activity creep."

Consider the case of Invisible Children Uganda, an advocacy and development organization. Invisible Children drafted theories of change for all of its programs in Uganda many years after the programs started. After conducting this exercise, the team found that not all of their activities and outputs could be directly linked to the key outcomes expected from their work. For example, the theory of change for a school scholarship program postulated that improved knowledge about reproductive health would lead to improved academic performance. Upon further reflection, the team realized that this connection was rather shaky. Realizing the program contained this extraneous activity, one staff member suggested the program might be more effective if it were simplified.

The team decided to cut reproductive health from the scholarship program, paring down its intervention to retain only those components most critical to their mission: to help kids stay in school and perform better.

---

the time is right for an impact evaluation, the theory of change provides a foundation for developing the right research question and identifying the correct data to collect to answer it.

Theories about why programs work also highlight the key mechanisms that drive change, the constituents that benefit most, and the right circumstances under which to rollout a program. This information is critical for those looking to scale a program to other settings (see Box 4.2).

TAKING THE NEXT STEP TOWARD RIGHT-FIT: MONITORING

The theory of change maps the territory for data collection and the CART principles provide guidelines for navigating the terrain. With these in place, organizations are ready to tackle the next step: developing a system for activity monitoring that demonstrates accountability and supports learning. We turn to this task in Chapter 5.

CHAPTER 5
Monitoring with the CART Principles

The Goldilocks approach counsels organizations to monitor their programs to manage operations, improve implementation, and demonstrate accountability to stakeholders. In practice, impact evaluation often gets more attention and takes up more organizational resources than monitoring. It should not. Both are critical.

Consider what happens if we boil the recipe for organizational impact down to a simple formula:

$$A \times B = \text{Social Impact}$$

In this formula, "A" means doing what you said you would do and doing it efficiently, and "B" means choosing good ideas.

If only life were that simple.

Monitoring and evaluation roughly align with the two variables in this formula. Think of *monitoring* as "A" and *impact evaluation* as "B." Then consider what happens if you forget about A. Even the best idea, which has been proved to work, will not have an impact if implemented poorly. This chapter focuses on variable A: how to use your theory of change and the CART principles (Credible, Actionable, Responsible, and Transportable) to understand whether you are doing what you set out to do and to improve how you do it.

We argue that if organizations develop accountable and transparent monitoring systems, they can not only meet external accountability requirements but go beyond them to use data to manage and optimize operations. By following the CART principles, stakeholders can hold organizations accountable for developing strong monitoring systems and reporting the data those systems generate. They will also avoid imposing systems with burdensome predetermined data collection requirements that do not support learning and improvement.

Of course variable B, impact evaluation, matters as well. And the push to evaluate can be hard to resist. At what point should organizations consider an impact evaluation? Given the cost and complexity of impact evaluations, we argue that several conditions must be met before proceeding. Most importantly, organizations should first be confident that the part they can control—their implementation—is happening with the fidelity they desire. And monitoring data can help make sure implementation is done well.

WHY DOES MONITORING MATTER?

Right-fit monitoring systems generate data that demonstrate accountability to donors and provide decision-makers with actionable information. They are every bit as important as proving impact. Credible and actionable data about program implementation is a critical but often maligned or ignored component of right-fit data systems.

Why is monitoring so often overlooked? In many organizations, monitoring data lack connection to critical organizational decisions or program learning. When data are collected and then not used internally, monitoring appears to be a waste—overhead that uses up resources without contributing to organizational goals. Instead of reassuring donors that their funds are being well spent, monitoring reports seem like mere bean counting. However, when monitoring systems provide credible and actionable data, organizations and donors gain important insight into how to manage programs and improve them—information that is far more valuable than the results of a poorly run impact evaluation.

Monitoring has two critical purposes. First, it demonstrates accountability, showing that a program is on track and will deliver the outputs it promised to deliver. Second, monitoring helps improve operational decision-making, allowing managers to learn, adjust programs, make course corrections, and refine implementation.

ACCOUNTABILITY AND TRANSPARENCY

Calls for organizational accountability seek the answer to a seemingly simple question: Did an organization do what it said it was going to do?

Transparency is a key component of accountability: By transparently exhibiting details of the implementation process, an organization allows stakeholders to evaluate whether the organization is living up to its commitments or has good reasons for adjusting those commitments.

Social sector organizations typically face a range of accountability demands from different stakeholders. Governments often require nonprofits to report on their financial and legal status. Individual donors and investors, large and small, want some assurance that their donations are making a difference. Charity watchdogs keep an eye on administrative costs and fundraising practices. And, finally, institutional donors and investors, such as foundations or development agencies, often require specific and detailed reporting on the use of their funds.

The challenge with many of these accountability demands is that they do not always produce information that is internally useful for organizations. This disconnect is another reason why monitoring data are often perceived as unhelpful or unconnected to organizational needs.

For example, in the United States, nonprofits must file an annual Form 990 with the Internal Revenue Services that reports basic financial data—revenue, program expenses, fundraising costs, and salaries of senior staff. These data allow stakeholders to calculate *overhead ratios*, which is the proportion of money spent on administrative expenses (sometimes including fundraising expenses, sometimes not).

Some charity watchdog organizations then use such ratios to "rate" charities on their efficiency, even though overhead ratios have little or nothing to do with overall organizational effectiveness. This is a known problem: even Charity Navigator, one of the charity watchdog organizations that uses overhead ratios heavily in their analysis, publicly states that overhead ratios as a measure of quality are a myth.[1] Overhead ratios are deeply flawed as a measure of implementation quality. Some things simply cost more to administer than others. Looking at overhead ratios is only good for identifying fraud, which is much rarer than most think: Out of 55,000 charities with more than $1 million in revenue, only 2.4% had overhead ratios greater than 50%. But, at lower levels of overhead (e.g., anything below 30%), there is little case to be made that those at 25% are less efficient than those at 5%.[2] One must look at the substance of what the organization does; some things simply cost more to do than others.

Similarly, while reporting requirements are important for funding organizations to track their work, they often require grantee organizations to collect information that does not help improve operations. Guidestar, a nonprofit organization which aims to be the data infrastructure behind the nonprofit sector, already provides easy access to 990 data for donors and is embarking on a new effort to also provide organizations' self-reported monitoring data. While this is an ambitious idea, it will be only as good as the data that are provided by organizations.

LEARNING AND IMPROVEMENT

To be useful, monitoring should go beyond just reporting credibly and actionably on program implementation, although that is an important first step. If monitoring data are to support program learning and improvement, they must be incorporated into organizational decision-making processes. We have discussed how monitoring has gotten a bad reputation, often serving external stakeholders more than internal organizational needs. All too frequently, monitoring data also go unused because even high quality data are not connected to actual organizational decisions. Often the data do not arrive in a timely fashion or are not appropriate for the decision that needs to be made. In the absence of appropriate data, decisions are often made on other criteria altogether, rather than on evidence from the program.

High quality monitoring that follows the CART principles helps to improve performance management. CART-based monitoring requires figuring out what credible data can be collected, committing to use these data, and ensuring the collection process is responsible and cost-effective (see Box 5.1).

BUILDING A MONITORING SYSTEM WITH A THEORY OF CHANGE AND THE CART PRINCIPLES

We now have two key building blocks of a right-fit monitoring system: the theory of change and the CART principles. With these in hand, we will walk through how to develop a monitoring system that drives accountability, learning, and improvement.

FIVE TYPES OF MONITORING DATA ALL ORGANIZATIONS SHOULD COLLECT

Five types of monitoring data are critical for learning and accountability. Two of these—*financial* and *activity tracking*—are already collected by many organizations. They help organizations demonstrate account-ability by tracking program implementation and its costs. The other

Box 5.1 FROM THE CASES: STRATEGIC MONITORING AT NATIONAL SCALE

Deworm the World works with governments to implement school-based treatment for parasitic worms on a national scale. Deworm the World was once part of Innovations for Poverty Action, but was spun out into a new nonprofit in 2015. The new nonprofit also took on other scale-up activities, and thus rebranded with a new name, Evidence Action. Evidence Action is committed to scaling up evidence-based ideas around the world to fight poverty.

In Kenya, Evidence Action supports the Ministries of Health and Education in their efforts to eradicate worms among school-aged children, providing technical assistance, training, and implementation support to reach around 6 million children a year. The organization faces the daunting challenge of monitoring this nationwide program, and could easily become bogged down in costly or low-quality monitoring data.

Evidence Action's monitoring plan aims to provide data on whether deworming medicine works as intended and deliver actionable data about program implementation to its government partners. By designing its monitoring system to align with the program's unique "cascade" structure, and by using its theory of change to identify data crucial for tracking the quality of implementation, Evidence Action is able to efficiently provide actionable data. Chapter 12 explains how an initial round of monitoring data revealed some implementation issues, which allowed program management to take concrete steps to improve implementation and reach more children.

three—*targeting, engagement,* and *feedback*—are less commonly collected but are critical for program improvement. We discuss each of these briefly, then show how they can be put to action using the CART principles. We return to the Nutrition for All (NFA) case to illustrate this process.

MONITORING FOR ACCOUNTABILITY AND PROGRAM MANAGEMENT

1. Financial Data

Financial information tracks how much is spent implementing programs. It should cover both costs and revenues, and it should be disaggregated by program and by site. Cost data includes spending on staff wages, equipment for the office, transportation, paper, and anything else needed for the day-to-day operation of the program. Revenues from grants and contracts must be tracked, and any organization that earns money, such as a bank or social enterprise, also needs to collect data on the revenues that programs generate.

The key to right-fit financial monitoring data is a balance between external accountability requirements and internal management needs. External accountability requirements often focus on revenues and expenses at the administrative and programmatic levels. Funders typically want organizations to report on use of funds by grant or by loan. External rating watchdogs often focus on the percentage of funds spent on programs versus overhead and fundraising. Organizing data in this way may make sense from the external stakeholder perspective (although, as we discussed earlier, "overhead" is a dubious measure of performance), but it often does little to help organizations understand how well their programs are being run.

To move beyond accountability to learning, organizations need to connect cost and revenue data directly to ongoing operations. This way, they can use financial data to assess the relative costs of services across programs and across program sites. External rating agencies are increasingly focusing on the cost-per-output of programs (rather than overhead ratios). These kind of operational data are intended for ongoing decision-making and differ from the financial data presented in annual financial statements or in IRS 990 filings. To contribute to program learning, data on operational costs and revenues must be credible, meaning that data are collected and reported in a consistent way across sites. Financial data must also be actionable, which requires that data are produced and reviewed on a reliable schedule. Timeliness is key for managers to be able to learn from successful programs or sites and address performance deficits early on.

Knowing how much an organization spends on specific activities, from program delivery to monitoring, also allows it to more accurately assess the opportunity costs of its monitoring choices and find a right-fit balance.

2. Activity Tracking Data

Activity tracking data give oversight on program implementation, especially the key activities and outputs identified by an organization's theory of change. These data could include information about everything from how many chlorine dispensers an organization distributes, to the number of trainings it conducts, to the number of financial products it offers to unbanked program participants. A clear and detailed theory of change supports organizations in pinpointing the key outputs of each program activity so that they can develop credible measures for them.

Output data on their own often do not convey much information on program performance, which is why they have come to have a bad reputation. Measuring an indicator like "number of trainings held" on its own does not, of course, show whether the trainings were well executed or generated a positive impact. When activity tracking data are made actionable, however, they can help indicate where there may be operational gaps: Were some regions not conducting as many trainings as they intended to conduct? Were some employees less productive than others?

Actionable activity tracking data require three conditions: first, the ability to disaggregate across programs and sites; second, the ability to connect activity and output data to cost and revenue data; and, third and most critically, the commitment to reviewing the data on a regular basis and using them to make decisions. With these conditions in place, organizations can, for example, learn from high-performing locations and use this information to support sites that are struggling.

Financial and activity tracking data are often the predominant forms of monitoring data collected by organizations, in part because external stakeholders often require them. Employing the CART principles helps ensure that these data serve not only external parties, but are actually used to improve program performance. As we mentioned earlier, three additional but less commonly collected types of data are also critical to improving performance.

3. Targeting Data

Targeting data help organizations understand if they are reaching their target populations and help identify changes (to outreach efforts or program design, for example) that can be undertaken if they are not. To be useful, targeting data must be collected and reviewed regularly so that corrective changes can be made in a timely manner.

Targeting data consist of information on the people participating in a program. These data have two purposes: identifying who enters a program and, in some cases, identifying the right service to provide a given participant. Basic program data might include information on an individual's age, gender, marital status, and socioeconomic status. But additional data on health status, educational achievement, and level of financial inclusion, among other characteristics, may allow an organization to carefully direct its programs or benefits to certain groups.

Targeting data are important for efficient program implementation, but they cannot and should not double as outcome data for reporting impact. A finding that 75% of a program's 1,000 clients are the rural, poor women that they are trying to reach is important information, but claiming that this is equivalent to program impact ("750 rural women's lives were changed by our program") is just plain wrong. Targeting data say nothing about whether the women in the program experienced any changes in their lives, let alone changes caused by the program.

Targeting data identify individuals or groups for participation in a program and allow organizations to learn who is receiving program benefits and who is not. With these data, organizations can figure out if they are reaching the group they told stakeholders they would. If they are not, they can consider where to focus extra resources to reach the target group or determine whether the programs or services they are offering are appropriate and desired by the intended users.

4. Engagement Data

We divide engagement data into two parts. The first part of this data is what economists call the *extensive margin*, meaning the size of the program as measured by a simple binary measure of participation: Did an individual participate in a program or not? Second is the *intensive margin*, a measure of how intensely someone participated: How did they interact with the product or service? How passionate were they? Did they take advantage of all the benefits they were offered?

Good targeting data make analysis of the extensive margin possible (who is being reached and who is not). "Take-up" data measure whether someone participated in a program, policy, or product. This is synonymous with the extensive margin. For example, take-up data measure the percentage of people who were offered a good or service and who actually end up using it. Take-up data also can be broken down by type of person: 35% of women took up the program, whereas only 20% of men took up the program. Take-up data support program learning and improvement because they help an organization understand whether a program is meeting client demand. If services are being provided but take-up numbers are low, organizations may need to go back to the drawing board—this could indicate a critical flaw in a program's design. Perhaps the product or service is not in demand, in which case organizations should focus resources somewhere else. If demand exists, then low take-up suggests that perhaps the program is not well advertised, costs too much, or does not match the needs of people it aims to reach.

Engagement data measure the intensive margin to provide important information to support learning and improvement. In particular, engagement data can help programs test assumptions behind their theory of change. If a program's take-up is high but usage is low, for example, it may signal that the benefits being offered are not easy to use or are a poor fit for the context. Suppose a program offers savings accounts to female rural small business owners to help them build working capital. If women open accounts but make only infrequent deposits, this suggests that the account design needs to be modified. Perhaps the travel time required to make deposits and withdrawals is too high, for example.

Engagement data are critical for program learning. Once organizations have collected activity tracking data and feel confident that a program is being well-delivered, the next step is to understand whether the program works as intended from the participant perspective. Collecting engagement data is an important first step before thinking about whether impact evaluation is appropriate for your organization. After all, if people do not use a service, how can it possibly make a difference?

5. Feedback Data

Feedback data give information about the strengths and weaknesses of a program from participants' perspectives. When engagement data reveal low participation, feedback data can provide information on why. While businesses often receive immediate feedback from customers in the form of sales because customers "vote with their feet," most social organizations are not in the business of selling goods and services and may need to be more intentional about seeking out feedback. For social organizations, engagement data provide information similar to that provided by private sector sales data. Low engagement typically signals that more feedback is needed from intended beneficiaries in order to improve program delivery.

Feedback data can be collected in a number of ways, such as through focus groups with clients or brief quantitative surveys that help identify adopters and nonadopters. Feedback can be gathered on various program dimensions, including the quality of the good or service, its importance to users, and the perceived trustworthiness of the provider. A number of organizations and initiatives seek to strengthen feedback processes and constituent voices in international development. These include Feedback Labs and Keystone Accountability. Program staff can be a valuable source of feedback as well. Feedback mechanisms that explicitly ask staff what parts of a program are and are not working well provide valuable information that might otherwise be missed.

Organizations should use feedback data to refine program implementation. Think again of our savings account example. Once such a program identifies low rates of account usage, it can contact account holders to ask why, thus providing guidance for potential changes.

Naturally, not all feedback leads to immediate prescriptions. Sometimes people do not actually understand their own decisions or have a clear rationale for their behavior. Two examples from recent research underscore this concern.

In South Africa, researchers conducted a marketing test with a microcredit consumer lending institution. The interest rate offered to potential clients varied and the offer was randomized, along with many marketing features on direct solicitations. Although the result is perhaps not surprising, its magnitude may be: including a photo of an attractive woman on the mailer was just as effective at getting men to borrow as dropping the interest rate by one-third.[3] Naturally, one is unlikely to hear feedback from a potential client that "what I really want on my loan, more so than a better price, is a picture of an attractive woman on the corner of my letter."

Another example comes from a study in Ghana, where smallholder farmers typically invest less in fertilizer than agronomy experts suggest is optimal and often leave land fallow that could be cultivated. Farm profits are considerably lower in Ghana than in other parts of the world. In focus groups, farmers typically report lack of cash as the principal reason they do not make agricultural investments. Investment in a farm enterprise typically requires money for fertilizer, seed, and additional labor. Land remains fallow, they say, because they do not have the money to invest. Some farmers, but many fewer, also report risk as a key hindrance. If they buy fertilizer, apply it, and then a drought hits, they lose their investment. So, according to these farmers, it is best not to invest much in agriculture that is sensitive to rainfall. Researchers, including this book's co-author Dean Karlan, then conducted a simple randomized test with four treatments: some farmers received cash, others rainfall insurance, others both, and others nothing.[4] It turns out that simply providing rainfall insurance led farmers to invest much more. Giving out cash led to higher investment as well, but not as much as insurance. So both constraints, cash and risk, were real. But the farmers strongly misstated the relative importance of the two when explaining their own behavior. Relying on feedback here may have led programs down the wrong path, thinking that their best option is to address the cash problem by, for example, setting up a microlending operation or cash transfers.

This should not be interpreted as a negative perspective on feedback data. No data source is perfect for all situations, and feedback data do have an important role to play in the monitoring process. We merely caution you to pay attention to the possibility of misperceptions by participants and to consider the incentives and knowledge base of those giving feedback. Multiple sources can help counter bias and triangulate data. Organizations should talk to program staff in addition to participants and balance such data against literature or other research. And, when interpreting feedback data, consider whether respondents have an incentive to answer in a certain way—such as existing jobs or future program benefits perceived as contingent on a positive assessment of a program. And consider whether there may be factors, like pictures on marketing materials, that could influence decision-making subconsciously in important and predictable ways.

Feedback on program design can also be collected through simple experiments embedded in program operations that provide immediate actionable information. These experiments, often called "*rapid-fire*" or "A/B" testing, compare how variations on an intervention affect a single, short-term aspect of program performance, such as product take-up, program enrollment, loan repayment, or attendance, among others. In rapid-fire tests, participants are randomized into treatment groups (and sometimes, but not necessarily, a pure control group) and exposed to variations in a program's design or message. The measure of interest (usually program take-up or use) is measured and compared across groups. Often these outcomes can be measured responsibly with existing administrative data so that there is no large survey undertaking necessary in order to compare the interventions.

Rapid-fire testing is most suited for answering questions that generate a fast feedback loop and for which administrative data are recorded. Because it answers questions about program design, it is particularly valuable in the design or pilot stage, or when expanding a program to new areas or new populations. It can provide credible insights into program design, produce highly actionable data, and do so at relatively low cost. Rapid-fire testing can be used to modify a program's design, a direct example of how monitoring can improve implementation.

The method provides evidence on how the design of a program affects take-up and use, and it eliminates the need to rely on guesswork or trial and error. Rapid-fire testing can be especially useful for answering questions about the early stages of a program's theory of change (i.e., the immediate steps that one expects to happen in the delivery of a program, service, policy, or product). We have emphasized that theories of change rely on a number of explicit and implicit assumptions about how a program will work. Early-stage assumptions describe the links between activities and outputs, such as the demand for a product or service. Whether or not these assumptions hold often depends on how information is conveyed to or received by the target population. Rapid-fire testing can be used to investigate these assumptions to see which design features or marketing techniques increase the take-up of a new program or product. The logic behind rapid-fire testing is important for all organizations to consider: piloting and testing inteventions and seeking immediate feedback will improve program design and effectiveness.

RIGHT-SIZED MONITORING, LEARNING, AND IMPROVEMENT AT NUTRITION FOR ALL

At this point, you may be thinking, "This is all fine in theory, but how does it work in practice?" Let's return to the hypothetical supplemental feeding program run by Nutrition for All (NFA) for malnourished children to see how the five types of monitoring data—together with the CART principles—can help NFA improve its program. We first revisit NFA's theory of change (Figure 5.1) to show how it can be used to set the priorities for data collection. Then, we will introduce the five different types of monitoring data we will need to collect to ensure the program is operating as intended.

What Information Should NFA Collect?

Using the theory of change to drive data collection, we identify information vacuums, key assumptions, and critical junctures.

To illustrate the five kinds of monitoring data NFA should collect, we focus on a critical link in their theory of change: connecting the activity of identifying malnourished children with the output of enrolling children and their families in the program. A number of assumptions connect this activity to this output.

Figure 5.2 suggests that community health worker (CHW) household visits are essential for identifying malnourished children the program's beneficiaries. If CHWs do not visit all households in the area, or they do not assess children according to the established standards, the program may fail to correctly identify its intended beneficiaries. Ensuring that families actually enroll in the program is also critical; otherwise, malnourished

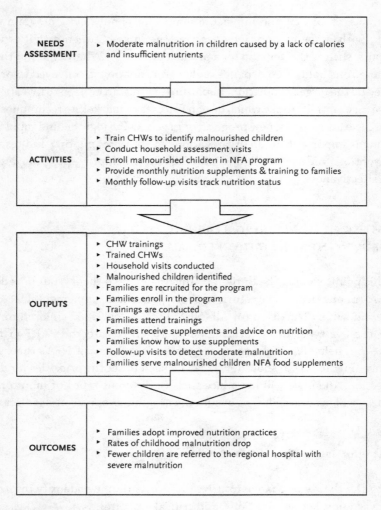

Figure 5.1 Nutrition for All's theory of change.

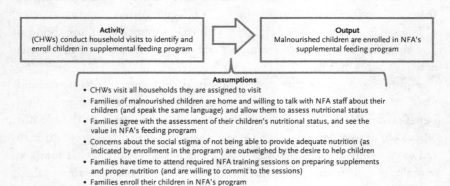

Figure 5.2 Assumptions connecting activities to outputs in NFA's theory of change.

children will not receive supplements and household nutrition practices will not change.

NFA's program also makes a number of assumptions about the links between elements in the theory change. The program assumes that the training provided will be sufficient to allow CHWs to correctly identify malnourishment. This assumes that CHWs attend trainings, that trainings cover necessary information, and that CHWs learn the training material. The program also assumes that families have the time and interest to attend NFA trainings on the use of supplements and proper nutrition and that they, too, can understand and learn the material presented. Once trained, the program assumes that families' behavior will also change—that families will be able and willing to properly administer supplements and prepare nutritious food.

Given the critical role that training plays in the program's design, NFA may want to gather additional information on these trainings in the field. The organization needs to know that CHWs are properly trained, that they are able to effectively communicate their knowledge, that families attend trainings, and that families are able to assimilate the information given.

Once NFA has used its theory of change to consider all the types of information it could gather and has identified the critical pieces of information it can afford to gather, it can begin collecting five types of monitoring data and using the CART principles to build a right-sized system.

THE FIVE TYPES OF MONITORING DATA AT NFA

Financial Data

NFA's financial data can support actionable decision-making. NFA regularly tracks implementation costs in each of the 10 villages in which it operates, which lets the program manage its finances in a timely manner and shift resources across villages as necessary. When combined with data on program implementation or the demographics of participants, NFA's financial data can be used to analyze the cost of specific activities, such as delivery costs per site or the cost of enrolling hard-to-reach individuals. This analysis can in turn be used to plan programming and more responsibly allocate resources. NFA may have to make hard choices between serving families in more costly, hard-to-serve areas versus reaching more families in more accessible areas. Having concrete data on the prevalence of malnutrition along with the costs of service provision can help the organization assess this tradeoff.

Activity Tracking

For NFA, a basic activity tracking system would measure the outputs of all of the program's core activities: the number of CHW trainings conducted, health workers trained, villages visited, households visited, malnourished children identified, families enrolled, family training sessions conducted, supplements distributed, and supplements consumed by targeted children.

To begin the activity tracking process, NFA needs to know how many CHW trainings were conducted and who was trained. Even more importantly, the organization would like to know that CHWs have actually learned the technical skills needed to identify malnourished children and that they can apply those skills in the field. Tracking training attendance could be done at relatively low cost; paper forms or tablets could be used to easily collect attendance information for CHW and family trainings. Credible data on whether CHWs have learned the skills would be more costly to obtain as it might involve testing CHWs or shadowing them on home visits. This may not be a responsible use of resources if the benefits of this additional data are not worth the costs. We return to this issue later.

Household visits and assessments are critical activities that need to be closely monitored. If household visits do not take place or assessments are not done correctly, NFA may fail to reach the malnourished children it aims to serve. NFA plans to use CHW assessment forms filled out in each village and after each household visit to track completed visits and gather data on the nutritional status of all children in the villages.

NFA needs to keep its eye on the credibility of all this data. NFA has two potential risks in using self-reported data on CHW assessment visits: poor quality assessments and falsification of data. To ensure the data are credible, NFA could randomly select households to confirm that a CHW visited and conducted an assessment. If NFA has reason to suspect poor quality assessments by one or more CHWs, the organization could validate the data by reassessing a random selection of children that the CHW had visited. However, this reassessment would burden children and families, and the *actionable* and *responsible* principles dictate that it should only be done if concerns about poor quality assessments are strong.

Targeting

NFA targets children with moderate malnutrition to improve their nutritional status. Fortunately for NFA, a well-tested, valid indicator for measuring moderate malnutrition already exists. Extensive work has been done to develop validated standard weight-for-age ratios that reliably screen children for moderate malnutrition.[5] If CHWs collect the weight-for-age ratios reliably using standardized and consistent methods of measurement, the data should provide a credible measure of malnutrition. During their household visits, the CHWs collect weight-for-age data on all children under five in the household using a standard method for measuring weight and height. NFA then uses this information to target children who fall below a predetermined threshold for their age.

The reliability of these data depends on the quality of the CHW training and their ability to put this training to use in the field. To verify the reliability of the data, NFA could choose to shadow CHWs to observe whether they are conducting measurements in a consistent and reliable way. This would be costly, but could help identify health workers who do not understand how to accurately do the measurements. Shadowing would not help, however, if the workers were sometimes taking shortcuts with the data and "guesstimating" weight-for-age instead of measuring, since workers would be unlikely to engage in this behavior while being observed. If NFA was worried about this possibility, it would need to conduct random spot-checks to validate the CHW data. While both of these options are relatively costly, they may be worth it, since identifying the children at risk of malnutrition is a critical component of the program.

At this point, you may be asking how far NFA can go in measuring its outputs and outcomes to ensure the program is working as intended. After all, have we not said that outcomes should not be measured without a counterfactual? Let's consider NFA's case. Weight-for-age ratio is a targeting indicator, but, in NFA's case, it is also an outcome. The link between the output (use of nutritional supplements) and the outcome (nutritional status, measured by weight-for-age ratio) is relatively straightforward. If children consume the additional calories provided by the food supplements, they should not be malnourished.

Does this mean, however, that if a child is malnourished, he or she did not eat the food supplements? No. Remember that there are many other possible explanations for changes in children's nutritional status. Perhaps there was a drought and malnourishment rates skyrocketed. Or a civil conflict disrupted markets. Suppose that the NFA program helped, but the rate of malnourishment stayed the same for the children because of the drought. If NFA tracked the weight-for-age data, it may incorrectly conclude that the organization had no effect and disband, when in fact it played a vital role in mitigating the consequences of famine.

And does it mean that if a child is *not* malnourished, it is *because* he received the food supplements? No! Perhaps there was good rainfall and the family earned an above average income that month. Perhaps there also was a school feeding program implemented for the first time that year. Perhaps NFA had no impact and was wasting money, yet with malnourishment rates on the decline, the program appeared effective and continued unchanged when it should have been modified or shut down.

In other words, we are back to the counterfactual problem.

However, there is a *targeting* reason to track two of NFAs outcomes. First, they should track weight-for-age to identify which children are still malnourished, in order to retarget them for additional support. Second, NFA should track whether families are adopting improved nutritional practices and are serving the supplements to malnourished children. This is a necessary step for the outcome of improved nutritional status, and NFA needs to know this is happening before they can consider measuring impact.

The challenge for organizations is clear. When outcome data are collected for targeting purposes, they should not be used for assessing impact. Yet the data are right there. Management and donors need self-control to avoid comparing before to after and making sloppy claims about causes.

Engagement

Once NFA is confident that targeting activities are working as intended, it can turn its attention to issues of take-up and engagement. Engagement data in particular may help NFA understand situations where enrollment does not appear to be improving nutritional status.

The enrollment (take-up) of families with children identified as malnourished is a critical component of NFA's theory of change. NFA's ability to provide food supplements to children in need depends on its ability to identify families with malnourished children (the targeting issue discussed earlier) and also on the assumption that these families will then enroll in the program. Enrollment depends on families seeing value in the program and expecting to have time to fulfill its requirements (attending nutrition training sessions, preparing nutritious food). Carefully monitoring these take-up rates will be critical for ensuring that the program is operating as intended. If take-up rates among eligible families are low, NFA will need to investigate the reason and ask eligible families about their decisions to enroll or not. Such data can inform improvements in program design.

Active participant engagement with the nutrition program is another critical component of the theory of change. Simply enrolling in the program is not enough to ensure that children's nutritional status will improve. The theory of change requires that families engage with the program's activities for rates of malnutrition to fall. They must attend training sessions to learn how to improve feeding practices at home and then actually adopt those practices. In addition, they must use the supplements they receive to feed their malnourished children. Tracking training participation through attendance sheets and practices in homes through simple surveys would allow NFA to understand if participants are acting as the theory of change suggests they will.

Understanding whether parents are actually feeding their children the NFA supplements—a key form of program engagement—will require data that are more expensive to credibly collect, but, given the importance of this part of the theory, it may be worth the cost. When we introduced our NFA example, we discussed a number of possible reasons that families may not feed supplements to their children as NFA expects. Perhaps some families are reselling supplements for needed income. Perhaps supplements are being consumed by other family members, instead of the targeted children. Perhaps children are consuming the nutritional supplements but eating less of other foods. Collecting credible data on these questions might require household questionnaires, although parents might be reluctant to report how supplements were used. Alternatively, NFA could try convening focus groups, checking in with knowledgeable community members, or asking program staff. Again, NFA has to be careful about using these outcomes data as results data. This is why specifying alternative explanations for outcomes in the theory of change is so important. NFA should also be sure that families aren't receiving nutrition supplements or nutrition education from other sources.

These data should have a wide variety of applications. If NFA is able to collect any of the preceding site-level data on engagement, for example, it can compare implementation and performance across sites to help understand where and why the program isn't working as expected.

Feedback

Gathering feedback from participants can help investigate program challenges or improve the quality of services NFA delivers. The questions the organization asks depend largely on the issues it observes or the assumptions it wants to test. If NFA collects engagement data that suggest that parents are not always feeding supplements to their children, feedback data can help understand why. What do participants think of the nutrition trainings? What challenges do they face in applying the knowledge they acquire? Feedback data could inform NFA whether the nutritional supplements are easy to prepare and appealing enough that children actually eat them. What could the program do better, and what services do participants value most? NFA can use household surveys and focus group discussions to collect these data, and it can also regularly ask field staff to relay the feedback they gather informally from participants.

The challenge of collecting engagement and feedback data raises the important issue of choosing sampling methods in monitoring systems. Does every client need to provide engagement and feedback data for the findings to be credible, for example? Probably not. Fortunately, the *actionable* and *responsible* principles help us think through these questions. Different data needs dictate different sampling strategies. With a clear understanding of how the data will be used, we can determine what type of sampling is appropriate.

Some elements of activity tracking data need to be collected for all program sites, for example. In our NFA example, the organization needs to know that supplements have been delivered and distributed at all program sites. Similarly, administrative data are often automatically collected on all program participants and can be used for targeting purposes (thus no sampling needed, since sampling only makes sense when collecting data is costly for each additional observation). Engagement and feedback data, however, can be more expensive and time-consuming to collect credibly. The responsible principle would therefore suggest considering a random sampling of clients, rather than the full population. A smaller sample may provide sufficient data to accurately represent the full client population at a much lower cost. Where data are intended to demonstrate accountability to external stakeholders, a random sample may also alleviate concerns about "cherry-picking" the best results. Data for internal learning and improvement might require purposeful sampling, like specifically interviewing participants who did not finish a training, or signed up and never used a service, or are particularly poor, or live in particularly remote areas. If organizations want to understand why lower income or more rural individuals are not taking-up or engaging with the program, for example, they will want to focus on those populations.

Data used for staff accountability (i.e., to track staff performance) likely need a full sample. (A high-performing staff member would likely not be happy to miss out on a performance bonus simply because the random sampling skipped her!)

Armed with these five types of credible monitoring data (accounting, activity, take-up, engagement, feedback), NFA will be in a strong position to understand what is working well and what needs to be improved in its program. Data systems built around key questions and aligned with the CART principles allow organizations to build right-fit monitoring systems full of potentially actionable data. But simply gathering sound data is not enough; organizations also need data systems that support action.

MANAGEMENT: BUILDING MONITORING SYSTEMS THAT SUPPORT ACTION

An *actionable* data collection system requires more than just creating an action step for each piece of information collected. Even if data create the potential for action, they are not truly actionable if the systems in place do not support timely usage of credible data. Far too often, a good piece of information will not get acted upon because it languishes in an information management system that is impossible to use or because junior program staff don't feel confident relaying uncomfortable findings further up the line. The most common complaint we hear from staff engaged in data collection is something along the lines of "it goes into a black hole and I never see it again."

An actionable system of data management does three things: collects the right data, reports the data in useful formats in a timely fashion, and creates organizational capacity and commitment to using data.

Collect the Right Data

The CART principles help organizations winnow the set of data they should collect. The *credible* principle reminds us to collect only valid and reliable data. This means ignoring data that cannot be collected with high quality, data that "would be nice to have" but realistically will not be credible. The *actionable* principle tells us to collect only data we are going to use. Organizations should ignore easy to collect data that do not have a clear purpose or action associated with them. We have demonstrated how a theory of change helps pinpoint critical program elements that are worth collecting data on. The *responsible* principle suggests that organizations should collect only those data that have greater benefits than costs—use must be weighed against the cost of collection and the quality with which data can be collected. *Transportability* may also help minimize costs. Where organizations can focus on widely used and accepted indicators, they can lower costs by building on efforts of others while creating opportunities for sharing knowledge.

Produce Useful Data in Timely Fashion

Actionable data systems must also resolve potentially conflicting data needs in different parts of the organization. Senior managers may want higher level aggregated data that speak to strategic priorities. Program staff need disaggregated data that help them assess how their programs are performing, and sometimes these program-level data do not neatly roll up into higher level indicators. Yet senior management buy-in is critical to obtaining the resources and commitment needed to sustain a data system. On the other hand, if data collected by program staff go up the ladder and into the proverbial black hole, staff will not commit to collecting credible data and important opportunities for learning will be lost. Additional demands for data may also be made by marketing and fundraising staff who need data to communicate with potential donors or investors. The critical role of nonprogram revenue in many organizations often privileges these data demands over others—after all, these are the people bringing in the money! Indeed, a recent study of international nongovernmental organizations (NGOs) suggests that priorities for data collection and reporting tend to favor the data needs of leadership over those of program staff.[6]

External demands for data can further complicate the situation. Donors often request data that align with their own needs rather than the grantee organization's. Organizations that are delivering services on a contract basis are often required to report on predetermined measures of service delivery (outputs) or performance (outcomes). We will return to these donor challenges, but note here that developing one data system to serve all these needs may not be possible, and organizations may face difficult choices about which data to collect. The CART principles are intended to help organizations identify data that improve performance and make the case both internally and externally for prioritizing them.

When conflicting requirements arise, we argue for first prioritizing program-level data that can be used by staff to improve performance. Program staff need to understand the value of the data and have access to these data themselves. Many program staff view data collection as a burden or simply as a reporting tool for donors. This is often because they are required to collect data that they never see put into use. As a result, it is no surprise that many staff try to minimize the time they spend collecting data. But there are many benefits to an actionable system. The field manager can learn about how his loan officers are doing. The hygiene training manager can see what happened at each month's events and the challenges in each session so that she can improve implementation in the next round.

Strong connections between program staff and monitoring staff are absolutely important. As data become more valuable to program staff, they are far more likely to use them.

Even if programmatic data are most important, organizational leadership have to see the benefit of these systems to justify spending adequate resources to build them. Satisfying both staff and managers requires a data system in which data can be accessed and analyzed in multiple ways. The system that houses and manages the data is crucial for making sure that the data are actionable. Consider the two most common types of off-the-shelf software available for this purpose. *Case management programs* focus on tracking individual clients through the system and beyond. *Constituent relationship management (CRM)* software programs, on the other hand, tend to focus more on external relationships. Ideally, any data systems should be able to provide data on costs, revenues, and clients by site and program. These data can be used to produce financial, activity tracking, targeting, and engagement data to support program learning. They can also be readily aggregated by program to provide external accountability reports. If it is appropriate for their organization, leadership will need to make additional commitments to collect information on engagement and feedback.

Create Organizational Capacity and Commitment

A fundamental challenge in creating an actionable data system is creating organizational capacity for using the data to make decisions. Here, we focus briefly on how organizations can develop systems that support actionability and data use.

Building organizational commitment requires sharing data internally, holding staff members responsible for reporting on data, and creating a culture of learning and inquiry. To do so, organizations first need to develop a way to share the data they collect. This can be as simple as a chalkboard or as fancy as a computerized data dashboard, but the goal should be to find the simplest possible system that allows everyone access to the data in timely fashion. Organizations often become enamored with complicated software or dashboard systems, thinking the system itself will solve all their problems. But often the simplest solution is the best and avoids building complicated systems that may be obsolete by the time they are complete.

Next, the organization needs a procedure for reviewing data that can be integrated into program operations and organizational routines. Again, this need not be fancy. Data can be presented and discussed at a weekly or monthly staff meeting. The important thing is that data are reviewed on a regular basis in a venue that involves both program managers and staff. At each meeting, everyone should be able to see the data—hence the chalk-board or the dashboard.

But just holding meetings will not be enough to create organizational commitment if accountability and learning are not built into the process. Program staff should be responsible for reporting on the data, sharing what is working well and developing strategies to improve performance when things are not. Managers can demonstrate organizational commitment by engaging in meetings and listening to program staff. Accountability efforts should focus on the ability of staff to understand, explain, and develop responses to data—in other words, focused on learning and im-provement, not on punishment. If the system becomes punitive or has strong incentives attached to predetermined targets, staff will have clear incentives to manipulate the data. The 2016 discovery that Wells Fargo bank employees were opening fake accounts to meet sales targets is one example of incentives backfiring.

The final element of an actionable system is consistent follow-up. Organizations must return to the data and actually use them to inform program decisions. Without consistent follow-up, staff will quickly learn that data collection doesn't really matter and will stop investing in the credibility of the data.

THE CART PRINCIPLES FOR MONITORING: A FINAL CHECK

We put forward a simple three-question test that an organization can apply to all monitoring data it collects. Clearly, as we have discussed earlier, there is more involved in right-fit monitoring than merely these questions. But we believe asking them will help management make sure their monitoring strategy is sensible:

1. Can and will the (cost-effectively collected) data help manage the day-to-day operations or design decisions for your program?
2. Are the data useful for accountability, to verify that the organization is doing what it said it would do?
3. If the data are being used to assess impact, do you have a credible counterfactual?

If you cannot answer yes to at least one of these questions, then you prob-ably should not be collecting the data.

We hope this chapter helps you design a credible, actionable, responsible and transportable monitoring system. Creating a right-fit monitoring system can provide you with the data needed to improve your program. We next turn to the process of building a right-fit system for measuring impact.

CHAPTER 6

The CART Principles for Impact Evaluation

In the mid-1990s, school enrollment in India was higher than ever and instructors were struggling to accommodate incoming students and their wide range of learning levels. While setting up preschools in the slums of Mumbai, an education organization called Pratham encountered a staggering number of elementary-age children not attending school or on the verge of dropping out. To make matters worse, many students who were attending lagged far behind appropriate reading levels.[1]

In an effort to get the mostly illiterate children on track with their peers, Pratham developed a program that recruited community members to tutor struggling students. The tutors, called *balsakhis*, met daily with groups of 10 to 15 children for two-hour lessons tailored to their reading level. These "bridge classes" aimed to bring children up to a minimum reading and math standard.

There were many advantages to this design. The *balsakhis* provided individualized instruction to students, could be trained easily and quickly, and could be hired at a lower cost than full-time teachers. And since the classes could be taught anywhere—in some schools, *balsakhi* classes were conducted in the hallways between classrooms—the program did not require any infrastructure investments.

Many stories emerged about the program's success, and Pratham's leadership decided they wanted to expand the program beyond the pilot cities of Mumbai and Vadodara. But, before doing so, staff at the organization wondered if they could get hard evidence about whether the *balsakhis* actually made a difference in students' lives.

Pratham began working in 1999 with economists at the Massachusetts Institute of Technology (MIT) to conduct a rigorous impact evaluation that randomly assigned some schools to receive the Pratham program for the third grade and others to receive it for the fourth grade. This allowed them to get a *credible* measure of the program's impact by comparing third-grade performance between schools that did and did not have *balsakhis* for third-graders and then repeating the process for the fourth grade.

The conditions were suitable for an impact evaluation. First, the timing was right: Pratham had refined the *Balsakhi* model operationally but had not yet undertaken a major expansion. Because the program had a clear theory of change, Pratham knew what it needed to measure. The organization was also able to find a sufficient sample size of roughly 200 schools for the evaluation. Finally, the program had measurable outcomes in the form of test scores. These conditions made it possible to conduct an evaluation that adhered to the CART principles.

After conducting a three-year evaluation and crunching all the numbers, the researchers at MIT's Jameel Latif Poverty Action Lab (J-PAL) found that the *Balsakhi* program more than met expectations: it substantially increased the test scores of students in the remedial education classes. They also found that since the program pulled the lowest performing students out of classrooms, the children who stayed in their original class also benefitted from more personalized attention.[2] When these findings came out, Pratham took *action* based on the positive results and expanded the program.

The evaluation of the *Balsakhi* program was a success for many reasons, and it illustrates how organizations can use the CART principles to successfully evaluate their programs.

Pratham's impact evaluation provided credible, actionable information on the merits of the *Balsakhi* program. The evaluation was also a responsible use of funding: other approaches to closing the learning gap among schoolchildren in developing countries, such as providing textbooks and wallcharts, lacked strong evidence or had been found to not work at all.[3,4] Finding an intervention that worked would potentially impact millions of children, not just those served by Pratham.

Furthermore, the results were transportable, not just because they were positive, but because the evaluation tested a theory of change that was applicable to other contexts. That is, it tested a general proposition: that community members, by providing additional instruction to small groups of low-performing students, can help those students improve basic literacy and numeracy skills. With this clear theory of change, the evaluation went beyond just rubber-stamping *one* program. Naturally, this does not mean the lessons can be taken everywhere, but the evaluation provided sufficient understanding of *why, how,* and *for whom* it worked so that others could learn from it in other settings.

Because the evidence was transportable, it not only helped Pratham learn where to focus resources, but also informed the development of similar education programs in other countries struggling with large education gaps. Policy-makers in Ghana, in collaboration with Innovations for Poverty Action (IPA), used the insights of the *Balsakhi* program along with evidence from other studies to create a remedial education program called the Teacher Community Assistant Initiative (TCAI), which also recruits community members to tutor lower-performing students.

Unfortunately, not all evaluations that claim to measure impact are designed and executed this well. As argued in Chapter 2, faulty claims about "impact" can range from simply reporting program deliverables, such as how many toilets an organization built, to assertions of impact that rely on before-and-after changes with no counterfactual, such as decreases in disease. In this chapter, we will explore the common biases to attribution that get in the way of measuring impact and explain what it means to conduct *credible, actionable, responsible,* and *transportable* impact evaluation. Before delving into those biases and methods to overcome them, however, we want to note that using a good method for attribution only gets you halfway to credibility. A credible evaluation of impact also requires high quality data, which demands expert fieldwork as well as sound analysis. We will present the characteristics of high quality data and discuss how to collect it in Chapter 7.

CREDIBLE

Before exploring the methods for conducting *credible* impact evaluation, we need to understand why credibility is so important and how bias threatens credibility.

Common Biases in Impact Evaluation

Bias can occur in any phase of research, including the design, data collection, analysis, and publication phases. The word "bias" may sound as if it refers to preexisting prejudice or ulterior motives that evaluators have toward their research, but in this case bias has a different meaning. *Bias* is a "systematic error introduced into sampling or testing by selecting or encouraging one outcome or answer over others."[5] And, in impact evaluation, one of the most important forms of bias is that of *attribution*. When evaluating impact, attribution bias occurs when we systematically misidentify the cause of an observed change; for instance, attributing changes to a program when in fact they were caused by some other factor correlated with a program's outcomes. As we have noted throughout the book, credible attribution requires a counterfactual. Three main attribution challenges can cause bias and reduce the credibility of data.

Bias from external factors. The outcome measured by an evaluation is likely to be influenced by many factors outside of a program's control, such as weather, macroeconomic conditions, governmental policy, or the effects of other programs. If the group that participates in a program is not compared to a group that is exposed equally to these same outside factors, the outside factors can generate a bias when estimating the program's effect.

For example, if we were examining the impact of a health-support program for babies, imagine we weighed the babies before and after the intervention, and the babies' weight increased. Can we then argue that the babies' weight gain was a result of the program? Of course not, that would be preposterous. The babies would have grown even if the health-support program had done nothing. In other words, the external factors of biology and the passage of time biased our results. While this is an extreme example in terms of its obviousness, it illustrates the problem with before-and-after analysis. Using "before" as the counterfactual creates bias since so many outside factors are changing over time. That is why we benefit from a treatment and a comparison group.

Here is a better way to evaluate that infant health program. We start with a set of babies whose families enrolled them in the program. We call that the treatment group. We then identify a bunch of other infants in the very same villages, and whose weight and length matches up fairly well with those that enrolled in the program but whose families did not enroll them in the program. We call this second group the comparison group. Now if the village experiences a bad harvest due to poor weather, for example, both treatment and comparison babies will have been exposed to the same external factors.

It seems like if we compare our treatment group to our comparison group, all from the same area, the bias from "outside factors" goes away. This is indeed a big improvement over before-and-after analysis, but the problem of bias is not solved. Two remaining drivers of attribution bias remain.

Credit: xkcd.com

Bias from self-selection. Individual characteristics that are hard to observe or measure may influence whether individuals participate in a program. If you compare those who choose to participate in a program, or
"self-select," with those who do not choose to participate, you may end up
with a biased measure of impact because your two groups are composed
of people who are fundamentally different. Families who choose to enroll
their babies in the health program are likely different in important ways
from those who do not.

Imagine we offer a job training program to a large group of people. We
follow a sample of those people over time and compare their subsequent
employment status to another group of people of the same age and income level from the same geographic area. But we fail to recognize that
the people who signed up for the program might be especially motivated
and entrepreneurial—maybe that is why they signed up! The program
participants' enthusiasm may make them more likely to find future employment than those who did not sign up, regardless of the program's intervention. We therefore end up overestimating the impact of the program.

It is important to recognize that many characteristics, like grit, desire, and entrepreneurial drive are hard, if not impossible, to measure.
That is what makes randomization and carefully crafted counterfactuals so
important.

Bias from program selection. Program selection bias is similar to self-
selection bias, except the problem is driven by the program allowing certain people to participate rather than others. Some potential sources of
program selection bias include staff incentives to target certain types of
people or program rules that allow peers to decide who gets to participate
in a program.

Suppose an organization started a program to provide agricultural
inputs and offered the program in the most agriculturally productive
area of a country. If we evaluate the program by comparing harvests of
participants in the program to harvests of individuals in another region,

we will get biased estimates of impact that likely overstate the potential for yield increases in the rest of the country.

Bias clouds our ability to see the impact of a program, either leaving us with no information or even worse off, as we may take inappropriate action based on wrong information. On top of that, we have just used resources that could have been better spent on programming. To eliminate these biases, and to determine that there is a *causal* link between a program and changes in outcomes that occur, organizations need a valid counterfactual. This brings us back to the *credible* principle.

RANDOMIZED CONTROL TRIALS

We discuss two groups of methods for generating credible impact: randomized control trials (RCTs) and quasi-experimental methods. As you will remember from Chapter 2, a counterfactual analysis is a comparison between what actually happened as the result of an intervention and what would have happened otherwise. For those unfamiliar with the concept, it may seem impossible to know the "otherwise." In our daily lives, we are rarely able to know what would have happened had we done things differently. But in research, we are able to design experiments that allow us to estimate with confidence what would have happened in the absence of an intervention and compare it to what actually happened. Conducting an impact evaluation with a strong estimation of the counterfactual helps avoid the biases just described, and there are several methods that allow us to do that.

RCTs are sometimes referred to as the "gold standard" in impact research[6] because, when appropriate and when designed and implemented properly, they successfully eliminate the biases discussed earlier. We want to put tremendous emphasis on the phrases "when appropriate" and "when designed and implemented properly." Just undertaking an RCT does not mean the study will be perfect, or "gold." There are certainly situations in which an RCT would be a bad idea and not worthy of the label "gold standard." And there are definitely poorly executed RCTs that do not live up to that label (indeed, this book's co-author Karlan previously co-wrote a book, *Failing in the Field*, containing many stories of mishaps in field research). The challenge, of course, is to know when an RCT is appropriate and how to execute one credibly.

First, let's talk more about what an RCT is. In an RCT, a large number of similar individuals (or households, communities, or other units) are randomly assigned to be in either a treatment group that receives an intervention or a control group that does not (or that receives a *placebo* or some other treatment). As long as the assignment is truly random and the sample size is large enough, it will generate two groups that are similar on average both in observable characteristics (such as gender, income, or ethnicity) and unobservable characteristics (like self-motivation or moral values). The only difference between the two groups will be that one will experience the program and the other will not.

Stratification can help ensure groups are similar on average for particularly important characteristics, but it is beyond the scope of this book. Stratification is a process by which one ensures that the randomization "worked," so to speak, by allocating the sample at predetermined proportions along certain observable characteristics, such as gender or age or income. One cannot stratify on everything of course, but one can setup the process such that treatment and control groups are similar along a set number of dimensions relevant to the intervention. See the Conclusion (Chapter 16) for further resources to learn about technical aspects such as stratification. Also note that organizations can verify the randomness of their group assignment by using observable information available prior to the study or data available at the end of the study as along as that information does not change over the study, or is easily recalled without bias (such as gender and marital status). The Dilbert cartoon below is a great example of how stratification could help avoid bad randomizations. At the risk of morphing E.B. White's famous line, humor is like a frog: dissecting it may help in understanding something, but you are then left with a bloody mess. Here, Dilbert always ends up with 9. Whatever other options exist never arrive. Stratification would most likely address this.

With two groups that are similar on average, one can measure the impact of a program by measuring the difference in outcomes over time between the group that received the program and the one that did not. Over the course of the study, the only difference between the two groups should be caused by the effects of the program.

When designing an RCT, or even deciding if it is feasible to conduct one, it is important to consider the potential validity of the analysis, which will depend on many factors, including the unit of randomization, the sample size, and the potential and mechanism for spillovers.

Unit of Randomization

The first consideration in thinking through the design of an RCT is the level at which you will randomly assign units to treatment and control groups. Typical choices include the individual, household, or community.

The unit of randomization should mirror how the program operates. If the intervention is implemented at the individual level—as vouchers for contraception would be, for instance—then the unit of randomization should be the individual. Other interventions are household-level interventions. Consider the example of Nutrition for All (NFA). In this program, health workers visit households, talk with them about their food choices, and provide supplements. It would be impossible to have one household member "in" the program and another one not. The unit of randomization can also be quite large. Some programs are implemented at the village level, and everyone in the village has access to the program. An evaluation investigating the impact of a rural electricity program, for example, might be randomized at the district level. Box 6.1 illustrates a range of example units of randomization.

The choice of the unit of randomization has to match the unit at which a program is implemented. The unit of randomization is an important factor in determining the sample size necessary for credible analysis and when considering possible indirect spillover effects from one individual or group to another.

Sample Size

A valid analysis requires a sample size large enough to create statistically similar treatment and control groups, on average, and to be able to distinguish "true" changes in outcomes from statistical noise with a reasonable probability. In some cases, a program's scale is too small to create large enough treatment and control groups. In other cases, the scale is large but there are not enough units of randomization. For example, a question like "What is the impact of opening up a country to free trade?" would be impossible to answer with an RCT. The unit of randomization is the country! Even if you could randomly assign free trade to different countries—and,

Box 6.1 UNITS OF RANDOMIZATION

- Providing contraception to women: individual-level intervention
- Distribution of bed nets to households: household-level intervention
- Subsidy for banking services or marketing of them to households: household-level intervention
- Teacher training program: school-level intervention
- Community-driven development grant program (a grant to a community typically accompanied by facilitation of community meetings to help the community decide how to spend the grant): community-level intervention
- Public radio campaign aiming to shift social norms on violence: the range-of-the-radio-coverage-level intervention
- Reform of countrywide legal procedures: country-level intervention (i.e., randomizing at the country-level is not viable as there are not enough countries and not enough control over country-level policy to implement such a strategy; however, if awareness of the reform is low, one could design an individual-level treatment in which people were made aware of the reform, to understand how it changes behavior)

logistically, you cannot—finding a group of observably similar countries to create valid treatment and control groups would be impossible. When an intervention is being implemented at the village level, randomization may require a large number of villages be included in the evaluation in order to create valid treatment and control groups.

Unfortunately, there is no magic number for a sample size that automatically makes a study valid. It depends on a number of factors: the unit of randomization, the type of analysis, and how similar groups are to each other, among other considerations. See, for example, *Running Randomized Evaluations,* by Rachel Glennerster and Kudzai Takavarasha (2013), or *Field Experiments* by Alan Gerber and Donald Green, for more in-depth discussions of these issues.

Spillovers

Indirect effects, also known as *spillovers* or *externalities*, refer to a program's effects on those whom the program does not directly target but who are nonetheless affected by the program. Failing to consider these indirect effects will bias the results of an impact evaluation.

For example, imagine an evaluation that randomly assigned village savings groups to treatment (those who receive financial literacy training) and control groups (those who do not). If there were treatment and control savings groups in the same village, some of the groups receiving the intervention might share lessons from the program with savings organizations in control groups. By raising financial literacy in the control group, this spillover would mute the apparent impact of the program, making it seem as if the program had less of an effect than it actually did. Consider an extreme version of this phenomena in which every treatment group, realizing the power of what they learned, immediately went to a control group and explained everything perfectly to them. A poorly designed study could ignore this spillover and erroneously declare the financial literacy trainings had no impact, when in fact the program had such a huge impact that it immediately spread to others.

To control for spillovers, researchers often change the unit of randomization to keep the treatment and control groups distant. In the financial literacy training example earlier, it would be wiser to randomize at the village level rather than the savings-group level. It is far less likely that someone would spread information about the financial literacy training to people in other villages than to people in one's own.

Some studies are designed to specifically measure the indirect effects of a program (especially health or education programs with potentially positive indirect effects). For example, when testing the impact of a deworming program in Western Kenya, economists Ted Miguel and Michael Kremer designed an evaluation that measured the program's effects on attendance (a key outcome) for control-group schools that happened to be located near treatment schools. Children from nearby schools play with one another, and worms can pass from child to dirt and then to other children—so reducing the prevalence of worms in one school could reduce prevalence more generally in the community. The economists found attendance in untreated schools increased, even though students had not directly received the deworming treatment, which suggested that spillovers existed for the program.[7] We will discuss this case in more detail in Part II of the book.

Organizations should have sufficient knowledge of program areas to describe potential spillover effects. Incorporating the measurement of these spillovers into research design, however, requires a combination of theory, data, and judgment. If you are not sure about design options for measuring these indirect effects, talk with an experienced researcher and see chapter 8 in *Running Randomized Evaluations* by Glennerster and Takavarasha.

QUASI-EXPERIMENTAL METHODS

In addition to RCTs, other methods can credibly measure the impact of programs if the right conditions are in place. These "quasi-experimental" methods do not set up the treatment and control groups beforehand through random assignment. Rather, researchers use different statistical techniques, explained briefly here, to build experimental groups.

Although quasi-experimental designs can be successful, they typically require many more assumptions than an RCT—such as a deep understanding of a program's selection process—in order to construct a valid counterfactual. They often require researchers with expert statistical and econometric analysis skills to crunch the numbers and assess the institutional facts. In many quasi-experimental studies we observe problematic designs, sample sizes that are too small, selection biases that likely determine entrance to a program, or other such issues. (Naturally, an RCT can also be poorly designed.) We highlight a few quasi-experimental methods here, but this is by no means an exhaustive discussion of the merits and pitfalls of quasi-experimental approaches.

Matching

With matching, researchers attempt to construct a comparison group that closely resembles those who participate in a program based on various observable characteristics. Common characteristics used in matching include basic demographic traits like gender, income, education, and age.

There are two different ways to create a counterfactual through matching methods. In *exact matching*, each program participant gets paired with someone who matches on age, sex, and other important characteristics, but who did not participate in the program. In *propensity score matching*, evaluators determine how likely someone is to participate in a program based on a set of characteristics and then assign a probability score to each person (participant and nonparticipant). Participants are then matched to nonparticipants with similar probabilities of participating. With program participants matched to similar individuals who did not participate, one can estimate the impact of a program by comparing the two individuals over time.

Inherently, this approach is only useful if the observable variables predict participation well. If participation is instead largely driven by unobservable characteristics, such as energy, drive, or passion, then a matching exercise will not get rid of the selection bias problem.

Quasi-Experimental Difference-in-Difference

The *"difference-in-difference" method* compares the outcomes of program participants and nonparticipants over time to measure impact. This method is often combined with matching. RCTs also often use difference-in-difference analysis since they can compare changes over time between treatment and control groups. In the quasi-experimental version, however, people are not *randomly assigned* to either participate in the program or not. Instead, changes over time for those who were *deliberately selected* to be a part of the program are compared with changes over time for those who were not. Creating a valid comparison group for this method requires data on a statistically representative group that did not participate in the program but for whom data over time are available.

A successful difference-in-difference analysis requires assuming that the treatment and control groups would have followed the same trajectory were it not for the program. For example, if researchers conducted an evaluation of a business training program and found that shopkeepers in the program started out poorer on average than those not in the program, they would need to assume that this initial difference in income did not influence the subsequent results of the evaluation (in other words, that the two sets of businesses would have grown roughly at the same rate if neither had participated in the program).

However, it is often hard to maintain the assumption that groups both in and out of a program would remain in similar circumstances in its absence. To overcome this problem, evaluators sometimes collect several rounds of data before the program starts to try to confirm that the overall trajectories of treatment and comparison groups are the same over time. This still does not mean, however, that the similarities will continue once the program starts.

Regression Discontinuity

Another method, *regression discontinuity analysis*, uses an existing eligibility cutoff for a program to help create treatment and control groups. The eligibility cutoffs for many programs, such as college admission or social welfare programs, are set in absolute terms, and individuals just above and just below the cutoff are often very similar. For example, a program offering food aid to those earning under $500 a year would accept those who earned $499 a year, but would not serve those who earned $501. Because there is likely little difference between those just over and under this line, those who just missed participating in the program may be able to serve as a counterfactual.

One challenge of using regression discontinuities to estimate program impact is deciding how to define the boundaries of the treatment and control groups. Are those who earn $515 similar enough to those just under the $500 threshold? What about those who earn $550? At what point do the differences become too large? Another challenge is that one often needs to sample a large number of people right around the cutoff to make a valid comparison, which is not always possible. A third challenge is accurate classification of individuals near the threshold. What if those with reported earnings just below $500 actually had earnings above $500 but figured out how to report a lower income, whereas those with reported incomes just above the $500 limit simply did not figure out how to do that? If "figuring out how to do that" is driven by a relevant but unobservable characteristic (such as motivation, persistence, or willingness to lie), this could lead to a critical bias—making those just above the threshold an invalid comparison group for those just below.

Last, even if it is done well, regression discontinuity only produces data on the impact of the program among people close to the cutoff, which may not reflect the full impact of the program for everyone it reaches. Those with very low incomes, for example, may experience different program effects from those at the top of the eligible income range. If so, regression discontinuity may not be very useful—or, it could be even more useful than a conventional RCT. If an organization is considering changing a program's eligibility threshold, for example, a study measuring the program's impact on people near the threshold could be far more valuable than one measuring the impact on everyone.[8]

Apart from RCTs and quasi-experimental methods, there are a couple of other credible approaches to measuring impact. We discuss these in the next section.

WHEN BEFORE-AND-AFTER COMPARISONS WORK

In Chapter 2, we explained the problems with simple before-and-after comparisons. These comparisons are essentially using "before" as the counterfactual, but "before" is almost always an entirely unsatisfying counterfactual. However, we can think of two instances when using preprogram measurements as the counterfactual may be useful. First, when the counterfactual can be deduced, which we call the *assumption-based counterfactual*, and, second, when the question is whether something did *not* work, rather than whether it *did* work, which we call the *shutdown rule*. We think these situations are rare, but they still merit discussion.

ASSUMPTION-BASED COUNTERFACTUAL

In rare cases, one can assess a program's impact on some outcomes by taking a deep look at the program context and deducing that a credible counterfactual for that outcome is the preintervention status of program participants. When this assumption is credible, an organization can measure its impact by comparing the outcome at the end of the program to what it was at the beginning. To make this assumption, the organization must be doing something that is entirely new in the program's geographic area and must be sure that that nothing apart from the program will influence program outcomes. These are big assumptions.

For example, if an organization is running a program that teaches people how to use chlorine to sanitize water properly, it may be possible to ascertain that this program is the only one in the area teaching this technique. If so, this organization can collect data immediately after the program ends on how individuals' knowledge changed after training and have some confidence that any changes reflect the impact of the program. Without anyone else in the region teaching chlorine-based sanitation, how else would people possibly gain that information in the short duration of the training? If the organization also knows that it is the only organization in the area that distributes chlorine, and no one would have access to new water sanitation strategies otherwise, it can also track its impact on chlorine usage and water quality without a counterfactual.

We refer to this as "assumption-based" counterfactual with a bit of tongue-in-cheek. This approach demands tremendous faith in one's ability to ascertain that nothing else could possibly have changed the outcome being measured other than the treatment. This requires a high level of local knowledge and full awareness of everything else going on in the program's setting. We rarely observe an evaluation where something is so truly new that an organization can make this argument.

And remember that this approach only applies to the immediate effect of a program. The minute one wants to know about *downstream* impacts—such as chlorine usage's impact on diarrhea, health, school attendance, or clean water usage in daily life—one cannot simply assume away the entirety of other possible influences on these outcomes. This faith-based approach is only good for immediate take-up of a practice. Note also that claiming to measure impact through these immediate outcomes is different from using immediate outcomes in monitoring as a measure of program uptake and engagement. For either use, however, organizations need to think carefully and critically about alternative explanations for outcomes.

SHUTDOWN OR REDESIGN RULE

The shutdown or redesign rule is an extreme rule that identifies situations of program failure but cannot be used to identify program success. Take a simple example. A program has designed a new solar power system for households. After rolling out the program and ensuring it is implemented as intended, a monitoring visit to the households found that no households were using the solar power system. This is a clear indication of failure. Thus, the choice is either to shutdown or redesign. But the opposite is not true. Think about the water chlorination example: seeing households use the water chlorination system does not mean success. For that, one needs a counterfactual: What would they have done otherwise? Perhaps there are other water chlorination systems available that are just as good. Or even better—meaning that the chlorination program was actually less effective than just leaving a household alone.

More conceptually, the shutdown or redesign rule states that for a program or policy to have an impact, some initial change *must* occur. If that initial change does not happen, then you do not need to measure impact: you know you had none.

A strong monitoring system helps organizations know whether to invoke the shutdown or redesign rule (and good feedback data can help if the decision is redesign rather than shutdown). For example, organizations can collect data on a short-term outcome, such as adoption of a new teaching practice or beginning to use a newly introduced savings account. These are simple because one knows people started at zero and usage could not go down. Data that do not start at zero are trickier. For example, using the shutdown rule for short-run change in income or consumption is a bad idea. Take a program that aims to increase short-run income. If income does not rise immediately, does this mean the program failed? Maybe not. Maybe there are bad economic times, or maybe there was a flood or a drought or something else bad, but not quite so observable. In that case, flat income may actually be a success. This is essentially back to the counterfactual problem. What makes the adoption-of-something-new situation different is that one cannot have negative adoption of something previously. Adoption started at zero, and it cannot go down. Thus continuation of no adoption is actually a bad thing. There is no counterfactual that could have a negative impact on adoption.

Let's return to our water chlorination example. In this case, the shutdown rule could apply if, in conducting a single round of data collection, it turns out that not a single household chlorinated its water. The data indicate that the program is clearly not working and should be shut down or redesigned.

Ruling out failure does not prove success, however. Imagine chlorine is being used. This could have happened for myriad reasons, not just because of the program. Thus, observing no chlorine use means the organization failed, but observing chlorine use does not mean it succeeded. Ruling out total failure is a good thing, though. It is better than marching on even if you are headed nowhere!

ACTIONABLE

We have spent a lot of time on creating a credible evaluation of impact. But creating a credible evaluation that is not actionable is pointless. An actionable impact evaluation must deliver information about a program that the organization or outside stakeholders are willing and able to use. At a minimum, this means answering the basic question of whether the program is effective enough that it should continue and delivering that answer in a timely enough fashion that someone uses the information. But, as we discussed with monitoring, actionability is more than just good intent. An organization should specify ahead of time what action it will take based on evaluation findings, have the resources to take this action, and have the commitment to do so.

An impact evaluation is only actionable if someone actually uses the results to make decisions about the program or others that are similar. Before investing in an impact evaluation, an organization needs to consider the true purpose of the evaluation: does the organization intend to *learn* from the results and potentially change its program, or is the evaluation simply an exercise to *prove* effectiveness? For example, if an evaluation showed the program was ineffective, would the implementing organization redesign the program or even end it? Or would it file the report away and continue doing what it was doing?

In some cases, programs do use impact evaluations to inform major actions and make tough choices. For example, this book's co-author Mary Kay Gugerty and Michael Kremer evaluated a program in Kenya run by International Child Support (ICS) that gave assistance to women's agriculture groups through a standardized package of training, seeds, and tools.[9] When the evaluation showed little effect on agricultural production,

ICS substantially revised its program, allowing groups to customize the packages of assistance and investing more in the program's agricultural training component.

The commitment to make decisions based on evaluation results should not be undertaken lightly. It requires the resources to implement resulting actions and the ability to generate organizational acceptance of potentially large changes. Finding additional funding to act on an evaluation can be difficult, whether for redesigning an ineffective program or scaling one that has proved its worth. Moreover, significant time and resources have likely been spent to run the program as it is, donors are likely invested in it, and managers may hesitate to change gears or scrap the program even if an evaluation suggests this is the responsible choice. Before undertaking an evaluation, an organization must be prepared to address these issues.

We recognize actionability is easy in theory but hard in practice. With all of the current emphasis on impact, many organizations conduct evaluations not because they consider them an organizational priority, but rather because of perceived or real pressure from donors. Changing this culture will be a long haul, but, depending on funder flexibility and responsiveness, organizations may be able to openly discuss which monitoring and evaluation activities will ultimately serve the dual purposes of learning and promoting accountability.

Once an organization has made the commitment to evaluate, three additional steps can increase the actionability of the evaluation:

First, use evaluation design to generate information on how to optimally run a program. Evaluations can demonstrate which program components are necessary to make the intended impact and which are not, or whether multiple program components have additive effects. For example, does offering an incentive *and* information result in better outcomes than just information? Conducting this kind of operational impact evaluation helps organizations use data to improve their programs, rather than to merely decide whether to implement them or not.

Second, create a plan to use the results. Having a plan can unlock resources that allow effective programs to scale or promising programs to improve. Ideally, the development of these plans should involve the stakeholders—such as potential partners, donors, or policy-makers—who can provide resources or enabling conditions to scale up if a program works.

Third, time the evaluation to correspond with the project cycle. This can be key to turning results into action because it introduces data into the decision-making process when the decision to expand, scrap, or refine a program would naturally be made. In our earlier *Balsakhi* evaluation example, researchers worked closely with the partner organization, Pratham, to evaluate the program just before expanding it to other cities. When the results came out, Pratham was able to expand with confidence that the program had a positive impact and was cost-effective.

RESPONSIBLE

Given the high cost of collecting and analyzing data, organizations have to weigh the costs and benefits of conducting an impact evaluation against those of *not* doing the evaluation. These costs and benefits have ethical and social components, in addition to a clear monetary consideration. Our discussion here covers how these issues relate to RCTs, although the issues are relevant for other impact evaluation methods as well.

WEIGHING THE COSTS AND BENEFITS

Two concerns are often raised about RCTs: price and ethics.

Many argue that RCTs (and other rigorous methods of impact evaluation) are too expensive to undertake. There are three points to remember. First, an RCT typically is not what costs money; collecting data drives costs, particularly if data collection requires surveys of individuals and households. Non-randomized studies often collect extensive data, too; the randomization is not the costly part. Second, many RCTs use data that are not costly to collect. In such a case, the RCT could be fast and cheap. Again, the "randomization" itself is not what drives costs; the data are. Third, while an RCT can have a hefty price tag, the question should not be how much it costs, but how much it costs relative to its expected benefits—and relative to the same tradeoff for other potential uses of the funds.

Researching the impact of an intervention has a range of potential benefits, all of which should be considered before undertaking an evaluation. First and foremost, information on program effectiveness gained from an impact evaluation provides critical information to organizations and donors on whether it is worth continuing to implement or fund a program. Results also reveal which elements of a program are working as intended, which can help organizations learn how to optimize their program. Finally, the knowledge gained from a well-designed impact evaluation provides useful knowledge to policy-makers or other organizations—that is, as long as it fills an important knowledge gap.

That knowledge gap has a technical name: *equipoise*. The principle of equipoise means that there is real uncertainty about whether or not a given intervention works. This uncertainty provides the basis for conducting an impact evaluation—the knowledge gained from such an evaluation justifies the cost of research. The flip side is important to remember: equipoise also means that it would be *irresponsible* to conduct an impact evaluation before taking a full look at the evidence that already exists. Previous research might have already validated or disproved the hypothesis of a study. In international development, a good place to start is the website of an organization called 3ie, which contains a searchable database of more than 600 impact evaluations and systematic reviews. Also check out the websites of organizations that regularly generate evidence, such as MIT's J-PAL (www.povertyactionlab.org) and IPA (www.poverty-action.org), as these websites house information about completed and ongoing evaluations, as well as policy memos that help make sense of the evidence. The Cochrane Iniative provides systematic review of health interventions, and the Campbell Collaboration summarizes studies across a range of social policy interventions.

If evidence about the impact of a program does not exist, the *responsible* principle means that the organization should consider pursuing an impact evaluation if it can responsibly commit the resources to do so, and the *credible*, *actionable*, and *transportable* principles are met. If the knowledge gap is large and the evidence relevant to many programs, the potential benefits of running such an evaluation may be huge. And, in these cases, *not* running an impact evaluation when these principles are satisfied carries deep social costs. Organizations may continue to run suboptimal programs, failing to make the best use of their resources. This has a clear future social cost: people in the future are potentially less well off than they could be with an alternate allocation of resources. If knowledge about the impact of the program already exists (even if it has not been fully disseminated) the potential benefits of an impact evaluation—to the organization, donors, or the outside world—are greatly reduced.

Under the *responsible* principle, an impact evaluation should also generate knowledge that benefits a broader set of programs. If an evaluation is so specific that it will not have any implications for other programs, then it may not be a responsible use of resources. We will discuss this in the context of the *transportable* principle later.

Ethics is the second concern often raised about RCTs. The common argument centers around "denying treatment" to individuals in a control group.

We have four responses to consider. First, though it comes from a place of concern for program participants, this argument assumes that we know how well an intervention works. The idea that it is unethical to "withhold" treatment assumes that we know the answer to the impact question already. But if we knew how well a program worked, we would not have to evaluate it in the first place. Remember that our principle of equipoise tell us that we should not engage in impact evaluation if sufficient evidence of impact already exists. What if the treatment has no impact? Or worse yet, what if the intervention has in theory some risk of making people worse off (if nothing more, perhaps it is ineffective and thus a waste of money and time that could be spent on other ideas that do work)? Perhaps the ethical concern should be for the treatment group, not the control. Why are they being provided a treatment that may or may not work, and may even make them worse off? The ethical argument regarding the control group requires knowing the answer to the question, and if that answer were already known then indeed the study would be wrong to do. But rarely is that the case.

Second, the idea that *randomization* reduces the number of people who receive treatment is also almost always unfounded. Nearly every program has limited resources and thus cannot serve everyone it would like. Inevitably, organizations must make tough choices about where to implement programs; it is impossible to reach everyone. The question to ask is not whether randomization holds back treatment from some, but whether fewer people received treatment in total because of the randomization. In most cases, the answer is no. All that differs is how those people were chosen, not the number of people who received a service.

Third, in some cases, randomization is actually a more equitable and fair way to allocate resources. In fact, some allocations are deliberately randomized for reasons of politics and transparency, and researchers merely discover the situation and study it. One excellent example of this is an evaluation of a school voucher program in Colombia, in which the government used lotteries to distribute vouchers that partially covered the cost of private secondary school for students who maintained satisfactory academic progress.[10] Researchers had nothing to do with the randomization.

Fourth, concerns about the ethical "cost" of control groups not receiving a service do not consider the people in the future who could be helped (or not harmed, if the program is bad). Ignoring future people could, ironically, lead those arguing against an evaluation on ethical grounds to actually do harm, not good. Imagine a simple situation. There is some program that provides a small but well-studied benefit to participants. For the same amount of money, a new program promises to double the per-participant impact for every dollar spent. A study is set up in which 2,000 eligible people will be randomly assigned to treatment (the new program) and control (the old program). The concern may arise that it would be unethical to withhold the new service from the 1,000 individuals in the control group because the new program is believed to be twice as good! But note that we said it is *believed* to be twice as good. What if the hopes are wrong, and the new program does not work? Now fast-forward a few years. Without the evaluation, the new program is rolled out to millions of people. Those millions are now worse off. They would have preferred the old program, which was known to generate some benefit. While this hypothetical contains many unknowns, it illustrates the importance of thinking of the potential long-run social benefits of discovering which policies and programs actually work.

Psychology has a lot to offer to help understand why these ethics issues are often raised. The control group is highly emotionally salient to us since we can see them and talk with them today, whereas the future lives that might benefit from increased knowledge are more abstract and thus less salient. But should we really let the emotional salience of a group influence our perceived ethics? This would be putting emotion in front of analytics when thinking through the ethical tradeoffs.

The biggest social cost to consider when deciding whether to do an RCT is the opportunity cost of the funds spent on the evaluation itself. These funds have up-front and real opportunity costs for organizations and potential beneficiaries. Money spent on an evaluation that is not credible could be used instead to deliver more of the program being evaluated (or some other program). Thus the money spent on this noncredible evaluation rather than the program itself is a social loss (as long as the alternative use of funds would have generated *some* benefit to society). Evaluations need to produce *credible* results and produce knowledge that does not already exist. Note that this point can be made about any type of evaluation, not just RCTs. And it gets at the heart of our point about costs and benefits. Any money spent on research or evaluation (or monitoring, for that matter) could be spent helping people instead, so make sure that an evaluation is filling an important knowledge gap or serves an important role for management and accountability. This means credibly answering questions and using the results to take action.

Conducting a responsible impact evaluation requires weighing the monetary costs of the evaluation against the potential benefits of having a real measure of impact, as well as against the cost of not measuring impact. According to the responsible principle, if evidence is lacking on the impact of their programs, organizations have an obligation to measure whether their programs are actually working. It is irresponsible to spend valuable resources on programs that may not be working. But, just as importantly, organizations (and donors) have an obligation *not* to spend money on an impact evaluation if there is already evidence that the program works.

REDUCING THE COSTS OF IMPACT EVALUATION

So far in our discussion of responsibility we have focused on understanding the opportunity costs and the true benefits of impact evaluation so that we can appropriately weigh the tradeoffs of evaluating. But there are ways to reduce the direct costs of evaluation as well. Because data collection is laborious and time-consuming, a major barrier to the widespread use of RCTs (and other rigorous evaluation methods) has been their high cost. Indeed, some RCTs of large-scale government programs can cost millions of dollars. However, researchers have found ways to conduct RCTs at a lower cost. One approach is to introduce random assignment to new initiatives as part of program rollout. This can involve randomly assigning some individuals to a program's old approach (for example, providing subsidized fertilizer to farmers) versus a new model that the service provider is testing (such as providing that fertilizer for free).

Another way of conducting low-cost RCTs is by using existing administrative data to measure key endline outcomes instead of collecting original data through surveys. Since the vast majority of the costs of an impact evaluation are survey costs, avoiding these can save a lot of money. For example, researchers conducted a credible three-year RCT of a New York City teacher incentive program for just $50,000 by measuring study outcomes using state test scores. The city already collected the scores, which eliminated the need for additional (and costly) endline data collection. After the study found that the program produced no effect on student achievement, attendance, graduation rates, behavior, or GPA, the city ended the program.[11] Evaluations like this show it is possible to create valuable evidence without breaking the bank.

Finally, some programs—such as marketing a savings product or distributing bednets—can be randomized at the individual level, which imparts high statistical power at relatively low cost (though, as noted earlier, one should be sure to manage spillovers when designing this type of evaluation). Apart from the approaches described earlier, quasi-experimental methods can be less expensive than RCTs when they use existing data to identify a comparison group, steering clear of expensive baseline survey exercises. In short, while the cost of an impact evaluation is an important factor in deciding whether it is a good fit, expectations about price alone should not dissuade organizations from running an impact evaluation.

In addition to weighing social and monetary benefits and costs, impact evaluations should generate evidence that is helpful to other organizations and policy-makers. This is the focus of the transportability principle, which we will explore next.

TRANSPORTABLE

THINGS GOT REALLY INTERESTING WHEN THE STATISTICIAN STARTED DOING WARD ROUNDS.

Credit: © Hilda Bastian

Some argue that every program operates in a unique context and that the fact that a program works well in one context does not ever imply it will work in another. That is true to some extent. Just because a job training program worked well in Bangladesh, the Government of Peru should not blindly implement the same program.

The cartoon above with the patient asking "Does it work?" makes this point in a different context: asking "does it work" can be open to many interpretations. For an evaluation to really be helpful, we need to understand what the "it" is that we are evaluating. That means having a theory of change and data to investigate that theory of change. That helps us understand why things are working. Understanding the *why* is critical for figuring out when lessons from one place can be helpful in others.

The ability to apply evidence to other contexts requires more than an estimate of impact. It requires an understanding of *why* a program worked and the conditions that need to be in place to get the same result. The *transportable* principle, or the extent to which evaluation results can be used in other settings and contexts, begins with a clear theory of change and an evaluation design that measures steps along that theory of change. Note that transportability also requires strong monitoring systems. A clear theory of change lays out the essential components of the program, while monitoring data tell whether the program is being implemented as intended. Suppose an organization conducts a credible impact evaluation with high-quality data and analysis and finds no evidence of impact. Remember our formula from Chapter 4: A × B = Social Impact, where A is effective and efficient implementation and B is good ideas. Without measuring both A and B, the organization cannot tell from the evaluation whether the results are due to poor implementation (A) or bad ideas (B)—a distinction that really matters, as we will see later.

The degree of transportability helps determine which programs ought to be scaled and where. The health sector has many clear examples. Since many treatments are effective regardless of context (such as vaccines), once an effective treatment has been found, it can be scaled to other areas with the expectation of similar outcomes.

Transportability can be more nuanced, though, requiring careful testing of a model before a program can be scaled up. For example, the design of the TCAI program in Ghana mentioned at the beginning of the chapter—which provides primary school students with remedial education in reading and math, in keeping with the *Balsakhi* model—was informed by three other evaluations, two in India and one in Kenya. All three evaluations had a clear theory of change and carried a similar message that teaching to the level of the child is what makes an effective program. Still, after using lessons from these three programs, the TCAI program encountered implementation challenges that limited its effectiveness. This is common in scale-ups. But with clear data on both implementation and impact (and evidence on impact from three other evaluations), the Ghanaian government was able to make the decision that it was worth working to fine-tune the model to optimize the program and deliver the largest impact.[12]

Transportability requires both theory and data. First, by having a theory as to why a program works, ideally with tests of that theory built into the evaluation, one can then understand the conditions under which the program will or will not work. A robust theory incorporates as much detail as possible and is thus better able to predict whether the program will work in other settings. Naturally, some ideas will have more legs, while others will be more resistant to contextual variations.

A second, complementary approach to transportability is replication in a variety of contexts, institutional frameworks, economic conditions, and sociopolitical environments. An example of this is a six-country study conducted by IPA on a multifaceted approach to building income for the ultra-poor.[13] The intervention was replicated in six countries (Ethiopia, Ghana, Honduras, India, Pakistan, and Peru) after seeing early results from an evaluation in Bangladesh.[14] Many factors differ across these seven sites, yet the studies showed fairly similar results in terms of benefits (higher consumption) relative to costs. The one site, Honduras, that sadly did not have benefits higher than costs was able to show with monitoring data that this was due to specific implementation problems, and thus the evaluation still supports the theory of change for the programs.

The goal of the *transportable* principle is to make sure that all impact evaluations generate evidence that will help others design or invest in more effective programs, rather than just providing a stamp of approval for a single program. In that way, policy-makers will have better evidence with which to design and implement more effective programs in the future.

DECISION TIME

Measuring impact is not always easy, possible, or necessary. As we explored earlier, sometimes the unit of treatment is simply too big to randomize, while, at other times, the sample is too small to allow for a valid analysis. Sometimes, the timing is not right for an impact evaluation. In other cases, the intervention itself is already tried and proven and no knowledge gap exists. For example, we would not recommend conducting more tests on the effectiveness of the measles vaccine as its efficacy is already well-established and documented.

For these reasons, some organizations will not be able to estimate the impact of their programs, nor will they need to do so. At first, it might seem irresponsible not to even try to find out the impact of a program. However, trying to measure impact when it is not appropriate will result in inaccurate estimates of program effectiveness and will waste valuable resources if evidence already exists. An insistent focus on measuring impact in these cases can be costly, both in terms of money spent collecting data and time that staff could have spent implementing programs.

When deciding whether an impact evaluation makes sense, donors and nonprofits should begin by thinking about whether or not an impact evaluation would meet the CART criteria. A good starting point is to ask several key questions:

1. Are we able to credibly estimate the counterfactual? (Would the evaluation be credible?)
2. Are we committed to using the results, whether they are positive or negative, and do we have the resources to do so? Is the timing right? (Would the evaluation be actionable?)
3. Do the benefits of impact evaluation outweigh the costs? Would this evaluation add something new to the available evidence? (Would the evaluation be responsible?)
4. Would the evaluation produce useful evidence for others? (Would the evaluation be transportable?)

If organizations can answer "yes" to these questions, they may be ready for an impact evaluation. There are many more questions that need to be answered when implementing an impact evaluation: How can an organization create a credible evaluation design? What are key elements of an effective survey team? How long will it take? How should data analysis be conducted? For the answers to these questions, we recommend reading *Running Randomized Evaluations: A Practical Guide* by Rachel Glennerster and Kudzai Takavarasha, *Field Experiments* by Alan Gerber and Donald Green, and *Impact Evaluation in Practice* by Paul Gertler, Sebastian Martinez, Patrick Premand, Laura B. Rawlings, and Christel M. J. Vermeersh. These resources will help answer practical questions all the way from design to data analysis.

If the answer to any of the preceding questions was "no," impact evaluation may not be appropriate for the program at this time. In that case, organizations should focus on developing monitoring systems that help them learn about how to best implement programming. The previous chapter explains how.

We can summarize our arguments about the timing of impact evaluation with a simple decision tree. When organizations are still tinkering with program design or figuring out implementation, clearly the timing is not right for impact evaluation. Organizations need to develop a theory of change, test it, and gather solid financial, activity tracking, targeting,

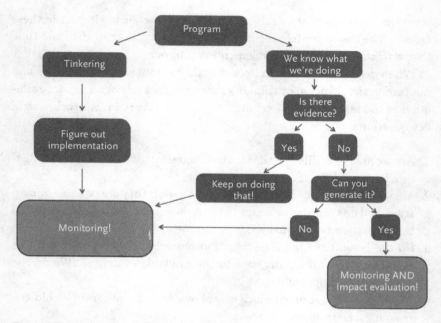

Figure 6.1 Decision tree for monitoring and impact evaluation

engagement, and feedback data until they are sure the program is running as intended. We elaborated this framework for monitoring with the CART principles in Chapter 5.

Once an organization is sure its program is operating smoothly, it is time to consider impact evaluation. As we discussed earlier, the organization should then ask whether evidence about its work already exists, whether it can gather the evidence credibly, whether it is willing to take action based on the results, whether an evaluation represents a responsible use of resources, and if the results will be transportable for others. This set of questions will help ensure that organizations take the appropriate approach to evaluating impact (Figure 6.1).

CONCLUSION

We have outlined the common biases in impact evaluation and explored why the CART principles are important. The CART principles not only guide organizations and donors on how to arrive at sound estimates of program impact, but they also increase the likelihood that implementing organizations will use the results and that others can apply them, too. And because the responsibility principle emphasizes conducting evaluations only when the circumstances are right, these principles encourage the creation of more valuable evidence to guide policy decisions.

We also explained that while impact evaluations have many benefits, they are not a right fit for all programs or organizations. To generate credible results, an impact evaluation should be conducted at an appropriate point in the project cycle, such as when an organization wants to pilot a new intervention that has been validated in practice. In addition, to be a good use of resources, the anticipated results must also be relevant to either an organization's future plans or a broader unanswered question in the organization's field of work. We recognize that many projects in the world do not meet these criteria. If impact evaluation is not the right choice, a great deal of learning can also happen through monitoring.

CHAPTER 7

Collecting High-Quality Data

So far, we have explored common monitoring and evaluation challenges and discussed how the CART principles (Credible, Actionable, Responsible, and Transportable data) help design high quality systems for decision-making and learning. But we have left out an essential piece of monitoring and impact evaluation: the data collection itself. Even the best-designed monitoring and evaluation systems will collapse without high quality data underpinning them.

High quality data are critical for credibility, the "C" in CART. And credible data are the lynchpin of the CART principles: without the "C" one really cannot have the "A" (why would an organization want to take action based on bad data?), the "R" (it sure would be irresponsible to spend money on bad data), and the "T" (why rely on bad data to make recommendations elsewhere?). So, without the "C," there is not even really the "ART."

Credibility requires both high-quality data and appropriate analysis. We have already addressed data analysis in detail: we focused on how to appropriately use monitoring data for accountability, learning, and improvement in Chapter 5; and we covered the essentials of conducting appropriate impact analysis in Chapter 6. In this chapter, we focus on collecting high-quality data for both purposes.

High-quality data need to be both valid and reliable. These characteristics matter for both monitoring and evaluation data: from regularly tracking program activities, gathering participant feedback, and collecting administrative data, to conducting an evaluation that measures changes over time.

Collecting high-quality data is not easy; many opportunities exist for data to go bad. These opportunities can emerge from errors in indicator design, translation, collection, management, or data entry—the list goes on and on. But the good news is that with some thought, careful planning, and sound management, organizations can minimize errors and increase their chances of collecting high-quality data.

This chapter works through the process of collecting high-quality data from start to finish. Beginning with the theory of change, we walk through how to strive for valid and reliable indicators. Then we go into some of the challenges of collecting high-quality data, such as dealing with measurement bias and measurement error. We suggest solutions to these challenges and identify where to find the data you need. We conclude with some thoughts on how to apply the *responsible* principle when deciding how much high-quality data is worth.

CHARACTERISTICS OF HIGH QUALITY DATA

We have covered how to use the theory of change to specify a project's key components (its activities, outputs, and outcomes), how they interact to produce the desired change, and the assumptions that must be true for that change to emerge. Developing a theory of change helps organizations to identify what they should measure—the most essential elements of the program, the most critical assumptions for program success, and opportunities for improvement—and choose which of these they can measure responsibly. These concepts apply to both quantitative and qualitative data collection efforts.

Once an organization has identified what it wants to measure, collecting high-quality data requires defining the concept an organization is trying to measure and the indicator or metric used to measure it. The first step is making sure that the concepts the organization wants to measure—the outputs, outcomes, and activities of interest—are clearly and precisely defined.

What do we mean by clearly defined? We mean that the concept is sufficiently and precisely specified so that one can construct clear metrics to measure it. Think back to Nutrition for All (NFA)'s key outcomes from Chapter 3. One of these outcomes is that "families adopt improved nutrition practices." But what exactly does "improved nutrition practices" mean, and how would NFA measure it? To measure this concept, NFA must detail which specific nutrition practices it considers "improved." Similarly, the organization must define what it means by "adopt." Is a practice adopted if it is practiced at least 50% of the time? Or must it be practiced 100% of the time to count? What if the practice is partially or imperfectly implemented? Clearly defining a concept like this is the first step in measuring it.

The second step in collecting high-quality data is developing a metric that will be used to measure the concept: *the indicator*. After an organization has defined what concepts to measure, it is ready to think about *how* it will collect data on those concepts. For example, if one component of NFA's desired nutrition practices is the consumption of green vegetables, then one indicator for measuring good nutritional practices may be, "How many dinners in the past seven days included green vegetables?"

High-quality indicators need to be both valid and reliable, criteria we introduced earlier in our discussion of the *credible* principle. This means that organizations can trust the data they collect because the data consistently provide accurate answers.

Validity typically refers to whether an indicator does a good job measuring what it is intended to measure. This is why it is so important to define concepts for measurement clearly and precisely; if organizations are not clear on what they are measuring, it will be hard to get a good measure for it! We will discuss two types of validity: construct and criterion validity. Criterion validity is often further broken down into concurrent validity and predictive validity. See Box 7.1 for definitions of construct and criterion validity.

To get a better sense of what validity means, let's look at three examples: one simple, one more complicated, and one downright hard. First, the simple one. Say an organization is measuring the impact of a job training program that seeks to increase employment rates for unemployed youth. The outcome is the percentage of trainees who currently have full-time employment. One obviously valid indicator is simply whether the person has been employed in a job for at least 35 hours per week for the past month.

Then consider the somewhat more complicated case of NFA's program: the organization's intended outcome is improved nutritional status in an area where malnutrition and stunting are common. Nutritional status can be measured in many ways. NFA measures whether children are underweight by using their weight-for-age, a good measure of moderate malnutrition. Being underweight is a fairly good proxy for whether or not a child has poor nutrition, but it is not a perfect measure. A child may be growing and maintaining expected weight but could still have other nutritional deficiencies.

Finally, consider this hard case. Suppose a program purports to increase the cohesion in a community (its "social capital"). How does one measure that? One option, from the General Social Survey,[1] is a qualitative question encoded into a scale from 1 to 5: "Do you think most people would try to take advantage of you if they got a chance, or would they try to be fair?" If people's belief in

---

Box 7.1

Construct Validity: An indicator captures the essence of the concept one is seeking to measure (the output or outcome).
Criterion Validity: The extent to which an indicator is a good predictor of an outcome, whether contemporaneous or in the future.

the good intentions of others is closely related to cohesion, then this would be a valid measure. But what if one was concerned that these beliefs did not really measure cohesion well (or that people might not answer honestly)? In that case, a more complicated but possibly more valid measure would ask people to demonstrate action based on their beliefs. One could play laboratory games with people in the field, such as giving people a small amount of cash and asking them to make contributions that would go to a community public good. In either case, measures of more complicated concepts such as community cohesion are often more speculative and require significant work to validate. To validate such an indicator, one can ask whether it accurately predicts some "real" behavior in the world. For example, in Peru, "trustworthy" behavior in a laboratory game played by microcredit borrowers successfully predicted repayment of loans a year later, suggesting that trust games are a good indicator of trustworthiness.[2] This form of validity sometimes goes by the name of *criterion validity*, meaning that the indicator is a good predictor of actual behavior.

Credit: © Hilda Bastian

Criterion validity can take two forms: concurrent and predictive validity. Concurrent validity exists when an indicator produces data consistent with closely related indicators. In the nutrition example above, we would expect all four of the indicators to be low when a child is malnourished. Predictive validity exists when an indicator is a good predictor of a future behavior, such as the trust game described earlier.

The idea of construct validity is crucial for much social science–based monitoring and evaluation work where generally accepted and validated indicators for concepts often do not exist. Researchers and evaluation experts often distinguish additional forms of validity as well. Content validity implies that an indicator (or set of indicators) measures the full range of a concept's meaning. Consider the NFA example again. A key targeting indicator for the organization is nutritional status or malnutrition (in an impact evaluation, improved nutritional status would also be a desired impact). There are two main types of malnutrition: protein energy malnutrition (generally characterized by symptoms such as stunting, wasting, or low weight-for-age) and micronutrient malnutrition (low levels of iron, vitamin A, and other key minerals). These different afflictions present varying symptoms.[3] A set of measures for malnutrition with full content validity would need to capture all these symptoms, which would require NFA to collect data on three or four indicators of malnutrition.

The point is that indicators should be a complete measure of the concept they are measuring (construct validity), related indicators should move in the same direction (criterion and concurrent validity), and indicators should be predictive of actual behavior (criterion and predictive validity).

Once we have a valid measure (or set of measures), we need to consider whether it is also *reliable* (Box 7.2) To see the difference, let's return to our height-for-age example. To get the height-for-age measurement, we need both a child's height and a child's age. We might consider age to be easy data to get, but in some communities, birth dates may not be precisely recorded. For younger children, being off by a month might matter. What about height? All we need is a tape measure, right? But consider what might

---

Box 7.2

Reliable: Data are consistently generated. In other words, the data collection procedure does not introduce randomness or bias into the process.

---

happen with a large number of data collectors traveling around to measure children's height. Some might have smaller children lie down to be measured; others may have them stand up. Enumerators may struggle to get a child to hold still and may end up just guessing his or her height by holding the tape measure near the child. If children are mismeasured, they may be incorrectly classified as stunted or not. Because the tape measure is not being consistently used, the measurements generated are not reliable—that is to say, they are not consistent.

Survey questions and monitoring indicators are a kind of instrument, just like a scale or a tape measure. They both pose large reliability challenges. First, the survey question or indicator has to be a good measure of the concept, as we noted earlier with our question on community cohesion. Then, it has to be asked the same way each time, and it must be specific enough that each respondent interprets it in the same way. Staff training is critical for producing reliable data. If each surveyor or data collector interprets questions and indicators differently, then each may be introducing his or her own special bias into the data collection process. Suppose in the community cohesion question some surveyors ask: "Don't you think most people would try to take advantage of you if they got a chance?" while others ask: "Don't you think most people would try to be fair with you, or would they take advantage of you if they got a chance?" These are nearly identical questions, but one emphasizes fairness and the other emphasizes the potential for being taken advantage of. They will not produce consistent measures of community cohesion. Naturally, reliability lies on a spectrum: there is no avoiding some inconsistency and noise in data collection procedures like surveys. The goal is to minimize this bias through good instruments and careful training of staff and enumerators.

Both validity and reliability are essential for generating high-quality, credible data. Indicator validity is fundamental to data credibility. Unless the indicators accurately capture the concept they aim to measure, all the reliability in the world does not matter. But unless each indicator captures that concept *reliably*, validity does not matter either. It is a two-way street.

So how does one assemble valid and reliable data? We break this discussion down into five parts: Avoiding Bias and Measurement Error, Primary Versus Secondary Data, Defining the Indicators, Finding Indicators, and Logistics for Collecting High-Quality Primary Data.

AVOIDING BIAS AND MEASUREMENT ERROR

Have you ever asked yourself why employers go to the trouble of drug testing employees rather than simply asking them "Have you taken any drugs in the past month?" Probably not, since it seems fairly obvious: a person who has used drugs has clear incentives to answer dishonestly. Even if they have not engaged in illegal behavior, respondents may not want to disclose information that is considered socially undesirable, so they provide answers that are false. This is why it can be very hard to measure anything "bad," like not practicing safe sex or engaging in corruption. If you ask politicians "Have you stolen any money this week?" they are highly unlikely to tell the truth.

High quality indicators not only capture the concept of interest on paper, but also collect truthful data in the field. Even indicators that look valid and reliable on paper can be tainted by bias during the data collection process, resulting in poor-quality data. *Measurement error* refers to differences between the value recorded through a measurement process and the true value. Measurement error can be purely random (some people estimate high, some people estimate low, with no pattern to their estimates), in which case the *average* answer is unbiased. *Measurement bias,* on the other hand, refers to *systematic* (i.e., not random) differences between the recorded value and the true answer. Measurement bias is particularly problematic because it results in data that are systematically incorrect, which can lead to decision-making based on flawed information.

Bias can come from a variety of sources and influence data in different ways (Box 7.3). Bias can influence both the *construct validity* and the *reliability* of an indicator.

A survey question may be biased with respect to its construct validity if the question systematically misses important elements or concepts. Suppose, for example, an organization wants to measure total household savings through a series of questions about ownership of financial accounts, balances, cash on hand, and even some informal savings options such as livestock and jewelry. In a developing country context, the inclusion of cash, livestock, and jewelry is important, but inevitably the estimate of savings will be systematically biased downward with respect to the true answer because some forms of savings will be missing. Many people

---

Box 7.3

Bias: In the context of data collection, bias is the systematic difference between how the average respondent answers a question and the true answer to that question

---

in developing countries save by lending money to someone else, or by buying farm inputs earlier than they need them, or by participating in informal savings clubs (called "ROSCAs," short for rotating savings and credit associations). In such a case, the survey questions put forward would result in savings estimates that are systematically biased downward; in other words, they would underestimate aggregate household savings. Similarly, responses to questions with high social undesirability bias, such as the corruption question posed earlier, would systematically underestimate the incidence of a socially undesirable behavior.

A survey question may be biased with respect to its reliability if, for example, the way the question was asked generated a bias. Suppose an organization wants to learn about mental health and stress, along with the use of financial services. If a survey first asks about loans and repayment of loans, and *then* asks about mental health and stress, the battery of questions about the loans may remind the respondent of stressful issues and lead to a higher reported stress. If the stress questions are asked beforehand, then maybe the survey would record a lower level of stress. Which is right? It is tough to say, as it depends on what the "true" stress level is. Regardless, if answers are volatile and predictable merely based on the timing of questions within the survey, they probably lack full reliability.

COMMON FORMS OF MEASUREMENT BIAS

Here, we highlight some of the most common forms of measurement bias organizations encounter when collecting data. These biases lead to systematic errors in the data by biasing answers in a certain direction. To create indicators that have construct validity in tough cases, like those posed earlier, one often has to be creative or carry out rigorous tests. One such approach is *list randomization*.[4]

Sometimes people change their behavior merely because they answered a question. For example, simply asking someone if he treats his water with chlorine may encourage him to go out and buy chlorine. This is called a *mere measurement effect*. Ironically, this can actually be a good thing: it could trigger a higher level of attention to positive behavior changes, helping people form a plan of action or stay on track toward a goal. However, it interferes with validity, and organizations should be aware of this potential bias when developing their data collection plan.

Anchoring, another source of bias, occurs when a person's answer is influenced by some number or concept accidently or purposefully put on top of the mind. The flow of a survey may unintentionally create "anchors" from one question to another, such as in our earlier example in which answers to questions about personal finance influence subsequent responses about stress. It is a bit tricky to write out a clear "prescription" for how to avoid such a bias, but it is something to consider. The best way is to think through how the ordering of questions may matter in a survey and to consult relevant literature.

Social desirability bias is the tendency of individuals to answer questions in what they perceive to be the socially desirable way. Individuals may hesitate to state negative opinions about the quality of a service because they do not want to offend or seem ungrateful. They may also report understanding a concept when they do not actually understand it. To address these biases, questions should be worded in a neutral manner and asked in a neutral way. And the incentives of individuals in responding to questions should be considered in question design.

A related issue is the *experimenter demand effect*, which occurs in the context of an experiment in which individuals, aware of their treatment assignment, answer in specific ways in order to please the experimenter. (This differs from a Hawthorne effect, in which participants actually *behave* differently, rather than merely answer a question differently. See Box 7.4 on Hawthorne effects and John Henry effects.) For example, in a business training program that teaches about recordkeeping, those in the treatment group may report that they are indeed keeping business records when in fact they are not. Eliminating this bias can be hard, and unfortunately one can often only speculate whether it is present or not. This risk can be minimized through neutral wording of survey questions and by concealing or deemphasizing the link between the person collecting the data and the organization using it.

COMMON CAUSES OF MEASUREMENT ERROR

We just discussed causes of measurement bias, which systematically shifts measurements in one direction or another. But responses can also be just plain "noisy," or plagued by random measurement error, which results in imprecise measurement. This is typically due to problems that arise in four main areas: the wording of questions, recall problems, translation issues, and management of data collection. Poorly or ambiguously worded questions or poor translation can result in questions that yield invalid and unreliable data. So can questions that ask people to remember things over an unreasonable amount of time. We discuss these three causes here. Unreliable data can also come from a lack of documented data collection procedures or inconsistent adherence to them, poor training

Box 7.4 ASIDE: HAWTHORNE AND JOHN HENRY EFFECTS

Some design issues apply only to evaluations, not monitoring. While they most directly relate to experimental design, they also affect the data collected and the causal inferences organizations draw from them.

The Hawthorne Effect occurs when people in the treatment group of an experimental study alter their behavior because they know they are in a study treatment group. For example, if an organization is evaluating the impact of teacher trainings on student skills, the teachers may perform better just because they know they are receiving the treatment. Their behavior will influence the results of the study, not because of the training itself but because they wanted to prove themselves in the experiment. Collecting data when the Hawthorne effect is present will yield data that systematically misstate the effect of the program or policy. To avoid this effect, researchers often try to separate the measurement from the intervention or policy. In our example, the organization would avoid telling teachers that they were being evaluated. This would reduce the likelihood that teachers temporarily perform better (to "prove" themselves) and yield a better estimate of the program's impact.

A related effect is the John Henry Effect. This occurs when members of the control group modify their behavior—either for the better or worse—because they know they are in a control group. Using the last example, teachers in the control group—who did not receive training—could perform better than normal to compete with the teachers who received the training. This would mute the real impact of the training program. It is possible to avoid this bias by ensuring that individuals are "blinded"—that they do not know their status in treatment or control.

An enumerator's knowledge of the study design or whether they are surveying someone in treatment or control can also influence how they behave toward respondents because they may consciously or subconsciously nudge respondents to answer or behave in a certain way. This observer bias can be avoided by blinding surveyors to the treatment assignment of the groups or individuals they are surveying and/or to the hypothesis of the research. Good enumerator training can also mitigate this bias.

of data collection staff, or inadequate supervision—anything that causes data collection staff to record the same responses in different ways. We discuss how training and logistics matter for collecting high quality data later on in this chapter.

Unclear Wording

Lack of precision and clarity in question wording leads to a range of interpretation by respondents. Unclear wording means that even though the same question is asked of respondents, they may in effect answer slightly different versions depending on how they interpret the question. A wider range for interpretation results in a wider variance in responses. Clarity in wording is essential for valid and reliable data.

Consider a simple example: an organization would like to ask a question that measures the number of times a person has sought medical attention in the past month. The concept the organization wants to measure is "care seeking." What are all the types of activities that could fall under this concept? Doctor and hospital visits? Homeopathy (hopefully not; if not sure why we say that, we suggest reading Ben Goldacre's book *Bad Science*.[5] Traditional healers? Massage therapists? What constitutes "care"? One visit? Multiple visits? Does it matter what happens at the visit? Depending on the context, the way this question is asked could yield many different answers.

Long Recall Period

Reliability can suffer when indicators ask respondents to remember detailed information over a long period of time (called the *look-back period*). An example would be an indicator that asks how much money a household spent on food in the past month. While the concept "amount of money spent on food in the last month" may be a valid measure of the concept on paper, it is unlikely to produce reliable data when used in the field. Without exact records on hand or a perfect memory, respondents are forced to guess, and the ability to make good guesses will not be the same for every person, every time. Appropriate look-back periods vary depending on the information being collected; consulting literature should reveal what is generally accepted.

Translation and Context

Poor or inconsistent translation and failure to account for cultural context can easily render the best-designed indicators invalid and unreliable. Many organizations do not translate their surveys into a local language, instead letting surveyors translate on the fly when they administer the survey to respondents. But if everyone is coming up with his or her own translation, it is unlikely that questions will be asked in the same way. Similarly, while many organizations translate their monitoring forms into a local language, if the translation is poor, the forms may not actually ask for the desired information. To ensure the indicators are reliable, it is necessary to translate the full survey or monitoring form into the other language, and then back-translate it to ensure that the translation is correct. We go into this in more detail later.

Failure to account for cultural or local nuances can also affect an indicator's reliability. Even a concept as seemingly simple as "household" may differ widely across cultures. In many Western cultures, the household denotes one's immediate family. In other cultures, the concept of "household" may include a variety of extended family members. So the answer to "How many people are in your household?" may vary widely depending on culture and context, and a question that doesn't clearly define household will produce unreliable data.

PRIMARY VERSUS SECONDARY DATA

When organizations think of monitoring and evaluation, they often think of collecting data themselves (or hiring external firms to do so). *Primary data* are data an organization collects for its own specific purpose, either monitoring or evaluation. Household surveys and focus group discussions are common types of primary data collection; so are administrative data collected by an organization. Data that come from outside sources are called *secondary data*. We most commonly think of government census data, tax records, or other information collected by government agencies as secondary data, but secondary sources include all data collected by anyone other than the organization itself. Both types of data have a role in monitoring and evaluation. They present different advantages and drawbacks in the data they provide and their implications for data quality.

Primary Data

Primary survey data give organizations insight into particular characteristics of the specific population they serve, from basic demographics and agricultural outputs, to knowledge and perceptions on a particular set of behaviors. Surveys can range from detailed household surveys conducted with thousands of individuals to targeted focus group discussions with just a few carefully selected individuals. Organizations often use survey data to explore specific issues facing program design or implementation or to assess a program's impact. When evaluating impact through a randomized evaluation, primary data collection is typically necessary in order to evaluate changes in the treated and comparison populations.

Primary data also include data collected through monitoring: activity tracking, take-up, and engagement data. Organizations collect administrative data on the day-to-day operation of a project, typically using it to monitor delivery of outputs and make operational decisions. Examples of administrative data can be found in the repayment records of microfinance institutions, health clinic records on the number and type of consultations, vaccination records, and student attendance at municipal schools. While administrative data are usually used for monitoring purposes, in some cases (and under certain circumstances), they can also be employed to measure impact.[6]

The main advantage of primary data collection is that it gives an organization control over the type of information it collects and its overall quality and credibility. Control over content can increase the actionability of data as well, as they are tailored to specific organizational needs. The biggest disadvantage—particularly for survey data—is that they are not cheap. Primary data collection requires time to develop and test collection methods, train staff in their use, and oversee data quality in the field. It also requires money to pay data collection staff. This implies high direct monetary costs, the cost of staff time, and the opportunity cost of foregone alternative uses for that time and money. The *responsible* principle reminds organizations to balance the full costs of primary data collection against the benefits it provides.

Secondary Data

While primary data are collected for an organization's unique needs, secondary data are collected by others to meet their own needs. Government agencies and organizations collect administrative data for use in administering their own programs. Examples include school test scores, hospital records, and financial data, among others. Under some circumstances, administrative data can be very useful for activity monitoring or evaluation. For an organization working in schools to provide free meals for low-income students, statistics about the demographic characteristics of the students—including how often they attend school, their parents' background, and some information about academic performance—may already be available. Other kinds of secondary data, such as demographic information from large-scale national surveys, can be extremely useful for informing the larger context surrounding a program.

The clear advantage of using this information is that it is far cheaper and easier for an organization than collecting primary data—an organization does not have to design a survey or pay a whole survey team to gather the information. However, organizations should confirm the accuracy of secondary information before using it. Statistical departments in many countries are severely underfunded and understaffed, leading to serious concerns over the reliability and accuracy of administrative data.[7] For instance, a recent study by Justin Sandefur and Amanda Glassman found that official administrative data in African countries inflate school enrollment by 3.1 percentage points on average. In Kenya, the gap between official figures and those from a household survey was a staggering 21.4 percentage points. While administrative data present many advantages, such data should be carefully assessed for quality before being incorporated into a data collection plan.[8,9]

DEFINING THE INDICATORS

There is no clear formula for defining valid and reliable indicators. Clearly defined *concepts* are the starting point. Organizations must then narrow these concepts to their key aspects that can be measured (observed, counted, and analyzed) and described by indicators. When a concept is clearly and narrowly defined, indicators will be more valid measures of the concept. To deliver high quality data, indicators should be specific, time-bound, and feasible to collect. They should also be collected with a frequency that corresponds to the concept they intend to measure. In addition to validity and reliability, several additional indicator characteristics are important for ensuring quality data.

Specific

An indicator should be specific enough to measure the concept it aims to measure and *only* that specific concept. We have already talked about how concepts such as "health" need to be defined more narrowly. Specificity also means avoiding "double-barreled" questions that contain two distinct metrics, such as "Please rate the level of quality and convenience on a scale of 1–5." (That question combines two concepts: quality *and* convenience.)

And it means avoiding questions that require respondents to choose one of two (or more) options, such as "Do you believe quality or convenience are important product characteristics?" Respondents might rate quality and convenience differently—so how should they evaluate both on the same scale? In the latter, it is possible that respondents believe both characteristics matter; again, they will have trouble answering the question. Specificity is important to both the reliability and actionability of the data. Without confidence in what the respondent intended to say with his or her response, there is neither credible data nor a clear path for action.

Sensitive

An indicator should be sensitive to the changes it is designed to measure, meaning that the range of possible responses should be calibrated to the likely range of answers. An example can be found in the use of tests to measure learning in certain populations. If school children in poorer areas of a city start off with test performance that is far below the average student, then a standardized test designed for the general population may not pick up on improvements for this particular set of children—that is, it will not be sensitive to the small changes needed to measure improvements in performance for these students. The same logic might hold for very advanced students. If such students got a perfect score the first time around, then the tests are unlikely to show any improvement in their performance! Indicators should be calibrated to reasonable expectations about the likely amount of change.

Time-Bound

An indicator should relate to a clearly defined time period and be measured with a defined frequency. Output indicators will typically be measured continually throughout a program or project, such as on a weekly, monthly, or quarterly basis. For impact evaluations, outcomes should be measured at times that correspond to when changes are expected to take place and how long they are anticipated to persist. Imagine asking farmers about the volume of a crop they have harvested "since the beginning of the year." If this question is on a survey that takes three months to complete, every farmer will be answering for a different time period! We might avoid this challenge by asking about harvests "over the past three months." But if we ask some farmers this question just after they have harvested, and ask others a month or two later, we will again get widely varying results.

Feasible

An indicator should be within the capacity of the organization to measure and the ability of respondents to answer. There is no sense in an organization asking a question on which it does not have the ability to measure an indicator or one that respondents cannot (or will not) answer. Making sure that each indicator is feasible is part of the *responsible* principle. Responsible data collection requires organizations to consider their capacity to collect each piece of data, taking into account staff capacity, time and resource constraints, and other barriers to credible data collection. It also requires organizations to ask whether respondents will be willing and able to provide the information the question requests. Often organizations try to use indicators that they lack the capacity to measure, resulting in poor-quality data. In these cases, it is worth considering whether it might be best not to measure these indicators after all.

Frequency

The most important determinant of the frequency of data collection is the nature of the question being asked. Different questions necessarily have different timeframes of collection. Consider a survey designed to provide information about how a program changed women's decision-making power. Given that attitudes and norms are slow to change, it would not make sense to collect that information a month after starting the program. Instead, one might have to wait a year or even longer after the intervention to measure changes. For some programs, additional rounds of follow-up surveys after two or three years may be conducted to measure the long-term impacts of the program. However, a long timeframe can also result in poor-quality data due to high attrition rates. Long timeframes may require intermediate points of data collection, since asking respondents to remember events from several years ago may also result in low-quality data.

To avoid this recall bias, data on many monitoring indicators must be collected frequently. An organization running a microfinance program should collect data on repayments when they happen, whether that is weekly or monthly. The same is true for collecting attendance numbers for trainings or other program events. Failure to align data collection with the timing of an event will result in less-actionable data.

Determining the frequency of data collection for a particular indicator requires using the *responsible* principle, balancing the need for the data against the cost of gathering it. Consulting with other studies that dealt with similar issues can help to get the frequency of data collection right.

FINDING INDICATORS

On the surface, coming up with valid and reliable indicators seems easy—and in some cases, it is. Sometimes widely used and validated indictors exist for a particular concept. Returning to our NFA example, recall that the organization targets malnourished children for enrollment in its nutrition program. "Malnourished children" is the concept to be measured. NFA conducts a literature review and learns that moderate malnourishment in children is widely defined as a weight-for-age ratio between two and three standard deviations below normal for a given age. This indicator is considered by most to be valid measurement of the concept.[10] The reliability of the indicator, however, will depend on the quality of data collection in the field. To collect weight-for-age data, NFA will use one indicator that tracks each child's age and another that uses a scale to measure their weight. To ensure the data it collects is reliable, NFA will have to regularly check that the scales it uses are configured in the same way: that they each register exactly 40 pounds when a 40-pound child is weighed. It will also have to establish some rules for its community health workers (CHWs) about how to estimate a child's age in case his or her exact birthdate cannot be determined.

If an organization is lucky, it can make use of existing indicators like this that have been widely tested and validated. Examples include widely used survey modules such as those in the World Bank's Living Standards Measurement Survey and the Demographic and Health Survey. A major benefit of using existing surveys is that they have usually been field-tested and validated, often in a number of countries and languages. They can save an organization time during indicator development and may allow for comparing data across countries or contexts. Use of validated indicators can also increase transportability of data since these measures will be readily recognizable for other programs.

However, while existing indicators and surveys have some benefits, we caution against using them without carefully checking that they are valid and reliable in the context where they will be used. Linguistic or cultural differences can make even the most widely used survey invalid or unreliable. And just because something is widely accepted does not mean that it is the best option. Think of the use of standardized test scores for measuring educational outcomes. They are widely used and easily available, but a debate exists about whether they are actually a valid and reliable measure student achievement.[11] Returning to the literature and conducting field tests (which we discuss in the next section) will help organizations sort through these questions.

Often, no existing indicators capture the concept an organization wants to measure, so it has to develop its own. Some textbooks suggest other checklists for designing indicators, but we prefer to focus narrowly on assuring validity and reliability. In addition to the features of high-quality indicators we discussed earlier, we also discuss some things to keep in mind during this process: biases and poor implementation that can hinder efforts at collecting valid, reliable data.

LOGISTICS FOR COLLECTING HIGH QUALITY PRIMARY DATA

The preceding sections focused on how to design indicators to collect high-quality data. But, as we have said before, even indicators that look good on paper can fail to deliver high quality data. We all know that humans are prone to error and may in some cases cut corners or cheat, thus compromising data quality. Fortunately, there are some steps organizations can take to minimize errors from the outset and catch and correct them as they go.

PRETESTING A DATA COLLECTION INSTRUMENT

Piloting or pretesting a data collection instrument is important to ensure its validity and reliability. Regardless of the care put into designing indicators, it is impossible to completely anticipate how they will work in the field. Sometimes a question that seemed perfectly fine in the office may still be overly complex or too sensitive for respondents to answer.

To address this uncertainty, organizations should pilot survey instruments—and to a lesser degree, monitoring tools—before they are used with the target population. Piloting gives valuable information about survey questions, such as whether they are culturally appropriate or difficult for respondents to understand. Pilots also provide information on how long each section of a survey takes and whether the flow between questions is logical or might result in anchoring bias—information that will prove vitally important later when planning field logistics.

Ideally, piloting consists of two phases: pretesting at the office and piloting the instrument in the field. Pretesting of the instrument starts at the office with some of the organization's field staff while the instrument is being designed and again as soon as it is translated. Pretesting gives organizations a chance to check the overall flow of the questionnaire and the quality of translation and to screen for questions that may not be appropriate in a given context.

The second phase pilots the actual instrument in the field to identify whether it will perform well when rolled out in full. This piloting offers information about instrument design, including whether questions appear valid, whether they are translated appropriately for the context, and whether the placement of different sections of the instrument is correct. You will be surprised how many issues a pilot turns up. (See the resources at the end of this book for more information on how to pilot a survey for validation.) It will also demonstrate which parts of the instrument are trickier to administer or more difficult for respondents to answer, which will let organizations focus on those parts during staff training.

MANAGING SURVEYS FOR QUALITY

Organizations can take a number of steps to ensure the reliability of their data, which we outline later. But quality controls themselves are not worth much without a plan of action. Before starting, organizations should define a response or action for each quality check, such as giving a warning or firing a surveyor if she is found prefilling answers.

Documentation

A first step toward ensuring consistency is documenting the detailed data collection plan, survey training materials, and standard operating procedures for surveys. These documents should define key terms from the data collection instrument and should also define any word, phrase, or concept that may be ambiguous. Details on how to collect the data, from whom, and when should also appear in the plan, with contingencies outlined for how to deal with unexpected situations. Data collection manuals should walk staff through the different kinds of questions they will ask; identify potential problems that may arise; specify key definitions; and outline protocols for locating respondents, which household member to speak with, and other such considerations. The manual can also serve as a useful guide or reference book, especially for less experienced data collectors, thus helping to prevent bias in the field.

Translation

Many organizations do not translate their surveys or data collection instruments into a local language, instead letting staff translate on the fly when they administer the questions to respondents. While that is certainly easier and less costly than going through a full translation process, it may also deliver less credible data and open the door to the biases we discussed earlier. If each staff member is creating his or her own translation of the survey, how can an organization know that everyone is asking questions in the same way—and getting reliable data?

As we discussed earlier, organizations should create a written translation of the full data collection instrument and then back-translate to ensure the translation was done correctly. It is important to keep a couple of points in mind: First, translation can be expensive and take a lot of time depending on the size of the instrument, so budgeting adequate time and money is necessary. Second, fluency in the local language does not guarantee a deeper understanding of the social and cultural context, so finding the right person to translate can be tough. Amazingly, translation firms may not always be right for the job. They often employ individuals who are not fully fluent in both languages, or who lack knowledge of the local context—meaning that important nuances are lost. And because they are for-profit firms, they may face incentives to reduce their cost. For example, their incentive to work quickly may outweigh your interest in accuracy. Use caution. If possible, organizations should find someone with a deeper understanding of respondents' social fabric to help develop a nuanced translation of the data collection instrument.

Once an organization has a translated version of a survey, it should back-translate that survey into the original language in which the survey was developed to learn if the translation accurately captures the intent of the instrument. To avoid biases, the person who back-translates should have no knowledge of the original survey. The two versions should then be compared to identify any discrepancies. This may not seem like a big deal, but small differences in language can completely change the meaning of a question and undermine the credibility of the resulting data. Talking with the survey team to work out the correct translation and refine the survey can help resolve any differences. If the original round of translation was way off for many questions, it may be necessary to retranslate the form to be sure that it is right.

Training Data Collection Staff

Careful training on administering a data collection instrument is critical. Even a change in tone can affect a respondent's comfort level or perception of what the "right" answer is, triggering a biased response. The way in which enumerators dress and interact with each other and with respondents can also affect how people respond to them. Enumerators should be trained to adopt a respectful but neutral style with respondents.

The data collection instrument itself should not leave any room for subjective interpretation of key concepts in the survey or ambiguity in definitions. Think of our discussion about how the commonly used term "household" could be interpreted differently, for example. Is a household people who are related and are residing in the same house, or is it people sharing meals together? Through expert training, surveyors learn key definitions, how to explain them to respondents, and how to maintain complete neutrality regardless of what question they are asking. Include key definitions in the instrument in case there is a question or a data collector forgets an exact definition. And testing data collection staff on key concepts and procedures before sending the survey to the field is a good way to assure data quality.

Oversight

Just as good data are integral to good program management, good management goes a long way toward producing valid, reliable data. Monitoring and survey activities should be subject to data quality assurance. We use the following three methods extensively in our fieldwork to ensure that surveyors ask questions consistently and deliver reliable data:

Accompanying: In the first few days of the data collection activity, a team leader should directly observe a surveyor for the duration of the survey. The team leader may also complete the instrument alongside the staff member and check the surveyor's work against her own; discussing any discrepancies helps the surveyor learn how answers should be recorded and helps improve reliability. The team leader should also discuss any issues— such as how the surveyor asks questions and his or her body language and tone of voice—that could result in inconsistently collected data. As data collection staff get more experienced, accompanying can be done for a smaller portion of the survey. For organizations using an external survey firm, the firm's staff will likely be responsible for accompanying surveyors. It is a good practice to accompany 10% of all surveys regardless, including those conducted by an external firm.

Random spot checks: Spot checks are unannounced visits by the team leader or the field manager to observe surveyors administering a survey. Spot checks help make sure that data collectors are actually out collecting data when they say they are (rather than fabricating surveys or monitoring forms under a tree near the office). While accompanying can be predictable, spot checks are surprise visits. One needs to vary the order of visits, times of day, and who does the spot checks so that data collection staff understand that any instrument could be checked at any time.

Back-checks: Back-checks (also called audits) are performed by an independent team that visits a random subset of respondents to ask them a few questions from the data collection instrument. The person responsible for analysis matches the answers to this subset of questions to the original ones to catch any discrepancies. This provides a way to check data reliability, acting as a check on both the quality of the data collection instrument and surveyor performance. A good rule of thumb is to conduct random back-checks for 10% of surveys. Back-checks may reveal patterns in the data signaling that surveyors are prefilling in the data or claiming that a respondent cannot be found. Back-checking is only useful if there is an efficient system for analyzing the data quickly and providing constructive feedback to the team. Therefore, planning for back-checking should start well before any field activities.

PERSONNEL CONSIDERATIONS

There are two additional considerations to keep in mind during data collection: the link between staff incentives and credible data and the implications of *who* collects the data on data quality.

Staff incentives: Staff incentives can influence the quality of the data collected. While incentives can be a helpful way to motivate staff to implement a program, they can also hurt the credibility of data. When staff get a small cash incentive for conducting a training, they might want to say that they conducted a few more trainings than they really did to earn a little extra money. That inflates actual implementation numbers. In the United States, for example, school systems often link teacher pay to student performance. In many cases, auditors have found that this encouraged teachers to alter test scores.[12]

Implementing a program with incentives requires careful auditing procedures to be sure the data are accurate. Later in the book, we will present the case of BRAC Uganda, an organization whose monitoring arm visited program volunteers to be sure that they were doing their jobs. Yet that information was not enough. Each monitor verified the reports of these volunteers by interviewing clients the volunteer claimed to help and by comparing those reports to physical receipts kept in the district office. In this way, BRAC could be sure that program managers got accurate information about the implementation of their programs.

Training Program Staff to Handle Data

In many cases, program staff, rather than monitoring and evaluation officers, will be collecting data about program implementation. If this is the case, it is necessary to be particularly careful about program implementation. Organizations cannot assume that forms are self-explanatory. Program staff need extensive training to ask the right questions and fill out the forms correctly. In addition, it is important that program staff have the time to collect data accurately. Since program officers have so many other day-to-day tasks, they may have an incentive to cut corners to get everything done. When presented with a choice between implementing a program and collecting good data, it is likely that data will lose out. In each case, these examples focus on making sure that information is accurate, regardless of where it comes from or who collects it. Program staff may also have incentives to alter data if they feel that it might reflect poorly on their performance or if they do not want a particular field officer to look bad. Independent data collection can help address these challenges, but at the cost of additional recruitment and training.

Program Staff or an External Firm

Particularly when conducting surveys (and sometimes in monitoring, when the perception of objectivity is crucial), organizations must decide whether to use their own staff or hire an external survey firm. Managing surveys is a demanding, time-consuming activity that requires a specific set of expertise and skills, which is why organizations often contract data collection activities to external survey firms. Survey firms can minimize some of the types of bias we discussed earlier, such as social desirability bias, because respondents do not have the same personal ties to surveyors that they might have to program staff. Respondents may therefore be less inclined to provide what they consider the "right" answer instead of responding truthfully. And in impact evaluations, where treatment and comparison groups must be interviewed in a consistent way for reliability, a survey firm can help ensure that data are collected consistently across both groups, which may be difficult for program staff to do. But survey firms often have different incentives, and organizations using survey firms often find evidence of cost-cutting and compromised data quality. There are benefits and costs to both approaches, and organizations must carefully weigh what makes the most sense in each case. *Impact Evaluation in Practice* goes into more detail about how to make this determination.[13]

DATA ENTRY

Just as humans are prone to error in collecting data, they are also prone to error in the tedious task of data entry. Fortunately, a few simple strategies can dramatically reduce error rates in data entry. When organizations use electronic data entry, some of these strategies can be programmed directly into the data entry form used by enumerators:

Skips: Skips are cues in data collection forms that direct surveyors to jump over questions that are not applicable, given respondent answers on preceding questions. For example, if a woman answers that she has never had children, the surveyor would skip over all questions related to pre- and postnatal care. On a paper survey, skip patterns are usually written into the data collection instrument; with electronic data collection they can also be programmed into the data entry tool. This is true for a range of data-entry tools, from mobile phone apps used to collect data in the field, data-entry software like CSPro, or even simple Excel sheets with predefined options for each cell.

Logical checks: Logic checks are programmed into the data entry tool to let the user know that an entry may not be reasonable. They compare responses in different fields for consistency and generate error messages when they find something strange. For example, a logic check would generate an error message if a man was accidentally noted to have received prenatal care or the age of a child was entered as 100. Logic checks help ensure credible data by preventing these common human errors. Such logical checks are harder to "hard wire" into paper surveys, but training and proper documentation can help.

Double entry: Organizations that use paper-based data collection forms should consider using double entry to correct for general data entry errors that cannot be prevented with skips and logic checks. Double entry requires that each piece of data be entered twice by two different people and then compared. Any differences in the data will be flagged, allowing data entry staff to refer back to the paper form and correct the data.

Personally identifiable information: While not related to data quality per se, appropriate treatment of data that can identify individuals should be part of any data collection plan. Respondents provide information on the intimate details of their lives—bank account balances, HIV status, political affiliation—with the expectation that this data be treated with utmost confidence. Particularly for more sensitive information, breaching this confidence can be devastating.

Organizations should do everything possible to ensure that individuals cannot be identified and associated with the responses they gave. Research institutions usually require any survey data that can be used to identify an individual be removed from the survey responses and stored in a separate encrypted dataset, linked only by an ID number. They also require that paper-based identifiable information be physically removed from the rest of the survey form (again, linkable only by an ID number) and then stored and locked separately from the rest of the survey.[14] Nonprofits and other organizations often have their own data privacy requirements, which may or may not adhere to such rigorous standards. We encourage organizations to take all appropriate measures to protect the privacy of people who have entrusted them with their data.

Quality control: Data should be entered and analyzed as quickly as possible to look for particular anomalies or patterns of bias among enumerators. Electronic data collection tools can speed this process by allowing survey managers to examine patterns of responses quickly and identify enumerators who may need additional coaching or support. Such checks can be done daily and problems identified quickly. Where paper surveys are being entered manually, organizations may want to select surveys across enumerators and enter them as quickly as possible to identify any issues.

A note on electronic data entry. Laptops, tablets, and mobile phones all provide convenient methods for conducting surveys that bypass the cumbersome process of data entry. But such methods are prone to their own challenges as well. In some contexts, staff are not comfortable with electronic data entry or find they can still record answers more quickly on paper. We know of one organization that provided its staff with tablets only to find out later that they were marking responses on paper and then later transferring these responses to the tablet in the office! Electronic data collection also provides many opportunities for things to go wrong. Devices can fail and connectivity can be a challenge. Ideally, data from electronic devices are collected, uploaded, and backed up on a daily basis.

CONCLUSION: DATA QUALITY AND THE RESPONSIBLE PRINCIPLE

This is all great, you may say, but ensuring data quality seems like an expensive and time-consuming endeavor. After the time and effort put into developing a data collection plan, ensuring indicators are of high quality, training data collectors, and instituting quality checks, will there be any money left to run programs? What about the *responsible* principle?

The *responsible* principle suggests that collecting high-quality data may not always be the best option. It may be too costly or may not be timely. One must think through the costs and consider how much better the higher quality data are relative to the cost incurred collecting them, or the timeframe for getting the data versus when they are needed for decision-making (to make them actionable). One can easily imagine situations where inferior administrative data can be much better (cheaper and faster) than survey data that require an entire infrastructure merely to collect, even though the administrative data do not provide rich information at the individual level.

Spending money to collect data that fails to credibly answer needed questions is futile. The costs of bad data are threefold: the direct cost to collect (that could have been spent on more programs), the management time to pore through reports, and the bad decisions that may get made by blissfully ignoring problems with the data or analysis. The *responsible* principle requires comparing the hoped-for benefits of getting good data to the costs and risks that the data are bad.

PART II

Case Studies

CHAPTER 8

Educate! Developing a Theory of Change for "Changemakers"

WHAT IS A CHANGEMAKER?

In 2011, staff in Uganda at the small nongovernmental organization (NGO) Educate! received an email from the organization's co-founder and Executive Director Boris Bulayev asking them to start building a theory of change for their flagship program, the Educate! Experience (see Box 8.1). In the email, he noted that the organization—dedicated to supporting youth entrepreneurship in Uganda—was struggling to define the program's main intended outcomes. Bulayev believed that a theory of change would help to clarify how the program was improving the lives of young Ugandans. He asked staff to focus on defining what it meant to be a "Changemaker," the organization's term for students who used lessons from the Educate! Experience to create positive economic and social change in their communities. The request challenged the staff to develop a more credible and transportable definition of its main intended result: turning students into social entrepreneurs, or Changemakers, with the knowledge and confidence to effect change in their own communities.

One clear example of a Changemaker was Lillian Aero. When Lillian first heard about Educate! she was in 11th grade (Form 5 in the Ugandan system). When she asked her teacher about joining, the teacher told Lillian that she was a year too old. Lillian approached the school's head teacher but got the same response. She then sought out James, the mentor in charge of the

Box 8.1 THEORY OF CHANGE

A theory of change can build consensus on program's vision and guide the development of a right-fit monitoring and evaluation system. In this case, we examine how the Uganda-based youth empowerment nongovernmental organization (NGO) Educate! used the theory of change process to clearly define its intended impact and decide how to measure it. After analyzing the process Educate! used to develop its theory of change, you will be able to discuss the value of gathering internal perspectives and conducting field research to develop a theory of change. You will also assess how successive iterations of the theory of change provide clarity on program design and objectives and determine whether the final theory of change is sufficient to design a monitoring and evaluation plan that adheres to CART principles (Credible, Actionable, Responsible, and Transportable).

program at her school. Although James had the same response as others, Lillian insisted that participating in the Educate! Experience was her "lifetime chance." Impressed by her determination, James finally accepted her into the program under one condition: that she fully participate even after she had graduated from school, even though that meant that she had to walk nine kilometers each way to join the weekly sessions with her mentor. Lillian held true to her word and used the ideas and lessons presented in the Educate! Experience to start the Namugongo Good Samaritan Project, which hired more than 60 widows who had HIV or AIDS to make and sell jewelry.

Staff admitted that Lillian's story was exceptional. Most Educate! participants or "scholars" engaged with their communities on a smaller scale. For example, some launched agriculture businesses at their local trading centers or sold crafts in urban areas, while others were advocating for local policy change or working on larger community development efforts. To build a theory of change and adequately capture what it meant to be a Changemaker, staff at Educate! would have to define the change that would indicate that their program was making a difference. Without a clear definition of what it meant to be a Changemaker, tracking program performance and measuring its impact would not be possible. This case focuses on how Educate! developed a theory of change that clearly defined the problems it seeks to address and the changes it aims to create.

Educate! was created by three US college students, Eric Glustrom, Angelica Towne, and current Executive Director Boris Bulayev, who believed in empowering other young people through education. They focused their efforts on Uganda, a country with one of the highest youth unemployment rates in the world. With this in mind, the Educate! team started asking youth they knew in Uganda what they needed most to succeed. The answer they got was always the same: opportunity.

In the beginning, Educate! tried to increase young Ugandans' opportunities by providing scholarships to secondary school students. However, the founders soon realized that with the severe lack of jobs in Uganda, scholarships by themselves were not enough. So they developed the Educate! Experience to teach secondary school students leadership and entrepreneurial skills they could use to create their own economic opportunities after graduation.

In the Educate! Experience, scholars attend a series of weekly extracurricular classes and mentorship sessions during their last two years of secondary school. The program intends to help students become leaders and entrepreneurs by meeting students where they are, building their confidence, and increasing their self-reliance. Each lesson includes project-based learning, case studies of successful role models, motivational speeches, and an emphasis on increasing students' self-efficacy to make a difference in their communities.

Classes in the first term of the Educate! Experience help scholars identify their passion and develop leadership skills. In the second term, the curriculum progresses from exploring personal leadership to becoming leaders in the community. The third term focuses on developing entrepreneurship and community awareness. In the final two terms, mentors help scholars develop business plans and solutions to community problems.

To help scholars bring these plans to action, Educate! pairs each scholar with a mentor who will support and refine the scholar's idea for a business or community initiative. In addition, scholars participate in one of the Educate! Clubs for school business, which bring students together to start school-based businesses and to solve local community challenges. Through the clubs, students create their own charter, identify a problem or market need they would like to address, and work together to create a solution to that problem.

Educate! started the Educate! Experience with a pilot class of 30 scholars in 2008 and expanded steadily. In 2009, the organization enrolled about 350 scholars in 24 schools across five districts. In 2012, Educate! expanded to reach 36 schools. By 2014, Educate! had adapted the program for scale and expanded into 240 schools across 18 districts.

DEVELOPING A THEORY OF CHANGE

Like many programs, Educate! started by identifying a need and a potential solution to address that need, then worked out the implementation details as they went. Bulayev's 2011 email highlighted the organization's need to fully develop its theory of change. To help staff begin, Bulayev attached a draft of the program theory in his message. This document identified the program's key outputs, expected short- and medium-term outcomes, and expected economic and social impacts (Figure 8.1).

According to this theory of change, Educate! expected scholars to develop a set of positive attitudes and skills in the first two terms of the program (T1 and T2), including increased confidence, awareness of community, social responsibility, and a sense of self-efficacy. The document suggested that scholars would internalize and exhibit resourcefulness by the end of the third and fourth terms. These key attitude and behavior-change outcomes would then mold young scholars into Changemakers during the fifth term of the program or shortly after they graduated from school.

Once these students became Changemakers and started their own businesses or other initiatives, Educate! expected to see changes in communities' economic and social outcomes, including higher incomes, increased employment, and greater self-efficacy.

> Analysis Question 1: Does the initial theory of change outlined in Bulayev's 2011 email help Educate! define the concept of "Changemaker" and clarify the processes of becoming one? Considering our discussion of the theory of change in Chapter 3, is there anything you would add or change?

FEEDBACK FROM STAFF

Although this draft theory of change showed when an individual was expected to become a Changemaker, staff realized it did not show *how* that change would occur. Without this pathway clearly mapped out, Educate! realized that its theory of change was incomplete. To answer that question,

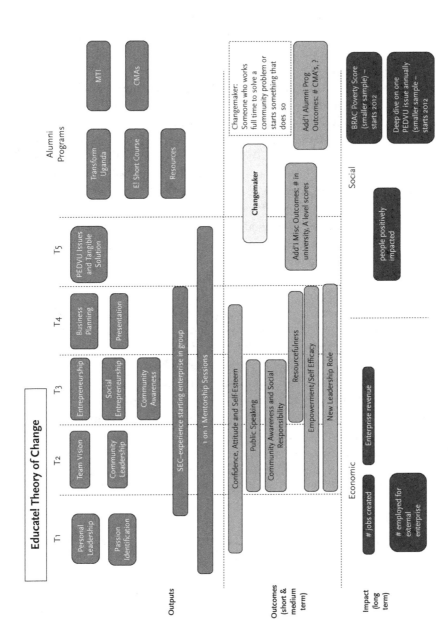

Figure 8.1 Educate! draft theory of change.

the Educate! monitoring and evaluation department asked the mentors to answer a simple question: "How do you know if your scholar is on the path to becoming a Changemaker?" Answering this question would help define the concept of "Changemaker," a key outcome that Educate! aimed to achieve. Defining the term would clarify how the organization would track its scholars' progress toward that outcome.

Mentors believed that scholars with Changemaker potential displayed many different attitudinal and behavioral changes during the Educate! Experience. These changes were key outcomes along the theorized path to impact. For example, many showed visible excitement and a stronger belief in their ability to create change in their communities—what some mentors called the "I can" stage. From there, scholars often started to take small actions, such as making changes at home (reaching out to build stronger relationships with their parents, for example), recruiting other students to join the program, and completing assigned tasks quickly and enthusiastically. By contrast, scholars who later dropped out of the program often did not engage with their communities or regularly complete the extra homework required by the program, which staff felt pointed to a lack of motivation and drive.

The mentors' experience highlighted an important component of the change Educate! wanted to see. The organization did not want to just increase the number of inspired and motivated young people in Uganda; it wanted to increase the number of young people who used that inspiration to take action to improve their communities. But how would the organization clarify this important difference?

Although most of the staff agreed that a scholar became a Changemaker once he or she had started a business or initiative that played a positive role in their community, they were less clear how to define the threshold for actions that indicated Changemaker status. For example, what if a scholar developed entrepreneurship skills and set up a successful poultry business in her backyard? Was she a Changemaker? What if she used the revenues from sales to pay her siblings' school fees? Or the business grew and she employed two friends to help collect and sell the eggs? At what point would her actions be substantial enough to count?

Staff also questioned whether Changemaker status could only be achieved through entrepreneurship. Educate! was founded on the belief that self-employment was an essential remedy to the rampant unemployment in the formal sector. But not every scholar wanted to start a business; some wanted to start community initiatives that would make their communities better places to live or to work for organizations that did so. In other words, is the scholar who raises chickens to earn income for her family really more of a Changemaker than the scholar who starts working for a local nonprofit that provides malaria treatment?

To answer that question and determine the types of change that met the bar for Changemaker status, staff at Educate! paged through the stories of real scholars:

> *Joan Nansubuga*: Joan started a jewelry business with capital from her father and her own savings. Her business expanded rapidly, and she hired two members of the community. Joan donated some of her profits to a local orphanage and supported the entrepreneurial efforts of other scholars in Educate! Clubs. She was also active in her school, sitting on the school cabinet.
>
> *Juliet Kabasomi*: Juliet started a community initiative that aimed to inspire youth to succeed in and out of school. To help kids pay for school and book fees, members of the community contributed to a fund that gave out loans at low interest rates. The initiative later expanded to include older women who mentor younger children while Juliet is in school.
>
> *Paul Sselunjoji*: Paul was an Operations Manager at Tugende, an organization that worked to promote increased profitability for "boda" motorcycle taxi drivers. While still a high school student, he won a nationwide business plan competition and has helped set up several small-scale businesses, including a venture that sells fertilizer to farmers on credit near his hometown.
>
> *Nathan Rugyemura*: Nathan had experienced firsthand the challenges that livestock farmers encounter in accessing markets and health care for their livestock. Nathan used the lessons of the Educate! Experience to set up a farming enterprise that offered veterinarian services. He also purchased local dairy products and sold them to buyers in the Ugandan capital Kampala, offering dairy farmers in his community access to more lucrative markets. The business generated an income of about 225,000 Ugandan Shillings (UGX) per month for Nathan, equivalent to about $100 per month.

THE SERIES OF OUTCOMES

Through their discussions, staff realized that they would like to recognize a wide spectrum of activities rather than restricting Changemaker status to just a few superstars. They captured their ideas in a diagram called

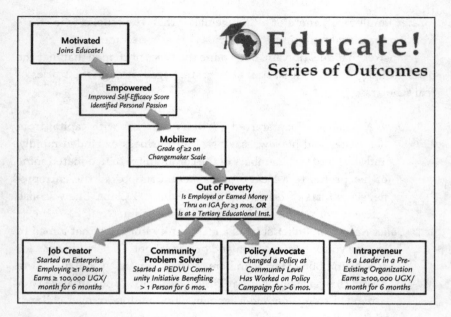

Figure 8.2 Educate! series of outcomes.

the "Series of Outcomes" (Figure 8.2) that showed the set of steps that Educate! expected scholars to move along before becoming one of four types of Changemaker: Job Creator, Community Problem Solver, Policy Advocate, or Intrapreneur.

The Series of Outcomes started when motivated students joined the program. Scholars became "Empowered" if they improved their self-efficacy score (a scale that measures belief in one's capabilities to organize and execute the actions required to manage prospective situations) and identified a personal passion. Students then became "Mobilizers" if they achieved a Changemaker score of at least two out of four when graded using a report card–like grading system at the end of each term. To achieve a score of two, scholars had to have a written business plan; a score of three indicated that they had a current, ongoing, and relevant project. Scholars moved "Out of Poverty" if they earned money from an income-generating activity for at least three consecutive months or were enrolled in a tertiary educational institution.

Once "Out of Poverty," a scholar could follow one of four paths to becoming a Changemaker. A "Job Creator" started a business that employed one or more people while earning 100,000 UGX, about $44.50 USD, per month for six months. Lillian Aero from the introduction and Joan Nansubunga were clear examples of Job Creators. Someone who starts a PEDVU community initiative (an Educate! designation that stands for Poverty, Environmental degradation, Disease, Violence, and Uneducated/Disempowered people) that helps more than one person for six months, like Juliet Kabasomi, would be considered a "Community Problem Solver." A "Policy Advocate" changed policy at the community level or worked on a policy campaign for six months. And, finally, an "Intrapreneur" (an Educate!-created term) was a leader who earns at least UGX 100,000 per month for six months in a preexisting organization with more than one employee. Paul Sselunjoji, the operations manager at the enterprise helping motorcycle taxi drivers in Kampala, exemplified this type of Changemaker.

> Analysis Question 2: How is the Series of Outcomes an improvement over Educate!'s first theory of change? What are its strengths and weaknesses compared to Bulayev's theory of change? How can it be used to develop metrics for monitoring and for impact evaluation?

MEASURING CHANGE

Although these workshops and documents helped the organization clarify intended intermediate outcomes and pathways of desired change, Educate! realized that it needed more capacity to develop its monitoring and evaluation system. Bulayev and Angelica Towne, Educate! co-founder and Country Director at the time, decided to make monitoring and evaluation an organizational priority. So, in 2011, as the organization continued reflecting on its theory of change, Towne hired an Evaluation and Research Officer named Rachel Steinacher.

Towne and Steinacher picked up the task of developing the theory of change. However, they quickly ran into another challenge: although the organization had made good progress in defining the outcomes it sought to achieve, it had not as clearly articulated the exact problem the Educate! Experience sought to address. The organization aimed to create opportunity for young Ugandans, but what was the root cause of their lack of opportunity in the first place? Steinacher believed that specificity in this area was fundamental to clarifying the theory of change. Without a clear conception of the problem, she would have a hard time determining what data to collect.

At first, Steinacher thought that defining the problem Educate! sought to address would be fairly straightforward. However, a short survey of staff revealed that everyone was not on the same page. Office-based leadership staff tended to think that education was the problem, noting that Uganda's secondary school curriculum was not well matched to the needs of students. Field staff, on the other hand, thought that youths were most constrained by deep financial poverty and the ensuing belief that they could not make positive change in their communities.

Towne and Steinacher saw the merits of both views and wondered which more accurately reflected the challenge at hand. After conducting a literature review, they realized that, rather than two competing theories, they had two similar and interlocking problems that could be reconciled in a concept created by the United Nations called "multidimensional youth poverty." This idea suggests that many youth face both unemployment and educational disempowerment that, together with risky behaviors, keep them locked in poverty. Steinacher circulated this draft problem theory for review and the majority of staff agreed that it accurately described the problem facing youth in Uganda.

QUALITATIVE RESEARCH

With the problem better defined, Steinacher returned to the theory of change. Towne and Steinacher believed that, to make a document that best reflected the change experienced by program participants, they needed to learn more from the students themselves. They designed a qualitative survey to get perspectives and beliefs about everyday life in Uganda, including money and income, family dynamics, personality, and threats to safety. They hoped that this information would help illustrate both the outcome-level changes that Educate! could hope to see from the program and some of the risks to realizing success.

Steinacher administered this survey to 72 young people in Uganda, split evenly between Educate! scholars and students outside the program. For an example of the information the survey gathered, see the excerpt in Figure 8.3 about how youth manage their money. This subject was particularly important to the organization as it would help staff understand how much capital youth had to start businesses and how they used the money they earned from their enterprises.

In addition to learning about key aspects of young Ugandans' lives, Towne and Steinacher also hoped to understand every step a student covered in the Educate! Experience—from the initial motivation to join to the process of becoming a Changemaker. For example, one survey module aimed to measure scholars' understanding of a community project that was clearly

YOUR MONEY

Tick ✓one box for each question

How much money did you receive as gifts for pocket money at the start of the term?
☐ Nothing (0 UGX)   ☐ 1-49,000 UGX   ☐ 50,000-99,000 UGX   ☐ 100,000 UGX or more

In the last month, approximately how much money did you spend on each of these items?

Clothes:	_____ UGX	Cosmetics (lotion, etc.):	_____ UGX
Shoes/footwear:	_____ UGX	Entertainment (movies/music):	_____ UGX
Snacks/food/drinks:	_____ UGX	Presents/gifts for others:	_____ UGX

While you are at school, do you have enough money to pay for **basic things** that you need (enough food to eat, school supplies, etc.)?
- ☐ No, I never have enough money
- ☐ No, I often don't have enough money
- ☐ Somehow, I sometimes have enough money
- ☐ Yes, I often have enough money
- ☐ Yes, I always have enough money

When you earn money, how much of your money do you share with your parents/family?

☐ I give them 1/4 (25%) of my money   ☐ I give them 1/2 (50%) of my money   ☐ I give them 3/4 (75%) of my money   ☐ I give them all of my money (100%)

What are the top three things that you spend most of your money on? **Put a tick ✓ beside three things**
- ☐ Helping to pay for my own upkeep (food, etc.) or school fees
- ☐ Helping to pay for my brother(s)/sister(s) upkeep/ school fees
- ☐ Giving money to my family
- ☐ Entertainment/fun things
- ☐ Saving it to pay for:_____
- ☐ Starting a business/project or making your business/project better
- ☐ Other:_____

Figure 8.3 Excerpt from Steinacher's Quality of Life survey.

differentiated from other types of Changemaking, such as volunteering, running a small business, or conducting other income-generating activities. Developing this understanding was an important part of the Educate! Experience curriculum. See the questions pertaining to this issue in the survey shown in Figure 8.4).

Main Questions	Additional Questions
25. This isn't a test question, but can you explain to me what a community project is?	a) How is a community project different from a small business or an income-generating activity? b) How many people does a community project have to involve? c) Can you give me a couple examples of a small business?
26. Again, this isn't a test question but can you explain to me what a small business is?	a) Can you give me a couple examples of a small business?
27. Do you currently, or have you ever had a community project? What was it?	IF YES, a) What was it? b) Why did you decide to start this type of project? c) Has anyone else ever helped you with your project? By help I mean more money, supplies, labour, advice, or helping you develop a relationship with someone who was important to help you start or run your projects? d) How many hours a week do you spend on your project? e) Does it ever take away time from your schoolwork or your work you have to do at home or for your parents(s)/guardian(s)? f) What does your father/guardian think about this project? g) What about your mother/other guardian? h) Has having this project ever caused trouble between you and your family (probe this further) i) What does your community think about your project? j) Has having this project ever caused any trouble between you and your community? (probe this further) k) If you go to University/when you are at boarding school, what happens/will happen to your project? l) How likely is it that your father/mother/guardian(s) will take over your business and make it theirs? m) Have you ever received training from an organization or person to help you with your project? What was it? IF NO, n) Why not?
28. Do you currently or have you ever done volunteer work or done work to help out in your community? (like cleaning wells, sweeping a compound, etc.)	a) What types of volunteer work do you do? b) Why do you do this type of work? c) How frequently do you do this type of work?
29. What are the biggest problems that your community faces? By 'biggest problems' I mean ones you worry about the most and have the biggest impact on your community.	a) Why do you think this problem happens? b) Who, in your community or in Uganda is the most able to solve this problem? c) Why do you think they are the best ones to be fixing the problem? d) What are they currently doing to fix the problem? e) What can a young person do to stop these things from happening?
31. Why don't more youth try to solve problems in their communities? What is stopping them?	

Figure 8.4 Learning about community projects.

FINDINGS OF THE RESEARCH

After administering these surveys, it took Steinacher and a team of three graduate students two months to code more than 3,000 pages of interview transcripts. Steinacher presented her findings to Bulayev and Towne as they reviewed the program's theory of change.

The data brought to light two important assumptions in the theory of change. First, Educate! learned that students who earned income were often expected to contribute to family expenses, meaning that 100,000 UGX would not necessarily move a family out of poverty, thus contradicting the assumptions of the Series of Outcomes.

They also learned that using a binary "yes/no" representation of a student's Changemaker status was not the ideal way to measure change. First, the process of becoming a Changemaker often involved a series of many small steps. In addition, students listed many different and worthwhile types of community projects that did not fit clearly into the existing Series of Outcomes. Towne and Steinacher hoped that this feedback would help Educate! move toward a more continuous measure of scholars' progress.

THE NEW THEORY OF CHANGE

What would it mean for Educate! to let go of the focus on creating Changemakers? The idea of molding scholars into Changemakers had, after all, been the foundational idea of change ever since the start of the Educate! Experience. If Educate! stopped using the term, it would mean dropping a key part of organizational thinking and motivation.

Nonetheless, Bulayev, Towne, and Steinacher agreed that the change was necessary. Steinacher's interviews indicated that the Series of Outcomes was missing a large part of the story. By expanding the range of outcomes measured, the organization could better track how scholars changed throughout their time in the program. But what would replace the Series of Outcomes? Educate! decided to create a theory of change aligned with their focus on multidimensional youth poverty. This new theory of change would more closely reflect the actual activities and outputs of the Educate! Experience and would show how these outputs fostered the wider set of outcomes anticipated from the program.

To start the process, Bulayev and Towne returned to the theory of change to consider what types of outcomes would reflect the changes Educate! expected from its program. Most importantly, Educate! wanted to be sure that its program was helping scholars create their own opportunities in the labor force, so the team felt that "improve youth livelihoods" was an important intended outcome. By tracking this outcome, Educate! would measure whether scholars were on track to move out of poverty. The team also decided that monitoring staff should capture whether the entrepreneurship element of the program was effective by recording whether scholars created businesses and job opportunities.

Steinacher's surveys also indicated that there was more to the program than entrepreneurship. To understand if the program was encouraging people to make a difference in their communities, Towne proposed adding outcomes to the theory of change to measure community participation and leadership and to track changes in soft skills, like public speaking, taught through the curriculum.

In the end, Educate!'s theory of change included the following four intended outcomes:

- improve youth livelihoods
- increase youth small business and job creation
- increase youth community participation and leadership
- increase youth practical (soft) skills

These intended outcomes incorporated the new organizational thinking about the diverse ways scholars could become Changemakers. The first two outcomes roughly corresponded to the Entrepreneur and Intrapreneur designations, while the third outcome, referring to community leadership, exemplified the "Community Problem Solver" and "Policy Advocate" types of Changemakers. The fourth intended outcome represented the skills that Changemakers of all kinds need to be successful.

When Towne brought these intended outcomes back to the monitoring and evaluation team, Steinacher pointed out that they were broad concepts that would be difficult to measure well. For example, what did a target like "improved youth livelihoods" ultimately mean? To measure that outcome, they would need to clarify definitions and create concrete indicators to track change. To build these indicators, Steinacher again turned to the qualitative surveys. For information about the important elements of youth livelihoods, she looked at the sections on students' income-generating activities and found that most students engage in the informal sector, making small products to sell for small profits.

With this information, Towne and Steinacher decided that the youth livelihoods outcome should be measured by the four indicators outlined in a final, revised theory of change (Figure 8.5). These metrics include the

	Directly after the Educate! Experience	1 year after the Educate! Experience	2 years after the Educate! Experience
Outcome 1: Improved youth livelihoods	[%?] graduates demonstrating social protection behaviours (should be one of these - likely just savings behavior): – savings behaviour – malaria prevention – water filtration	Graduates have increase their net monthly income of at least 125%	Graduates have increase their net monthly income of at least %
	[%?] graduates are able to make at least two products (examples: liquid soap, beads, chapattis, etc.)	Graduates that are employed or that have a business have a mean net monthly income of 125000 UGX	Graduates that are employed or that have a business have a mean net monthly income of 150000 UGX
	[%?] of graduates have a net income of [#?]/month		
	[%?] of graduates score [#?] or higher on the Economic Status Index	[%?] of graduates score [#?] or higher on the Economic Status Index	[%?] of graduates score [#?] or higher on the Economic Status Index

Figure 8.5 Educate!'s draft theory of change: outcome measurement.

number of graduates demonstrating what Educate! defined as "social protection behaviors" (savings building, malaria prevention, and water filtration), the number of students who are able to make at least two products to sell in the informal market, the number of scholars who earn more than 140,000 UGX/month, and the percentage of students who improve on an overall Economic Status Index.

> Analysis Question 3: Is it possible for Educate! to credibly measure the early outcomes of the Educate! Experience, such as the number of students that become Changemakers and their progress toward the targets laid out in the Educate! theory of change? What are some of the challenges of measuring Educate!'s contributions to these outcomes?

With their intended outcomes more clearly defined, Educate! staff turned their attention to program monitoring. Towne and Steinacher wanted to make sure that this latest theory of change clearly showed how program activities would lead to outputs and outcomes. To do so, they would need to track implementation for each of the four main elements of the

Inputs (Program Components)	Indicative Statistics		Outputs	Indicative Statistics
Program Component 1: Entrepreneurship and Leadership Course — All mentors teach 90% of Entrepreneurship lessons	94.14% of Entrepreneurship and Leadership Lessons Taught		All scholars attend 75% of the Entrepreneurship lessons	81.81% of the possible attendances (Scholar/Lesson) happened. This number was obtained doing the average of the % of attendance of all scholars for all terms.
Program Component 1: Entrepreneurship and Leadership Course — All mentors teach 90% of Leadership lessons			All scholars attend 75% of the Leadership lessons	

Figure 8.6 Revised theory of change: monitoring program implementation.

Educate! Experience: the curriculum and classroom experience in the Entrepreneurship and Leadership course, teacher training, the mentorship program, and Educate! Clubs for business planning. Each element of the program now connected to both activity-level targets—which would make sure that the program was implemented according to plan—and output-level indicators, which would track attendance and performance.

By connecting each stage of the program to benchmarks for success, Towne and Steinacher hoped to collect more informative data about how the program was proceeding. Figure 8.6 contains an example of these benchmarks for one component of the program: the Entrepreneurship and Leadership course. These data would allow Educate! to track activities, ensuring that programs were being delivered as intended. Educate! could also measure take-up and engagement, tracking things like scholar attendance at courses and participation in mentorship and club sessions. Before Educate! could think about engaging in an impact evaluation that measured outcome achievement, however, they first needed to be sure that the program itself was optimized.

THEORY REALIZED

Since Bulayev's initial email in 2011, Educate!'s understanding of its program goals had evolved from a loose set of hard-to-measure behaviors to a more refined set of expected outcomes. As we have seen, the process began with staff discussions and multiple versions of theories of change, which provided a foundation for the organization to build upon. When these ideas were coupled with detailed qualitative research, the organization was able to create a theory of change that more accurately reflected the pathways of change the program sought—pathways that the organization could quantify and track over time.

CASE ANALYSIS

Analysis Question 1: Does the initial theory of change outlined in Bulayev's 2011 email help Educate! define the concept of "Changemaker" and clarify the processes of becoming one? Is there anything you would add or change?

The initial theory of change Bulayev outlined focused on the ways the Educate! Experience would create positive long-term social and economic change. He theorized that the curriculum would boost traits like confidence, self-efficacy, and resourcefulness. These qualities would turn scholars into Changemakers by the end of the two-year program.

By articulating the changes that Educate! wants to see in scholars as a result of the organization's curriculum, this theory of change is a great start for Educate! However, this initial theory of change has a number of weaknesses.

First, many of the outcome-level changes outlined in the theory of change are vague and hard to quantify. This is not to say that organizations should only conceptualize their work with ideas that can be easily tracked and verified with data. However, including indicators such as "resourcefulness" or "community awareness" could result in imprecise data collection and incomplete understanding of program progress. Instead of an opaque metric like "resourcefulness," Educate! should think about more concrete ways to track resourcefulness, breaking it down into the measurable behaviors that would show a scholar is resourceful.

Second, this theory of change fails to note the assumptions that must hold for students to progress as intended. For example, in implementing the program, Educate! assumes that students will actually want to start their own businesses or become more engaged in their communities. Without clearly identifying these types of assumptions, Educate! misses key areas to track with data.

Finally, the document fails to show the connections between program activities and their related outputs and outcomes. For example, does the organization expect that starting an enterprise will support all of the near-term outcomes in the theory of change, or just a few? The same issue applies to the connections between short- and long-term outcomes. Changes in empowerment or resourcefulness, for example, do not necessarily have to translate into the business outcomes noted in the document.

> Analysis Question 2: How is the Series of Outcomes helpful to Educate!? What are its strengths and weaknesses compared to the original theory of change?

The Series of Outcomes—the document that emerged from staff discussions that identified the four types of Changemakers—is an improvement over the original theory of change. Rather than focusing on expected attitude changes, this document defines a series of concrete steps that must occur for a scholar to become a Changemaker. In addition, the Series of Outcomes also distinguishes between different types of Changemakers, which the first theory of change did not do. This clarifies the definition of the Educate! Experience's key intended outcome. However, because it does not outline how specific program activities intend to create specific changes, this iteration of the theory of change still lacks a critical component.

> Analysis Question 3: Is it possible for Educate! to credibly measure the early outcomes of the Educate! Experience—such as the number of students that become Changemakers and their progress toward the targets laid out in the Educate! theory of change? What are some of the challenges of measuring Educate!'s contributions to these outcomes?

Educate! should collect data on the number of scholars who become Changemakers, which scholars do so, and what type of Changemakers they become. These data would help check the theory of change's logic. For example, what if Educate! finds that only a few scholars become policy advocates? Educate! may want to rethink that arm of the program and learn why so few scholars are choosing that path.

Although these data can help refine the program, Educate! cannot use them to prove its effectiveness without a counterfactual. There are many reasons that scholars may start to make meaningful changes in their lives, especially because Educate! selects students who are highly motivated to participate in the program. Therefore, measuring Changemaker outcomes will not yield credible information on how Educate! contributed to them.

> Analysis Question 4: How would you critique the final Theory of Change?

The final theory of change structures monitoring around four intended outcomes for Changemakers. It is the first to connect Educate! activities with the outcomes expected as a result. Not only that, many of the pathways outlined in this document are supported by the extensive qualitative research conducted by Steinacher and her team, which is a rare and commendable undertaking.

We offer a few suggestions to strengthen the theory of change. First, while this document ties metrics to theory, it stops short of mapping the pathways of change between specific program activities and later outcomes, which a complete theory of change would do. For example, the theory considers all program outputs, defined as attendance in mentorship sessions or participation in the Educate! Experience, to connect to all expected program outcomes. Is it realistic to expect that students will learn all of the same material in mentoring versus working with peers in the Educate! Club? Why does Educate! have these two separate programs if it expects both to produce the same result?

Additionally, the final theory of change fails to register a number of assumptions, such as the knowledge changes that must take place for the program to achieve its goals. Just because mentors teach the sessions and students attend them does not mean that students are actually learning in these sessions. For example, say that Educate! conducted an impact evaluation that found that many students failed to display the social protection behaviors taught in the program. Without information about knowledge change, Educate! would have no way of knowing whether scholars did not know how to adopt these behaviors, did not want to, or simply could not.

CHAPTER 9

BRAC

Credible Activity Monitoring for Action

INTRODUCTION

In Mbarara town in Western Uganda, Jovex, a Monitoring Officer from the nongovernmental organization (NGO) BRAC, hopped off the back of a motorcycle taxi and approached a group of women milling around a small store. Jovex hoped the women could help her locate Patience Okello, a Community Livestock Promoter (CLP) implementing BRAC's Community Livestock and Poultry Program in the district (see Box 9.1). Jovex wanted to speak with Patience about her work in helping community members vaccinate their poultry. The women at the store confirmed that Jovex was in the right place, pointing to a housing compound just down the hill where Patience could be found.

Inside the compound, Jovex sat down to interview Patience about her role in helping farmers in the area obtain poultry vaccinations. This information would help BRAC to better understand whether CLPs were actively engaged in supporting local poultry producers. CLPs are critical to implementation of the livestock program, but they work as individual entrepreneurs rather than paid staff. BRAC provides CLPs with the training and tools needed for their work. The opportunity to start a small business in poultry vaccination provides the incentive for CLPS to do the work, but if the incentives are not working properly, CLPs may not act and the program will suffer. Jovex's task today was to try to obtain accurate information about CLP activities and report her findings to program management

so that they could identify and fix any problems with the program. This
case focuses on the gathering of actionable data and on the difficulties organizations often face in turning actionable data into concrete change.

BRAC

BRAC started in 1972 as the Bangladesh Rural Advancement Committee,
a relief operation for refugees from the Bangladeshi Civil War. Two
years later, the organization began to transition from providing direct
postconflict relief to longer term antipoverty efforts, such as microcredit
lending. This economic development work would become the foundation of
BRAC's approach. Today, BRAC (Building Resources Across Communities)
is one of the largest NGOs in the world, serving 110 million people in 11
countries.

The organization aims to address the "interlinked and manifold causes
of poverty" through a wide range of programs that focus on human rights,
social empowerment, education, health, economic empowerment, enterprise development, livelihood training, environmental sustainability, and
disaster preparedness. BRAC distinguishes itself from other NGOs in three
main ways: a focus on sustainability, the use of "microfranchises," and a
sustained commitment to monitoring and evaluation.

The focus on sustainability began with BRAC's first social enterprise, a
dairy business that purchased milk from farmers. These farmers, many of
whom had purchased cattle with BRAC microcredit loans, processed and
sold the milk to urban consumers. This enterprise, known as BRAC Dairy,
allowed BRAC to pass on more of the proceeds from milk sales to farmers,

and the profits it generated could also be used to support other projects in the BRAC portfolio. In 2007, BRAC Dairy earned $1.17 million in profit. The success of the dairy business encouraged BRAC to start other revenue-generating enterprises, including tea estates, salt production, and chicken farming.

The "microfranchises" are another distinguishing component of BRAC's approach. While many organizations expand by hiring full-time paid staff, BRAC's microfranchise model recruits community members to take on key roles (such as agricultural extension agents and community health workers). These entrepreneurs sell reasonably priced goods or services to community members and receive a small share of the proceeds as profit. BRAC believes that microfranchises can integrate such work into community life more seamlessly, efficiently, and sustainably. This more flexible model allows BRAC to expand its reach at a fraction of what it would cost to hire paid staff and offers community members opportunities for income generation.

BRAC's approach to monitoring and evaluation also differentiates it from other NGOs. Rather than housing monitoring and evaluation in the same unit, BRAC separates the functions into two units—one for Monitoring and one for Research and Evaluation. This split recognizes the fundamental differences between the two functions. BRAC also stands out as one of the first organizations to start monitoring and evaluation activities; the Research and Evaluation unit was created in 1975, and the Monitoring Unit started in 1980. The monitoring unit collects essential information about program implementation, which gives program managers the data they need to make operational decisions. The research unit focuses on demonstrating program impact, which ensures that BRAC programming is evidence-based and effective. Both the Monitoring and the Research and Evaluation units work independently of BRAC's operational programs, serving as critical voices that guide program design and implementation.

> Analysis Question 1: From a management perspective, what are some of the advantages and disadvantages of BRAC's decision to split monitoring and evaluation into different departments?

BRAC IN UGANDA

BRAC opened its Uganda office in 2006. In less than seven years, BRAC became the largest development organization in the country, operating in a wide range of sectors including microfinance, agriculture, livestock husbandry, health, and education. By 2014, these projects were implemented across 94 branches in nearly half of Uganda's 111 districts, and BRAC had reached more than 3.4 million Ugandans—about 10% of the country's population.

Agriculture is a large part of BRAC's Uganda portfolio. BRAC seeks to provide farmers with affordable seeds, fertilizer, and other high-quality inputs to increase their farm yields. As a part of this effort, BRAC's Poultry and Livestock Program seeks to reduce livestock mortality, increase farm income, and boost agricultural employment.[1]

Like many BRAC programs, the execution of the Poultry and Livestock Program relies heavily on community members running individual microfranchises: these are the CLPs we introduced at the beginning of the chapter. CLPs act as agricultural extension agents, providing advice to neighbors on how to improve livestock practices as well as selling veterinary supplies such as vaccines and medicines. To ensure that CLPs have the expertise necessary for the job, BRAC gives them 12 days of initial training, as well as ongoing supervision from paid Project Associates who are trained by government and BRAC specialists on essential agricultural techniques. A key premise of the program's theory of change is that CLPs can generate a modest profit by selling BRAC-subsidized vaccines and other agricultural products to local farmers.

BRAC's theory of change assumes that the profit from vaccines and agricultural products will be sufficient motivation for CLPs to implement the program with enthusiasm. But many CLPs are farmers themselves or have other jobs and roles within the community. What if the BRAC incentives were not enough? In that case, a key link in BRAC's theory of change would break down, CLPs might not implement the program as planned, and BRAC might not achieve its goal of improving livestock health.

MONITORING PROGRAMS AT BRAC

Because BRAC often works at a regional or national scale, the organization must carefully consider the amount of monitoring data it collects. On the one hand, if BRAC tried to engage in detailed activity tracking for every one of its programs all of the time, it would risk flooding program staff with more data than they could manage. It would also risk overwhelming headquarters with more information than it could possibly process without huge resource and personnel commitments. On the other hand, insufficient monitoring would leave BRAC programs without the information they need to track implementation, learn, and improve. With the organization operating at such a vast scale, undiagnosed problems could result in a massive waste of resources.

To arrive at the right balance, the monitoring unit utilizes a rotating schedule of data collection. Monitoring officers work in two-month periods during which they focus on a specific set of issues in three BRAC programs. After two months, officers switch their focus to another set of issues in three other BRAC programs. With this cycle, they are able to work on all 12 BRAC Uganda programs by the end of the year.

At the start of each two-month cycle, monitoring staff meet with program staff to identify the issues and challenges to focus on during the cycle. Once the list is set, the monitoring department gathers data on these issues. Each cycle also follows up on problems identified in previous monitoring cycles. If, for example, program staff identified that a low attendance rate at trainings was a significant and widespread challenge in one year, the monitoring plan would include this issue the following year to track progress.

Once the learning priorities for each program are clear, the monitoring department deploys full-time monitors to 15 of BRAC's 95 Uganda branches to learn about these issues. Each monitor is responsible for auditing program activities and collecting the necessary information at a single regional office.

At the end of the two months, the process begins again. Over the six two-month stints, the annual monitoring plan covers all of the organization's program areas and monitors the activities of each branch office in Uganda.

THE CRITICAL QUESTION: ARE CLPS ACTIVELY IMPLEMENTING THE LIVESTOCK PROGRAM?

Once CLP effort was identified as a key link in the theory of change for the livestock program, the next step was to find a way to learn whether CLPs were implementing the program as intended. Uganda's Monitoring unit, run by Program Manager Abul Bashar, led this effort. Bashar worked closely with a monitoring coordinator to oversee 13 monitoring officers, including Jovex, who collected data about BRAC's Uganda programs.

The monitoring department had two priorities. First, to understand whether CLP volunteers were reporting their efforts accurately and, second, to assess whether CLP efforts were sufficient to achieve the outputs and outcomes expected from BRAC's theory of change. The first step was to understand how many CLPs were "active." To be considered active, a CLP had to purchase 2,000 Ugandan shillings (UGX) worth of medicine (approximately $0.80) and at least one vial of vaccine (enough to vaccinate 500 birds), train or interact with at least three local groups (typically BRAC microfinance groups), and vaccinate at least 250 birds each month.

BRAC understood that setting a threshold for active status created an incentive for CLPs to misreport their work to maintain their standing. Recognizing this challenge, Bashar often instructed his officers not to take a volunteer's report about his or her own activities at face value: "If [a CLP] tells you something, do you just write it? No. You have to cross check. It is not just that someone simply tells you something and you write it down."

The process of collecting and cross-checking data began with interviews, as Jovex sought to do with Patience at the beginning of the chapter. In the interviews, BRAC monitoring officers listed the number of vaccines that a CLP reported giving as "reported." Monitoring officers then verified the data, either through the receipts that CLPs were supposed to keep or through the testimony of clients that CLPs reported to have served. After verification, the officers then recorded the actual number. As a final check, monitors were also supposed to ask the office accountant for the previous month's sales to verify both figures against internal records. In addition to this activity tracking data, officers gathered feedback from less-active CLPs on why they did not invest in medicine or vaccines. Key tracking questions are illustrated in Figure 9.1.

Data	Unit	CLP Reported	Verified Number
Did CLP receive initial CLP training?	Yes/No		
If yes, how many days of training did the CLP receive?	# of days		
Value of medicine purchased by CLP in the last month	Uganda Shillings		
If CLP did not buy medicine, opinion of CLP about why	Text response		
Number of vials of vaccines purchased by CLP in last month	# of vials of vaccines		
If CLP did not buy vaccine, opinion of CLP about why	Text response		
Number of groups CLP visited in last month	# of groups		
If no groups visited, CLP opinion as to why	Text response		

Figure 9.1 Community Livestock Promoter (CLP) activity data gathered by BRAC monitoring officers.

In the interview with Patience, Jovex wanted to determine whether Patience was "active." Patience reported to Jovex that she bought almost 3,000 UGX worth of medicines in the preceding month. When asked to show the receipts for these purchases, however, Patience said they were at the home of a CLP who happened to be very far away. Jovex worried that Patience might have been inflating her numbers. She was right: When Jovex checked with the accountants' office, she found that Patience had in fact purchased less medicine and vaccines than she had claimed.

Patience also reported that she had vaccinated more than 500 chicks that belonged to her neighbor. Jovex went to the neighbor's home and again found a different story. The neighbor reported that while her chicks had been vaccinated almost three months prior, she had done it herself with the help of her husband. In addition, the neighbor reported using a different brand of vaccine than the one subsidized by BRAC. The investigation confirmed what Jovex had suspected—Patience probably did not vaccinate the birds.

In the end, Jovex found that Patience was not active by BRAC's standards. Through similar interactions with CLPs throughout the region, Jovex learned that Patience was not the only one:

- Only 3 of the 10 CLPs Jovex visited had purchased enough medicine to be considered active, although all 10 had reported purchasing the minimum requirements.
- All 10 CLPs reported interacting with at least three groups in the previous month, but none had actually visited and trained a single group.
- Of the 10 CLPs sampled, only three confirmed that they had vaccinated any birds. They had claimed to vaccinate an average of 85 birds per person, but Jovex was only able to verify the vaccination of 21 birds per person on average.

In short, none of the CLPs that Jovex surveyed qualified as active.

Other monitoring officers found similar results. Of the 150 CLPs sampled from 15 of 95 branches across Uganda, monitoring data showed that only 11 CLPs (7.3%) qualified as active. These findings suggested that program implementation was not going as planned, and some of the program assumptions needed to be examined.

The correct organizational response would depend on how BRAC interpreted its findings. Is the problem lazy or dishonest CLPs? If so, should BRAC take drastic measures, such as penalizing or firing inactive CLPs? Should BRAC adjust its recruitment process to identify harder working or more honest CLPs? But the widespread issues identified suggested a more systemic problem. Perhaps the incentive system put in place for CLPs was not working as expected and BRAC's theory of change itself might need reevaluation.

INVESTIGATING THE RESULTS

Jovex had developed a number of theories about why activity levels were so low. She suspected that the CLP incentives might not be correctly tailored to communities' needs, noting that there was little demand for immunization, resulting in low uptake. For many farmers, money for feed took priority over vaccinations. Even when farmers did have money to vaccinate their birds, Jovex suspected that they had little reason to buy the vaccines from CLPs because local suppliers offered them at about the same price. With low community demand, CLPs often vaccinated far fewer birds than the 500 that could be treated in the 24 hours before the vaccine went bad, which meant that CLPs often incurred a net loss after a vaccine purchase.

Although this staff feedback was valuable, BRAC needed more than the opinion of one monitoring officer to be confident about why the CLPs were so inactive. To help assess the causes, BRAC developed a survey that solicited feedback from CLPs through a series of open-ended questions. The form asked CLPs to detail the challenges they faced in their work, as well as a number of other questions about the challenges and successes of CLPs implementing the program. "We ask this to know the difference between the demand and what we provide," Jovex explained.

REPORTING FINDINGS

After the monitoring team collected the feedback data, Jovex wrote a written summary of the findings and shared it with the Uganda Poultry and Livestock Program team. Jovex and other officers noted that this could be the hardest part of their job due to resistance and resentment from branch-level staff who sometimes felt that monitoring was designed to get them in trouble. "Sometimes [project staff] call us police," she said. Although Jovex acknowledged that presenting her findings to the team was "uncomfortable," she also recognized its necessity. Since the project associates were in charge of training and supervising the CLPs, this feedback would provide important information about how well they were doing their jobs.

Even though the project team leader for western Uganda was dismayed to learn that only 7.3% of her CLPs were active, she signed off on the report and Jovex sent her data to Bashar at BRAC Uganda headquarters in Kampala. In Kampala, Bashar used the data to create two reports: a detailed report intended for project staff and management in Uganda and a brief that distilled the same information into graphics for program heads at BRAC's headquarters in Bangladesh.

The first report aimed to inform day-to-day decisions in Uganda. It displayed all of the information about CLP activity collected for that period, summarized at the branch level in a series of Excel spreadsheets. It also summarized instances when CLPs may have misrepresented their activities, information that project associates could use to better manage and support CLPs.

The brief sent to Bangladesh (included in the Appendix to this case) distilled the same information into charts and graphs for program heads in Bangladesh who had to sign off on any programmatic change. This report, intended to inform decisions about big-picture program design and implementation, included statistics on the number of active CLPs (Sections 4 and 5), qualitative information about the appropriateness of the vaccines (Section 8), a list of materials that could help CLPs better do their jobs (Section 7), and the survey feedback from CLPs (Sections 6 and 7).

Bashar always tried to be impartial when presenting data to program management. Rather than drawing conclusions about how to improve the program, he aimed to simply report the data to program staff, who would then figure out how to use it to make changes.

Analysis Question 2: What elements of this reporting process created actionable data? What barriers to action remain, and how can they be addressed? In what ways can reporting be improved?

IMPROVING THE PROGRAM

This was not the first time Bashar had reported concerns about CLP activity to management: the issue of inactive CLPs had first been investigated two years earlier. When those initial findings indicated a gap between expected and actual performance, the same issue was monitored the following year, and again a third time, as described in this case. Bashar observed that "sometimes it takes time, but action is mandatory—there is no alternative way." He was therefore pleased when he heard that the program heads in Bangladesh had decided to take action.

To address the issue of vaccine waste due to expiration, the Community Livestock and Poultry Program manager in Kampala found a smaller

100 mL vial that could be imported from Kenya. The new vial was smaller and could be used for 72 hours before it spoiled—rather than just 24 hours for the previous vial—which should result in less wasted vaccine. The manager expected this smaller vial to allow CLPs to better meet demand for poultry vaccinations in the communities. BRAC management expected the new vials to provide a greater incentive for CLPs to vaccinate birds, which would in turn improve outcomes for farmers in the region. Understanding whether the new vials alone would create sufficient incentives for CLPs given all the other issues they faced would require another round of monitoring by Jovex and the rest of the team.

Analysis Question 3: Based on what you know from the case, do you think the change to small, longer-lasting vaccine vials will be enough to improve the activity rates of CLPs? Which of the performance challenges does this change address, and which challenges remain? Consider the five types of monitoring data presented in Chapter 5: Which of these five does BRAC collect for this program, and what monitoring data might help them further understand the situation?

APPENDIX: SELECTIONS FROM THE SHORT REPORT

CLP Activities in Preceding Month (150 CLPs)

Particulars		Results	
		Number	Percentage
Bird treatment	CLP	26	17
	Birds	1103	—
Model poultry rearer visit	CLP	12	9
	Rearer	12	—
Key rearers visit		14	9
Chick rearer visit		2	1
Animal treatment	CLP	11	7
	Animals	83	—
Dewormers sold (Number of CLPs)		1	1
Active CLPs (bought ≥200Ush of medicine and 1 vaccine vial, and visited 3 groups)		11	7.33

Figure 9A.1 Community Livestock Promoter (CLP) Activities in Preceding Month (150 CLPs).

Necessary Additional Support Reported by CLPs

Particulars	Reported By:	
	Number	Percentage
T-shirts, umbrellas, gum boots	55	37
Should give CLPs poultry items on loan	18	12
Reduce prices	18	12
Provide refrigerators for vaccines	12	8
Torches	11	7
Flasks	8	5
Bicycles due to long distances	8	5
Involve community members in trainrigs	7	5
Put up shops selling P/L products	5	3
Need poultry drinkers	3	2
Chicken feeds/always in stock/Vanety vaccine	3	2
Should provide vaccines for free	2	1

Figure 9A.2 Community Livestock Promoter (CLP) Activities in Preceding Month (150 CLPs).

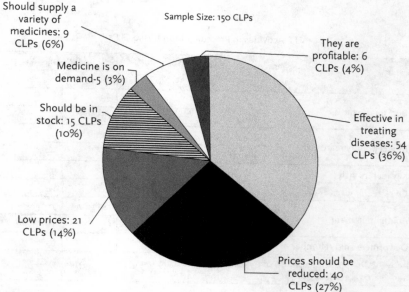

CLP Opinions on Medicines

Sample Size: 150 CLPs

Should supply a variety of medicines: 9 CLPs (6%)

They are profitable: 6 CLPs (4%)

Medicine is on demand-5 (3%)

Should be in stock: 15 CLPs (10%)

Effective in treating diseases: 54 CLPs (36%)

Low prices: 21 CLPs (14%)

Prices should be reduced: 40 CLPs (27%)

Figure 9A.3 Necessary Additional Support Reported by Community Livestock Promoters (CLPs).

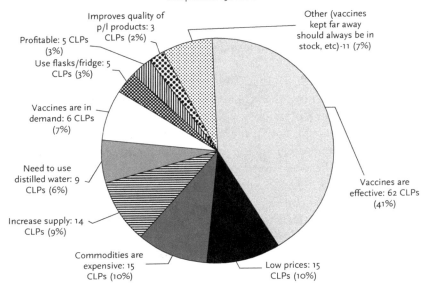

Figure 9A.4 Community Livestock Promoter (CLP) Opinions on Medicines.

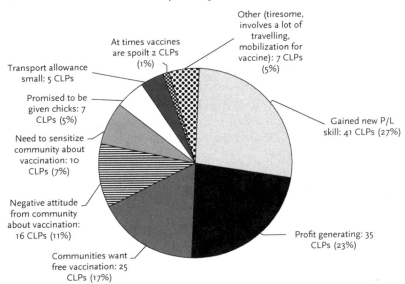

Figure 9A.5 Community Livestock Promoter (CLP) Opinions on Vaccines.

CASE ANALYSIS

> Analysis Question 1: From a management perspective, what are some of the advantages and disadvantages of BRAC's decision to split monitoring and evaluation into different departments?

The main advantage is that the split recognizes the fundamental differences in learning that come from monitoring versus evaluation. At many other organizations, a single department is responsible for collecting data about both program operations and program impact. Housing both functions in the same department can blur the crucial differences between outputs and outcomes that we described in Chapters 3 and 5. BRAC needs to continually monitor programs to be sure that microfranchises are implementing the program as planned, which it does by conducting a deep, two-month dive into data collection. Separating this monitoring function from the evaluation function also allows the monitoring team to time data collection to maximize actionability. Since the monitoring department is also separate from the program implementation team, the credibility of the data is enhanced. Monitoring staff are more likely to report honestly because they do not report to those managing the program.

However, the emphasis on making sure that programs are being correctly implemented can undermine the monitoring team's mission to understand the program more comprehensively. Monitoring in this way inevitably makes program staff wary about visits from monitors—the "police," as one project associate called them. These staff may be hesitant to offer honest information about program implementation, and any staff trepidation could harm the credibility of the data. In these situations, there is a real danger of creating division in an organization in which different departments lose sight of the fact that they are working toward the same goals. In addition, program staff may not feel ownership of the data and may view it as being useful to the central monitoring team but not for improving programs.

> Analysis Question 2: What elements of this reporting process created actionable data? Are there still barriers to action? In what ways can reporting be improved?

Presenting monitoring data to the project team is an important first step to spurring action. This gives the team implementing the project the chance to understand, interpret, and respond to the data. BRAC's livestock program leader signed off on the CLP report, but it is easy to imagine an alternative scenario in which the project team and monitoring team really clash over the data's meaning and credibility. To avoid such distractions and conflicts, organizations need to create a culture of program learning and avoid punishing program managers when projects are not going as intended. To do so, organizations need to share data locally with managers and to reward adaptation, learning, and improvement, rather than blindly setting targets with predetermined consequences.

The graphics from the briefing reports to management (shown in the Figures A9.1 through A9.5) provide some insight into potential implementation gaps and areas for improvement, most notably in the low number of active CLPs. Feedback data from CLPs (shown in the pie charts) help to identify potential causes for low activity. For example, many CLPs complained about the high price of vaccines and reported that communities had a negative opinion of them. These reports indicate that the products may require more sensitization or that perhaps BRAC should reconsider its pricing structure.

Although it does present a lot of actionable information to program managers, this briefing report could present information in a more effective manner. Instead of these pie charts, BRAC should simply code these responses and present the raw numbers to program leadership. This simple change would help convey some important findings that get lost in the pie charts (for example, that very few CLPs report that the vaccines are actually in demand) and could increase the actionability of the monitoring data.

BRAC has developed a monitoring system that reduces the "drowning in data" problem that is common at so many NGOs. The organization decided on this system after asking program staff to help set the monitoring agenda. This system in turn delivers targeted, actionable information to decision-makers at the program level and in management.

While the system supplies actionable information, actionability is hampered by the long decision-making chain. Information must make its way back to Bangladesh, where managers are empowered to make program decisions. Program managers in country may not have the authority to make even minor changes to their programs. BRAC has invested in developing credible and, in theory, actionable data. However, the organization may need to change its system to fully actualize the data's action potential.

BRAC could take several approaches to increasing actionability. First, the organization could clarify which decisions can be made at the country level and which require approval from program heads in Bangladesh.

Perhaps straightforward implementation questions, such as how to source vaccines, could be addressed at the country level. Structural changes that impact the overall theory of change may need to be decided upon in Bangladesh. In addition, BRAC could work to define in advance the possible actions to be taken based on monitoring data, which could speed up response times to the briefing reports. For example, they could decide that CLPs' relationships with BRAC will not be renewed if they go more than six months without being active, or they could agree to reexamine performance in a given region if more than 50% of CLPs are not active.

> Analysis Question 3: Based on what you know from the case, do you think the change to small, longer lasting vaccine vials will be enough to improve the activity rates of CLPs? Which of the performance challenges does this change address, and which challenges remain? Consider the five types of monitoring data presented in Chapter 5: Which of these five does BRAC collect for this program, and what monitoring data might help them further understand the situation?

The change in vaccine vials addresses one key challenge for CLPs: ensuring that CLP-delivered vaccines are price-competitive with other vaccines. The feedback gathered from CLPs and presented in the Appendix suggest some other challenges: farmer demand for vaccines may be quite low, and a number of farmers may feel that vaccines should be free. The CLP data also suggest that some CLPs may need loans in order to access poultry products to sell to farmers. BRAC may need to gather additional data to see how serious these problems are and whether they affect all CLPs or just those in certain areas.

Overall, BRAC is doing a good job of activity tracking by collecting data on CLP activities and sales and verifying that information to ensure that it is credible. Actionability is supported by having a separate monitoring unit that is responsible for reporting the information to project management, but the long feedback chain through headquarters in Bangladesh slows down this process. BRAC is collecting good engagement and feedback data from CLPs but might want to consider additional takeup and engagement data from the poultry producers themselves. This would help them better understand whether performance challenges are the result of assumptions of the CLP microfranchise model, product characteristics and demand, or some other factor.

CHAPTER 10

Salama SHIELD Foundation

The Challenge of Actionability

INTRODUCTION

Jackson Matovu, a program officer at the Salama SHIELD Foundation (SSF), was visiting self-help groups in a community a 20-minute drive outside the town of Lyantonde in southwestern Uganda (see Box 10.1). He had come to learn more about *Finance for Life*, a small microfinance program designed to help women get the credit they needed to start businesses or pay for productive assets. He was interested in one feature of the program in particular: for each of the five years of the program's existence, SSF's data showed that everyone repaid their loans in full. Matovu and SSF staff believed the high repayment rates reflected the success of the program and indicated that their model, built to leverage group incentives to repay, could be scaled to other parts of Uganda. But they also wondered what factors contributed to these rates and if there were any untold stories behind them.

Matovu located the self-help groups and asked some of the group members about why they repaid on time. He heard a consistent message: group members respected SSF's work and wanted the program to continue. "We all want the next round of lending," replied one group member. "SSF loans on good will, so we feel like we should repay," added another.

Although encouraging, Matovu believed that these statements did not tell the whole story. And they did not give him confidence that similarly high repayment rates would continue if SSF scaled up across Uganda.

Box 10.1 SALAMA SHIELD FOUNDATION

Monitoring data at the Ugandan Salama SHIELD Foundation revealed perfect repayment rates in its microfinance program. But rather than take these data at face value, a diligent program officer set out to determine if the data might be concealing other stories. In his efforts to investigate the truth behind the data, he made a number of decisions about what data to collect—and, importantly, what not to. But, as this case demonstrates, actionable data are only half the story; right-fit resources and systems are necessary to turn data into action. As you read this case, you will think critically about what data are necessary to answer key operational questions and will design data collection instruments to deliver these data. You will also consider ways of applying the CART principles (Credible, Actionable, Responsible, and Transportable) to strengthen the data collection system and determine where the organization should focus its monitoring efforts.

Matovu wanted answers to two questions. Were repayments always made on time? And, if they were, what forces were driving these exceptional numbers? Back in the office the next day, Matovu and his team started thinking about how they would answer these questions. They knew they would have to look beyond anecdotes and gather the right kind of hard data.

ABOUT SALAMA SHIELD FOUNDATION

SSF was founded in 1994 by Dr. Dennis Willms, a Canadian medical anthropologist who had been conducting behavioral and ethnographic research on HIV/AIDS in southwestern Uganda. Willms and his co-investigator Dr. Nelson Sewankambo focused on Lyantonde, a town on the main trucking route through Uganda to the Democratic Republic of Congo, Rwanda, and other countries. Through their research, Willms and Sewankambo found that the HIV/AIDS problem in Lyantonde was multifaceted: limited economic opportunity outside of the "hospitality" industry catering to truckers, combined with limited health infrastructure and awareness, resulted in one of the highest HIV rates in Uganda.

Willms began thinking of culturally relevant interventions that would attend to the needs of the most at-risk individuals. In 1994, with the help of a generous donor, Willms formed the Salama Shield Foundation, and his colleague, Dr. Sewankambo, the Principal and Dean of the College of Health Sciences at Makerere University in Kampala, joined the Board that same year.

Over time, SSF's mission grew from providing HIV/AIDS prevention education to addressing the broader determinants of risk for HIV transmission. The goal of this expanded focus was to promote "sustainable, healthy communities in Africa" through four program areas: income support; health counseling; food security, water, and sanitation; and education.

This case focuses on the monitoring and evaluation challenges in SSF's *Finance for Life* program, a group microfinance program that gives loans to women who are, according to SSF, "honest, hard-working, and just in need of an opportunity." The program consists of groups of 5–25 women who each take individual loans ranging from $20 to $315, repaid along with 12% interest over six months.

SSF expects that women in this program will use the capital to start businesses, generating income that families can use to increase savings and pay for health care, education, or other expenses. In 2013, the fund gave loans to about 750 women in 80 groups in Lyantonde and Rakai Districts in southwestern Uganda.

To identify the most creditworthy borrowers, SSF conducts an extensive vetting process before disbursing any money. This process starts with a community meeting that introduces the program and explains the program's rules and who can participate. The organization emphasizes the importance of repayment: the program will only continue disbursing new loans if groups pay back the loan within a six-month cycle. If a group repays, SSF allows them to bring five new members into the next cycle. If the group is unable to repay the loan in full, SSF will put the whole community on probation. If a second group of borrowers fail to repay, SSF will not offer any more loans in the village.

The program proceeds in the following sequence:

1. In a community meeting, and after outlining program rules and eligibility, SSF asks community members to select people who need capital and would put the money to good use. Meeting participants nominate individuals to receive the first cycle of loans.
2. SSF evaluates the nominees by collecting data on the current income-generating activities of nominated individuals. The organization assumes that those who already have a stable source of income are less likely to default on a loan. "We select women who we know have the ability to repay," explained one of the field officers.

3. Using community recommendations, its own assessments of the women's ability to repay, and informal credit checks, SSF selects those who will receive a loan.
4. SSF then trains new members in financial skills like business management, savings, and income generation, as well as in sanitation and health. In these trainings, SSF also helps future borrowers identify group and individual projects to start with the loan funds and the appropriate loan amounts for each project.
5. When training concludes, SSF disburses the loans to borrowers.
6. After disbursing funds, SSF gives borrowers a one-month grace period before they begin to repay the loan. This enables borrowers to use the loan to make productive investments without worrying about generating immediate returns. Thereafter, SSF collects payments monthly on a specified due date. Payments must be made in full on behalf of the whole group; partial payments are not accepted. Once a group has made the full set of payments, it can enter into a new lending cycle.

QUESTION-DRIVEN MONITORING AND EVALUATION

To supplement the information gathered from the client focus groups in Lyantonde, Matovu asked SSF staff about their ideas on what might be driving the high repayment rates. The first explanation supported what he had heard in the field: many program officers had worked in communities long before *Finance for Life*, implementing SSF's other programs in health and education. Because borrowers knew their program officers well, they were more likely to repay. The importance of relationships in loan repayment has been supported in research. A study conducted by Dean Karlan, Melanie Morton, and Jonathan Zinman on the effectiveness of different SMS loan repayment reminders found that SMS reminders including the name of the borrower's loan officer were more effective than those that did not.[1]

However, SSF staff also believed that the rule that missed payments would result in termination of lending to groups was creating strong peer incentives to repay loans. Matovu worried that this pressure could have two consequences. First, given the high stakes, he suspected that if an individual group member was not able to make her monthly repayment, other group members would lend her money to enable full group repayment. While this was good for the organization's bottom line, it could also indicate problems with the screening process and reflect poorly on the health of the system. Second, Matovu worried that program officers were letting late payments go unrecorded to help borrowers stay in good standing in the program. Although he respected the need for flexibility and understood that SSF did not want to punish borrowers for small infractions, Matovu also recognized that SSF would have no way of knowing how well the program was truly functioning without accurately recording the timing of repayments.

Matovu and the SSF team revised Matovu's initial query to guide additional investigation into repayment rates. They wanted to know:

1. Are the group repayment rates really received on the scheduled date 100% of the time? What proportion of groups repay, but late?
2. Where does the money for repayments come from? How often do members pay on behalf of those who cannot pay in order to avoid group default?
3. If repayment rates are genuinely high, what motivates people to repay their loans?

> Analysis Question 1: How would you find the answers to SSF's key questions? Think about the information you need, the frequency of collection, and the unit of analysis. How would you collect this information and ensure the validity and reliability of the measure?

ASSESSING DATA COLLECTION

With these guiding questions and several possible explanations, Matovu began to think about how to collect more detailed information on repayment rates. He started by assessing current data collection tools at SSF to see if they could be used in his effort.

The organization used three forms to collect all *Finance for Life* data. To monitor group progress, SSF used a Loans and Savings Tracking Sheet (Figure 10.1) that gathered financial data on three indicators. A *Loan Repayment* section collected information on the total amount of each payment, identifying how much went to principal and interest. A *Savings* section noted the amount of money deposited and withdrawn from the borrower's savings account during a given month. The *Balance* section tracked the remaining principal and interest on the loan, as well as the savings balance the borrower accumulated.

SSF also conducted a baseline survey of its borrowers before they entered the program to learn about the program's participants. The survey generated a basic profile of borrowers, including their loan history,

Name of group..

No	NAME	LOAN REPAYMENT			SAVINGS		BALANCE		
		PRINCIPAL	INTEREST	TOTAL	DEPOSIT	WITHDRAW	LOAN	INTEREST	TOTAL
1									
2									
	TOTAL								

Figure 10.1 Initial loans and savings tracking sheet.

what they planned to do with their loan, and how they planned to pay it back (see Appendix A). SSF also administered a follow-up survey at the end of each lending cycle (Appendix B). This survey included a series of open-ended feedback questions designed to capture how borrowers used their loans, what benefits they gained from the program, the challenges they faced, and how they thought the program might be improved in the future.

Finally, to learn about the experiences of successful borrowers in the program, SSF developed a "Guideline Questionnaire for Success Stories" form (Appendix C) that gathered more detailed qualitative feedback data about how standout borrowers used their loans and their overall opinions about the program.

DESIGNING TOOLS TO ANSWER TARGETED QUESTIONS

After surveying these forms, Matovu realized that SSF had to develop a more robust and targeted system of data collection in order to fully understand the high repayment rates. Matovu determined that the best approach would be to revise the Loans and Savings Tracking sheet introduced in the previous section. Program officers were already using these sheets to track program activities, and adding a few more questions would not be much of a burden.

To find out whether borrowers were really repaying on time, Matovu added a column titled "Delinquency" (see the final form in Figure 10.2), which tracked whether or not the borrower was late that month. To learn more about how borrowers were repaying, he added a section called "Support for Repayment." One column in this section catalogued money that borrowers had received to help repay their loans, and another tracked the amount a borrower had lent to those in need. These data would help

SALAMA SHIELD FOUNDATION (MICRO-CREDIT)

DAILY LOANS AND SAVINGS TRACKING SHEET

(version 2, 11/15/11)

Village: _____

Date Scheduled: _____   Date Received: _____   Month Number: _____

Particulars			Loan Repayment				Support For Repayment			Savings			Delinquency
No.	Client Name	Amount Disbursed	Principal	Interest	Total	Amount Repaid (Loan)	Amount Support Received	Amount Support Given	Days to Repay Previous Support	Accumulated	Deposit	Total	Ready to pay on scheduled day?
1													Y / N
2													Y / N
3													Y / N

TOTAL AMOUNT RECEIVED: _____ UGX

Chair Person _____   Signature: _____
(for group)

Received By: _____   Signature: _____
(for SSF)

Figure 10.2 Final loans and savings tracking sheet.

SSF understand how pervasive and severe the repayment problems were. Matovu also wanted to know how long it took those borrowing from friends to repay them, so he created a third column in the same section titled "Days to Repay Previous Support."

Matovu considered adding a column to record the number of people who supported another group member's repayment. If many people needed lots of support to repay, that could indicate that the loans were too costly and put too much pressure on borrowers, in which case SSF would think about decreasing the size of loans, extending the grace period, or even revising the borrower selection criteria. But Matovu realized that SSF wouldn't learn enough from a simple count of the number of lenders. For example, if a borrower was 10,000 Ugandan Shillings (UGX) short and asked two people to help—one loaning 2,000 UGX and another 8,000 UGX—the column would register that in the same way as if the borrower had received just 2,000 UGX from the same two people.

Matovu also considered tracking how much of each repayment was drawn from profits generated by the enterprises borrowers started with their *Finance for Life* loans. Although this information would quantify a critical part of SSF's theory of change, in the end Matovu decided not to pursue it. He realized that it would be hard, if not impossible, to get accurate data from that question because few borrowers were likely to have records with this level of detail.

The final version of the form, shown as Figure 10.2: [Final] Loans and Savings Form, included information about the amount and duration of support and was tested by staff in the field before SSF rolled it out to all groups in the *Finance for Life* program.

> Analysis Question 2: Does the final version of the tracking form solicit the data necessary to answer SSF's questions on repayment rates and sources? If not, what kind of form would? Describe the changes you would make and the reasons you would make them.

FAST FORWARD

Just one year after the new tracking sheet was finalized, stacks of completed sheets containing repayment information about each program group had piled up in the *Finance for Life* office. Even though the data had been diligently collected, none had been entered or analyzed. Why? "It is a problem of systems," said one staff member. "Even resources," added another.

To process the data, a staff member would have to enter information from the paper tracking sheet into an Excel spreadsheet by hand, a long and tedious process that would have to be completed for each of the program's 750 borrowers every month. Because SSF does not have dedicated monitoring and evaluation staff, the responsibility of entering and analyzing the forms falls on the program officers, whose primary responsibilities lie elsewhere. SSF staff admitted that they barely have time to collect the data on the tracking forms; any time spent on data entry or analysis would take time from program activities.

Even so, staff recognize that their failure to enter data represents six months of lost learning that could help improve their microfinance program. As the organization moves forward, it is working to develop more robust monitoring and evaluation systems so that it can make a more responsible commitment to answering key questions in the future.

Analysis Question 3: What does the lack of data entry and analysis say about how SSF's monitoring system holds up to the CART principles of credible, actionable, responsible, and transportable data?

Analysis Question 4: Where should SSF focus its monitoring and evaluation efforts going forward?

APPENDIX A: BASELINE QUESTIONNAIRE FOR THE MICROCREDIT WOMEN BENEFICIARIES

Date (dd/mm/yy): _____ Village _____

Interviewer: _____ Interviewee: _____

1.0. What is your Sex?   1. Female   2. Male
    1.0.1.   What is your age? __years

1.1   What is your tribe?

1.2.   For how long have you been a resident of this place? ___years
    1.2.1.   Have you shifted residences in the past one year?   1. Yes   2. No

1.3.0   Have you ever gone to school?   1. Yes   2. No *(If no skip to 1.4)*
    1.3.1   *(If Yes)* What is the highest level of education you have completed?

1.4.   Do you consider yourself to be a religious person? [] Yes   [] No (Skip to 1.5)
    [] Not sure (Skip to 1.5)
    1.4a.   What is your religion?

1.5.   What is your **current** marital status?
    1.5a.   **If currently married or cohabiting:** Are you in a monogamous or polygamous relationship?
    Circle one.   1. Monogamous *(go to 1.6)*   2. Polygamous *(Go to 1.5b.)*
    1.5b.   **If female in polygamous relationship**: How many wives does your husband have, including yourself?

1.6.   Have you had any biological children?   [] Yes   [] No *(If no, go to 1.6.c)*
    1.6.a.   How many are alive?   (M/F)
    1.6.b.   How many have died?   (M/F)
    1.6.c.   Do you stay with any orphaned children in your home?   [] Yes   [] No
    1.6.d.   *If yes,* how many? _____
    1.6.e   Apart from the orphaned children, do you have other dependants?   [] Yes   [] No
    1.6.f   *If yes,* how many? _____

1.7.   Do you stay in your own house?   [] Yes   [] No, I rent

1.8.0.   Are you the head of the household you live in?   [] Yes   [] No
    1.8.0a.   If no, who are you in relation to the head of the household?

1.9   What is the nature of your work/**main** occupation

2.0.   What is your **most important** source of income?
    2.0.a.   What are your **other** sources of income?

2.1.   What is your **main** expenditure?
    2.1.a.   What are your **other** expenditures?

2.2.   Have you ever taken a loan?   [] Yes []   No
    2.2a.   *(If Yes)* Where have you ever taken a loan from?
    2.2b.   *(If Yes)* What was the last loan amount?
    2.2.c   *(If Yes)* What did you use the money for?
    2.2.d   *(If Yes)* How much of the loan did you pay back?
    2.2.e   *(If Yes)* How much have you not paid back yet?
    2.2.d.   *(If No)* Why have you never taken a loan?

2.3   How much do you hope to get from the Salama SHIELD Foundation?

2.4   How do you plan to use the money?

2.5   How do you plan to pay back the money?

APPENDIX B: ENDLINE ASSESSMENT QUESTIONNAIRE

Assessment Questionnaire

Date: _____   Village:. _____
Interviewer: _____   Interviewer: _____

1. What is your age?
2. What was your project?
3. How much money did you get first cycle?
4a. What benefits did you get from your project?
4b. What benefits did you get from the Program?
5. What challenges did you find?
6. How did you overcome the challenges?
7. How can we improve the program?

APPENDIX C: ENDLINE ASSESSMENT QUESTIONNAIRE

Personal Information:
1. Name
2. Age
3. Marriage Status
4. Occupation
5. Level of Education
6. Number of children (M/F)
7. No of children go to school (M/F)
8. Avg. Age of children (M/F)

Group Information:
9. Name of the group
10. No. of members in the group
11. What role do you play in the group
12. How did you and other group members came to know SSF Micro credit
13. What benefits do you get from a group
14. What are some of the challenges of being in a group

Project Information:
15. What is your project
16. How many cycles have you received money and how much: (1st: 2nd: 3rd: 4th:)
17. What improvement have you made in your project after receiving a loan
18. How have been paying back the loan
19. What benefits have you got from the program
20. What challenges have you encountered
21. How can we improve on the program (suggestions for improvement)
22. Any other concern that need urgent attention

Previous loan performance:
23. Had you ever received any loan before joining SSF Micro credit program
24. Do you have any other loan from any other financial source

CASE ANALYSIS

> Analysis Question 1: How would you find the answers to SSF's key questions? Think about the information you need, the frequency of collection, and the unit of analysis. How would you collect this information and ensure the validity and reliability of the measure?

To answer this question, first recall the three key questions SSF would like to answer:

1. Are the group repayment rates really received on the scheduled date 100% of the time? What proportion of groups repay, but late?
2. Where does the money for the repayments come from? How often do members pay on behalf of those who cannot pay in order to avoid group default?
3. If repayment rates are high, what motivates people to repay their loans?

Then, think about the indicators SSF needs to measure to understand its key questions: when loans are repaid, how borrowers make repayments, and what the underlying motivation is for those repayments.

SSF should use activity monitoring data to learn about when loans are repaid. Let's consider issues of validity and reliability first. Survey data are likely more credible than periodically collected qualitative data due both to recall (borrowers may not remember when they made each repayment) and bias in self-reporting (respondents may not want to admit how long it took them to repay because SSF will end the program if borrowers fail to repay). To collect these data, SSF could add the date of repayment to the delinquency questions on the new Loans and Savings Tracking Sheet. Program officers should also record:

- How much each individual borrower repaid on the scheduled date each month.
- And, for borrowers who didn't pay in full, did they pay the full amount by the end of the month?

To find out where borrower money for repayment comes from, SSF could add questions about the amount and source of support to existing monthly tracking forms, as we saw Program Officer Jackson Matovu do in the case. Or the organization could use the endline survey to ask structured questions. In either case, SSF should be sure that it is collecting reliable information and design its questions to minimize bias. For example, because SSF pledges to end the program in a community that fails to repay, people who are in danger of becoming delinquent may underreport the amount of support they receive from others. Rather than asking borrowers how much support they needed to make the repayments, asking group members how much they contributed to help others repay may result in less biased data. SSF should ask each beneficiary about money received and given in support every month. Furthermore, to minimize bias and maximize the reliability of the questions, SSF should consider pretesting the wording of the question and conduct thorough staff training to limit the extent to which people hold back the truth. To summarize, the questions would be:

- How much support did you receive to make a repayment?
- How much did you give to someone to repay their loans?

Finally, SSF can learn about the motivation for repayments through both qualitative and quantitative feedback data. Focus groups of borrowers would provide detailed qualitative information about how they feel about the program and what motivates them to repay. A simple multiple-choice question ("What is the most important motivation for you to repay your loan on time?") asked during the endline survey could gather this information, with the benefit of providing a large, representative sample. Keep in mind, though, that either form of feedback data could be biased by participants praising the program because they want to keep it around. Multiple-choice questions might mitigate this risk somewhat but could also artificially constrain responses.

Although both qualitative and quantitative approaches are valid, the choice of method does influence the unit of analysis. If SSF conducted focus groups, it could lead a discussion with whole communities, interview different groups (groups that have consistently made repayments and groups that have not, for example), or talk one on one with borrowers. Quantitative data collection, on the other hand, happens at the individual level, though SSF could collect and analyze data for the whole program.

When considering how to collect data, SSF should ask itself what action it will take based on what it learns. As Matovu noted, it might be enough for SSF to know the degree of difficulty borrowers face in repaying their loans. Knowing their motivation for doing so might be interesting, but would it influence decision-making within the organization? If so, then the cost of data collection may be justified. But if management can't define an action it would take based on this information, then the responsible step may be to scrap this line of investigation.

> Analysis Question 2: Does the final version of the tracking form solicit the data necessary to answer SSF's questions on repayment rates and sources of repayment funds? If not, describe the changes you would make and the reasons you would make them.

The progression in data collection Matovu followed—articulating key questions, conducting field interviews to better understand the problem, and then designing forms to better capture the information needed to answer those key questions—is a sound way to gather credible, actionable data. Although the form Matovu created is a step in the right direction, it misses some information about the nature of repayments and collects some information that might not hold any value for the organization. We have included a sample form that corrects these imbalances in Figure 10.3. To create it, we did the following:

1. Removed the questions on savings. Since participants' savings are an outcome-level change, SSF has no way to know whether they changed as a result of their intervention or because of a number of other possible factors. What if someone in a participating family got sick and the family needed to pay for medical bills out of savings? The form would register a sharp decrease in savings that in no way reflects the impact of the "Finance for Life" program. Data on savings are not credible without a counterfactual.

2. Changed the delinquency indicator to the question "Paid in Full?" and moved this column to the appropriate section. The term "delinquency" has a negative connotation. Beneficiaries might see it and respond negatively to their inclusion this category. It could also bias Program Officers' behavior, resulting in inaccurate reporting or additional pressure on borrowers as they do not want to report that they have delinquent groups.

3. Created clearer questions for repayment amounts. This meant separating the question into two parts: "Principal Amount Paid" and "Interest Amount Paid." It is more reliable to ask about the balance at the beginning of the month because the amount will change if a woman pays some on time and some at the end. Adding the loan balance gives the total balance owed by each beneficiary.

DAILY LOANS AND SAVINGS TRACKING SHEET

(version 3)

Village: _____

Date Scheduled: _____   Date Received: _____   Month Number: _____

No.	Particulars				This Month's Loan Repayment						This Month's Support For Repayment		
	Client's Name	Loan Amount Disbursed (Loan+Interset)	Principle Amount Paid (as of last month)	Interest Amount Paid (as of last month)	Total Paid on Scheduled Date		Total Paid at Follow-up Visit		Paid in Full?		Amount of Support Received	Amount of Support Given	# People Owed for Past Support
					Principal	Interest	Principal	Interest					
1									Y/N				
2									Y/N				
3									Y/N				
4									Y/N				
5									Y/N				
6									Y/N				

Chair Person _____   Signature: _____ (for group)

Received By: _____   Signature: _____ (for SSF)

TOTAL AMOUNT RECEIVED: _____ UGX

TOTAL AMOUNT OWED: _____ UGX

Figure 10.3 Proposed loans and savings tracking sheet.

4. For the amount paid during the current month, we separated out how much was paid on the scheduled date and how much on a program officer's follow-up visit. This will help SSF find out how much women are struggling to repay, as we outlined in Question 1.
5. Removed the "Days to Repay Previous Support" column due to concerns about its credibility. The goal of this indicator is to measure how much people struggle to repay the support they received. However, if people received support from two people for one monthly repayment, would they have to add the days together? It is unclear how SSF staff would interpret this. We considered other indicators, all of which had similar flaws. Given that the findings would be vague, we think it is best to remove this indicator altogether.
6. Added "Total Amount Owed" at the bottom of the form to track the group total and make it readily available for program officers to share with members.

These changes should make the form easier to understand and help SSF collect better data about its programs.

> Analysis Question 3: What does the lack of data entry and analysis say about how SSF's monitoring system holds up to the CART principles?

The repayment data were not analyzed in the six months after the forms were designed, which could indicate a lack of organizational capacity. Indeed, program officers indicate that they do not have time to process the forms. It could also indicate lack of buy-in throughout the organization, misaligned incentives for program officers, or poor planning and staff management. Regardless of the root cause, the system as described in this case did not adhere to the *responsible* principle. Resources were being spent on data that were not being used.

Ideally, SSF would think through a series of questions before collecting the data to determine if the expanded data collection would really help staff learn. For example:

- Who will be responsible for entering the data from the forms into Excel? Do these people have the time to do so? If so, what responsibilities might they have to set aside? If not, will management hire the necessary staff to process the forms?
- Has SSF management bought into the need for these data? How can management support data collection and analysis efforts?

- What incentives do program officers face in their daily tasks? How can they be aligned to adequately incentivize entering the data they collect?
- What systems exist for extracting and analyzing the data? How often will the data be analyzed? With whom will the data be shared, and with what frequency?

Answering these questions beforehand should increase the chance that SSF would be able to enter and use the data. However, to make its monitoring system more responsible, SSF needs to increase its capacity to process repayment data and find more efficient ways to gather it.

Improving organizational capacity to process these data should be the first step. Gathering good financial data about repayment rates should be the primary monitoring goal of any microfinance program. Without knowing who is repaying and when, SSF will not be able to credibly identify problems if they occur or use data to improve the program in the future.

Mobile data collection, using tablets or smart phones, could improve the efficiency of data collection by eliminating the need to transcribe paper forms. However, it would likely require significant investment—reconfiguring SSF's information management system to interact with mobile software would be costly, as would purchasing equipment and training staff. Without the ability to analyze collected data, mobile technology would not be a responsible use of resources. However, once SSF improves its analytical capacity, the organization could consider more efficient forms of data collection such as tablets or smart phones.

No matter what data SSF ultimately collects, it will have to make some investments to make the data credible and actionable. In addition to investments in staff to make the data more credible, SSF should consider developing a system for reviewing the data on a regular basis. Monthly staff meetings could be used to share results, identify problems, and brainstorm responses.

> Analysis Question 4: Where should SSF focus its monitoring and evaluation efforts going forward?

Considering the organization's small size and limited data collection abilities, SSF should focus on the basics of it monitoring system—credibly collecting key repayment data and strengthening its capacity to process these data in a timely manner.

But repayment rates and timely analysis are just a start. SSF is missing a few indicators that would give the organization greater insight into the sustainability of the program: it should define what it considers to be the key aspects of a healthy microfinance program and focus on collecting and analyzing those data. In general, all microfinance institutions should collect data about their reach, repayment rates, sustainability, and similar indicators.[2]

CHAPTER 11

Invisible Children Uganda

An Evolving Monitoring and Evaluation System

KONY 2012

In early 2012, the nonprofit organization Invisible Children created a 30-minute video called *Kony 2012* to raise awareness about warlord Joseph Kony's crimes during the civil war in Northern Uganda that began in 1987 (see Box 11.1). *Kony 2012* went viral. By March 15, just 10 days after it was posted, the video had attracted more than 80 million online views.

The popularity of the video translated into action on the part of many viewers. People all over the world started wearing t-shirts and armbands in support of *Kony 2012*. Messages of support for the *Kony 2012* campaign took over Facebook feeds. The video also swayed members of Congress. In the words of Republican U.S. Senator Lindsey Graham:

> This is about someone who, without the Internet and YouTube, their dastardly deeds would not resonate with politicians. When you get 100 million Americans looking at something, you will get our attention. This YouTube sensation is [going to] help the Congress be more aggressive and will do more to lead to his demise than all other action combined.[1]

The *Kony 2012* campaign showcased the types of advocacy campaigns that Invisible Children had conducted for years, but it brought the organization a new level of visibility. At the time of the video, the organization was already expanding its programs focused on recovery efforts to rebuild local

Box 11.1 INVISIBLE CHILDREN UGANDA

Monitoring and evaluation systems rarely begin as right fits; instead, they evolve over time, often to meet the demands of internal learning, external accountability, and a given stage of program development. In this case, we follow Invisible Children Uganda as it formalizes its monitoring and evaluation system in response to increased visibility, the demands of traditional donors, and an internal desire to understand impact. As you read the case, consider how Invisible Children's first logical framework—a rough equivalent of a theory of change—lays the foundation for a right-fit monitoring and evaluation system. You will also analyze the broader challenges of commissioning high-quality impact evaluations and the importance of clearly defining them.

communities. These programs required different data collection strategies and reporting than advocacy campaigns funded largely by individual private donors. As part of this transition, the organization would need to rethink its approach to data collection and build a new system from the ground up. This case focuses on the early steps Invisible Children took in rethinking its approach and some of the challenges it faced along the way.

BACKGROUND

Invisible Children was started by three young filmmakers who traveled to East Africa to document the conflict in the Darfur region of Sudan. Their travels took them through Northern Uganda, where they found that thousands of young children were walking from villages to nearby cities to sleep every night to avoid forced conscription as soldiers by Joseph Kony and the Lord's Resistance Army (LRA). The filmmakers shifted their focus to this issue and produced a video called *Invisible Children: The Rough Cut*. The video quickly gained attention, and they decided to start a nonprofit organization that would raise global awareness about the conflict in the region.

Although videos and media were always a large part of Invisible Children's work, it was just one arm of a four-part model for addressing the problems caused by the LRA in Central and East Africa:

- *Media*: The media arm of the organization produced films and campaign videos about various aspects of the LRA crisis.

- *Mobilization*: Mobilization activities rallied grassroots popular opposition to the LRA through large-scale demonstrations conducted in major cities around the world.
- *Protection*: Protection activities included a radio network that broadcasted information about the LRA and other armed militia activities in the regions where these groups were still active.
- *Recovery*: Recovery efforts were designed to help rebuild areas affected by the LRA. This arm of the organization ran livelihoods, savings, and education programs.

This case focuses on a program within the Recovery arm called Schools for Schools (S4S). Started in 2006, the goal of the S4S program was to "holistically improve the quality of secondary education in Northern Uganda." The S4S program had two components: a "hardware" component and a "software" component. Through the hardware component, Invisible Children built and renovated school structures such as classrooms, water systems, dormitories, and science labs. In the software component, the organization trained and hosted an exchange program for teachers and helped students with career guidance and counseling. In total, the S4S program cost about $2 million per year, which represented about 7% of Invisible Children's revenue.

THE EVOLUTION OF MONITORING AND EVALUATION

Kony 2012 enhanced a unique feature of Invisible Children: a large, flexible funding base raised primarily through individual donations. According to an independent financial audit, Invisible Children had $17 million in unrestricted assets in fiscal year 2012, largely generated through the sale of merchandise like t-shirts and armbands. General donations in 2012 totaled $4.6 million, while the organization only received $357,252 from institutional donors: foundation grants and partnerships (about 8% of all donations).

Given that it received such a small proportion of funds from institutional donors, Invisible Children did not face strong external pressure to develop a solid system of data collection and reporting. Instead of collecting data on program operations, staff created narrative work plans that outlined activities and their intended dates of completion. Although these documents reflected the organization's desire to be accountable, they did not have clear targets and did not use data to compare actual accomplishments against intended objectives.

Invisible Children first began to think about how to improve its monitoring and evaluation systems in 2011. Two factors motivated this desire. First, the organization knew that it needed better program data to attract traditional donors. "Ultimately we will have [institutional] donors, so we want to learn the language and get the systems in place," explained Adam Finck, the International Programs Director. Second, the staff and leadership were eager, after five years of work in Northern Uganda, to learn about the impact of the programs they worked so diligently to implement.

To improve data collection efforts, Invisible Children hired Collins Agaba as its first Monitoring and Evaluation Department Head. With the help of a Monitoring and Evaluation Assistant, Renee Jones, Agaba started by developing a theory of change that would be used to guide the organization's data collection system. To develop their theory, Invisible Children used a Logical Framework, or LogFrame, a variant of theory of change used by many international donors. These logframes were the organization's first attempt to systematically lay out program activities, outputs, and outcomes, and to develop indicators and targets for each of the four Recovery programs, including S4S.

Staff found that this process helped them refine overall program logic. And Monitoring and Evaluation Director Agaba believed that the logframes would help measurement, but also noted the difficulty of clearly outlining elements of the program:

> I see something so key in terms of indicators. But what was challenging was that you have outputs but you don't know if it is leading to an outcome. So those backward-forward linkages—the causal linkages. Getting a clear distinction between activities, outputs, outcomes [is] still a bit challenging.

The logframe developed for the S4S program (shown in Figure 11.1) maps the pathways of change expected from the program. The document argued that by providing lab equipment, computers, latrines, and teacher trainings, Invisible Children would create adequate school infrastructure, improve the quality of teaching, and motivate students and teachers, which would achieve the end goal to "Improve quality of life of youth in Northern Uganda through education." Though not as clear about the connections between activities, outputs, and outcomes as a theory of change should be—and without identifying assumptions and risks—the logframe was a good first step toward mapping the changes Invisible Children intended to create.

Narrative summary	Objectively verifiable indicators	Means of verification
Goal: Improve quality of life of youth in Northern Uganda through education.	Life after graduation • Percent gainfully employed • Percent enrolled in a further level of school	Life after graduation: Random sample (~30) of graduated students from S4 and S6 at each partner school one year after graduation.
Outcome: Holistically improve quality of education at selected secondary schools.	Academic performance • Percent of senior 4 students achieving Division 1 or 2 on UCE; scoring C6 or better in each core subject on UCE • Percentile ranking of partner schools nationally. • Percent of S6 students awarded government sponsorship for university degree. Dropouts/repetitions • Percent of students who dropped out or repeated	Academic performance: UNEB results; UNEB rankings; Ministry of education and sports Dropouts/ repetitions: district education reports; DOS.
Outputs/expected results: 1. Quality teaching in core subjects	Quality teaching: • Percent of syllabus covered in core subjects • Teacher attendance in core subjects • Student evaluation of teachers in core subjects	Quality teaching: DES, DOS
2. Motivated and prepared students	Motivated/prepared students: • Student attendance • Dropouts due to indiscipline, pregnancy • Administration/teacher evaluation of student attitude.	Motivated/prepared students: DES, MOE, school disciplinary committee, media reports
3. Adequate facilities and equipment	Adequate facilities and equipment: • Classroom: students • Secure male/female accommodation: male/female students • Male/female latrine: male/female students • Water source: students	Adequate facilities and equipment: engineering evaluation/reports
Activities		
Teacher training and support: • Hold head teacher's meeting • Support recruitment of 5 teachers • Train teachers in KOBs, computer usage, and staff saving scheme • Core subject-based review meetings		Assessment report
Procurement and supplies • Procure and supply science equipment • Procure syllabus books • Supply t-shirts with READ words		Assessment report
Other educational activities • Hold an Essay writing competition (targeting S1 to S4) • Hold (at least 1 at @ school) career guidance sessions using role models/OBs/OGs • Teacher Awards and Recognition for best performed core subjects		• Essay poster, results from the competition and minutes • Session reports • List of awards
Construction • Laboratory block at Keyo SS and Pabbo SS • Girl's dormitory at Gulu High School, St. Mary's Lacor, Awere • Remodel and refurbish staff houses at Sir Samuel Baker SS • Remodel classroom at Pope Paul VI Anaka • Establish 30 workstations in computer labo		Signed contracts, site handover report
Note: The original logframe also contained information on frequency of data collection; the parties responsible for collecting it; and assumptions that included continuing political stability, that adequate teachers will continue to be posted by government, that similar numbers of students will be admitted, and that parents will be willing to provide financial support.		

Figure 11.1 M&E Logical Framework (Abridged)

Analysis Question 1: In what ways does the logframe in Figure 11.1 set a clear foundation for the organization's monitoring and evaluation system in the S4S program? What is missing? What changes would you make to improve it?

THE CHALLENGES OF EXTERNAL EVALUATION

The logframes were a start, outlining a monitoring and evaluation system that would track the completion of S4S activities and provide information about the program's outputs. With these documents in place, Invisible Children started thinking about how it would use the logframes to consider the impact of its programs.

Staff wanted to know if their programs were making a difference, but the organization simply did not have the experience or the systems in place to manage data or conduct a credible impact evaluation. Undeterred, Invisible Children decided to use an external evaluator to conduct an impact evaluation. In October 2012, Invisible Children released a Terms of Reference (TOR) giving the framework for an evaluation and seeking firms or individuals that could assess the impact of its S4S program over the previous five years. The TOR specified using mixed methods of data collection:

> Both quantitative and qualitative assessment methods should be employed. The impact evaluation will collect primary data from both direct and indirect beneficiaries of the program and will also use secondary data. Use of key informant interviews, focus group discussion, and other methods such as pictures, diaries, and case studies would all be useful methods.

The TOR specified that consultants would collect data in 9 of the 11 targeted schools over a one-month period. Using these data, Invisible Children expected the consultant to:

1. Determine if ICU (Invisible Children Uganda) has successfully achieved its desired results at the outcome and output levels.
2. Determine the impact and/or potential impact of the programs at all levels
3. Look at the following dimensions of the program's impact: (i) relevance; (ii) efficiency; (iii) effectiveness, (iv) outcomes, and (v) sustainability.

4. Assess performance in terms of shared responsibility and accountability, resource allocation and informed and timely action.
5. Determine strengths (including successful innovations and promising practices) and weaknesses of the planning, design, implementation and M&E.
6. Determine factors that led to the change/impact and the extent to which all the institutional arrangements (partnership relationships, financial management systems and coordination function) contributed (or not) to this impact.
7. Provide actionable, specific and practical strategic recommendations on how ICU and its partners can use the learning to strengthen future work.

> Analysis Question 2: This first Terms of Reference document outlines an ambitious set of goals. What challenges do you see in achieving these goals, given the data that might be available through the process?

UPDATING THE TERMS OF REFERENCE

Shortly after releasing the TOR, Agaba met with a consultant who was helping Invisible Children define the terms of the impact evaluation. The consultant reviewed the TOR and noticed that many of the listed objectives included measurements of impact even though the TOR didn't require collecting information on a comparison group in order to credibly estimate changes in outcomes. Realizing that what Invisible Children had called an "impact evaluation" would not actually deliver credible estimates of the organization's impact, Agaba revised the TOR to focus more on learning about the program implementation process. He decided to call this a "Process Evaluation of Invisible Children Uganda." He changed the overall aim, goal, and scope of the project from "The purpose of this evaluation is to assess the impact of ICU program interventions in both schools and communities in northern Uganda" in the initial TOR to read "The purpose of this process evaluation is to take stock of ICU programs interventions in both schools and communities in Northern Uganda, in order to promote organizational learning for effective program implementation in the future."

In addition to revising the overall goal of the evaluation, Invisible Children revised the objectives of the evaluation to focus on the process of the Recovery Programs.

The consultant will:

- Determine if ICU has successfully achieved its desired results at the outcome and output levels.
- Determine if the results contribute to ICU Thematic Goals of Education and Livelihoods.
- Assess the programs in terms of: (i) relevance, (ii) efficiency, (iii) effectiveness, (iv) outcomes, and (v) sustainability.
- Assess performance in terms of shared responsibility and accountability, resource allocation and informed and timely action.
- Determine strengths (including successful innovations and promising practices) and weaknesses of the planning, design, implementation, and monitoring & evaluation.
- For the Schools for Schools program, the consultant will assess the following:
  - Outcome of trainings in schools
  - Contribution of hardware interventions towards the needs of the school
  - School community satisfaction with hardware and software interventions
  - Relationship between hardware interventions and academic performance

The requested method of data collection stayed the same, relying on activity tracking data supplied by Invisible Children, which would be supplemented by case studies, in-depth focus groups, and other types of qualitative data collection.

After reviewing bids, Invisible Children contracted a local evaluation firm to conduct the evaluation on the basis of its expertise and promised timeline. Working within the budget permitted by the contract, the consulting firm planned for 5 days of document review and 20 days of data collection to meet the intended objectives.

MONITORING THE EVALUATION

Not long into the data collection process, Invisible Children began to worry about the performance of the firm it had chosen. From the start, the firm failed to submit weekly updates as required in the TOR. After not hearing from the firm for more than two months (the whole exercise was supposed to take less than a month), Renee Jones, the M&E assistant, went to the field to see how the survey work for the evaluation was progressing.

What she found was disappointing: the firm had started taking serious shortcuts. The data collection plan made by the firm and Invisible Children sampled schools from the diverse areas where Invisible Children worked. Rather than conducting surveys as outlined in that plan, the firm instead conducted surveys according to a "convenience sampling method," visiting those schools that were easiest to reach. This sampling process risked biasing the findings because the easy-to-reach schools were probably quite different—in the children they served and challenges they faced—from schools in more remote areas. In addition, Jones found that only two of the four data collectors spoke Luo, the local language. Such a language barrier would negatively affect the validity and reliability of the data. Jones was most shocked when the firm asked if she could help conduct interviews, particularly because she was from the United States and did not speak Luo!

The problems were not solely the fault of the survey company. Agaba admitted that Invisible Children could have planned better for data collection. By the time the firm was selected and the agreement was finalized, schools were nearing the end of the academic year, and many of the beneficiaries in the S4S program were on holiday, making it more difficult to find available and willing survey respondents.

THE EVALUATION REPORT

The firm finally delivered the evaluation report months after the deadline. The report discussed the overall relevance, effectiveness, and efficiency of each of Invisible Children's Recovery programs in a long, 151-page document.

Staff were disappointed in the final report for a variety of reasons. First, it was clear that the findings borrowed heavily from Invisible Children internal reports and documents rather than relying on the firm's own data collection. For example, the evaluation report considered the fact that 22 teachers had participated in the teacher exchange program as a clear success of the program. But Invisible Children already had counts of exchange participants from its own activity monitoring data.

Agaba believed that since the evaluation company did not spend much time collecting data, the report simply used whatever information it could to affirm Invisible Children's hopes that its programs were relevant and effective. "You would hardly see a serious recommendation that you could rely on. Where they were recommending they wrote a recommendation that was out of context. Recommendations were not being informed by [research] findings," Agaba explained.

The S4S Program Manager concluded that Invisible Children "did not get value for money on this evaluation." He said that if Invisible Children had designed and managed the evaluation in-house, the organization would have learned more from the process. Having learned nothing new from the evaluation, the S4S Program Manager felt he had little choice but to carry on implementing his program as he had before. It was a missed opportunity to learn about implementation, improve programs, and demonstrate accountability to a growing list of institutional donors.

For Agaba, the biggest lesson learned was that external evaluations require a lot of resources and might not pay off: "This has given us a good lesson. Somebody gives you a good technical proposal, but they cannot deliver." In the end, Invisible Children announced in December 2014, that it was going to disband, ending all operations except for a small lobbying contingent. S4S and other Recovery programs have been passed on to local Ugandan nongovernmental organizations (NGOs).

CASE ANALYSIS

> Analysis Question 1: Does the logical framework in Figure 11.1 set a clear foundation for the organization's monitoring and evaluation system in the S4S program? What changes would you make to improve it?

The logframe outlines the basic information Invisible Children would need to collect to track program implementation and measure progress. This rough conceptualization of monitoring is an improvement over workplans and narrative reports, which do not address data collection at all. The logframe also shows the general logic behind the S4S project, which helps administrators decide what needs to be measured.

However, some of the items in the logframe are classified inaccurately, which could potentially create a misunderstanding of program impact. For example, of the "outputs" listed in the logframe, only "adequate facilities and equipment" is truly a deliverable of the program. The other listed outputs—quality education and motivated students—are actually outcomes because they reflect changes expected from program outputs.

In addition, some of the terms within the elements are not clear. For example, what does it mean to "holistically" improve secondary education? Holistic improvement could have many meanings that are hard to measure, such as happier students, more time spent on lessons, or a more open and collaborative learning environment. Although these qualities are important to the overall educational environment, ICU could drop the term "holistically" so that the intended outcome reads "improve the quality of education at selected secondary schools" and use test scores or other objective means of verification to get credible data about progress on this outcome.

These critiques are more than semantics. Clearly defining the outputs of the program is important for a number of reasons. First, clearly tracking all of the program's outputs is necessary to show that Invisible Children actually accomplishes what it promises to do. Second, clearly defining outputs allows the organization to track the connection between the activities and outputs in the S4S program. Take, for example, the activity "Train teachers in computer usage" mentioned in the logframe. Without measuring a corresponding output like "number of teachers trained in computer usage" (with "trained" clearly defined), ICU will not know how many teachers complete the training and how competent they are after finishing the program.

Another reason that outputs and outcomes should be distinguished is to ensure credible data collection. "Quality education" is not well-defined, making it hard to develop indicators that are valid and reliable measures of the concept. In addition, by including "quality education and motivated students" as outputs, Invisible Children might be tempted to collect data on these outcomes. Without a counterfactual, such data are not credible.

> Analysis Question 2: The original Terms of Reference outlines an ambitious set of seven goals. What approaches and types of data collection would you use to measure them?

The goals in the first TOR included assessing the impact of all programs, assessing the strengths and weaknesses of monitoring and evaluation, and providing recommendations on how to improve data and learning in the future. Meeting these objectives requires a wide variety of approaches and data collection strategies. A starting point is to group these objectives by those that would require an impact evaluation and those that could be answered with monitoring data.

Generally, parts of goals 1, 2, 3, and 6 would require an impact evaluation because they involve assessing longer term causal changes in outcomes. For each, the evaluator would need to compare the outcomes of Recovery program beneficiaries with the outcomes of a similar population that did not participate in Invisible Children's programming (this is not written into the TOR). Conversely, points 4, 5, and 7 could (and likely should) be part of regular monitoring activities. Here, we cover these items in more depth.

1. Determining if Invisible Children has achieved its desired outputs and outcomes would require a mix of approaches. The goal is to learn whether ICU holistically improved the quality of secondary school education in

Northern Uganda and delivered all the outputs of the program—quality teacher instruction, motivation of students, and adequate school facilities—according to their logframe. But, as we discussed, instruction quality and student motivation are outcomes rather than outputs, and Invisible Children's impact on them cannot be measured without a counterfactual. Invisible Children simply cannot claim that it has improved the quality of teacher education without understanding what would have happened if S4S did not exist. The last output (adequate school facilities) is actually more of a monitoring question. Invisible Children could learn whether S4S provided adequate school facilities by defining that term (such as schools with a working latrine, solid construction, etc.) and collecting data to confirm that these outputs are provided as specified.

2–3. Item 2 directly asks about the impact of Invisible Children's programming, and Item 3 defines impact as the program's relevance, efficiency, effectiveness, outcomes, and sustainability. The goal of assessing the effectiveness of the S4S program requires impact evaluation, but the evaluator might be able to learn about relevance, efficiency, and sustainability in this evaluation (depending on how they are defined) by using process data. Relevance could be assessed using data on whether outputs are used and on whether beneficiaries thought that program elements fit their needs well. Efficiency could be assessed by comparing output data (number of labs rehabilitated and latrines built) with the cost of these interventions. Assessing sustainability would need more involved data collection and analysis that would seek to understand how investments made by the S4S program would be maintained after Invisible Children's involvement ended.

6. This asks a question that would require a counterfactual—and should be abandoned in this process evaluation. Without a credible comparison group, Invisible Children will not be able to answer this question.

4, 5, and 7. The consultant could assess each of these items through a process or formative evaluation, although Invisible Children could also learn a lot about each by including them in a monitoring plan. Item 4 seems to ask about the efficiency of the program, making sure that resources are delivered cost effectively and on time. Item 5 looks at program weaknesses, which could be explored through interviews with beneficiaries to assess program plan versus program reality: What did Invisible Children do well, and what did the organization fail to achieve? The final item asks the consultant to provide overall recommendations for the program based on outcomes and earlier elements of the theory of change. If the evaluation is conducted well and data collection narrowly focused on the organization's learning needs, the external evaluator could realistically deliver these recommendations.

CHAPTER 12

Deworm the World

From Impact Evidence to Implementation at Scale

DEWORMING DAY

In a small primary school in Western Kenya, the day started off much as it had for the rest of the term—the students in each class stood up together and greeted the head teacher with a loud "Good morning, teacher!" On a typical day, the students might have proceeded to a lesson on Kenyan geography, recited a poem, or learned how to calculate the area of a circle. But today they were about to participate in one of the largest school-based public health initiatives ever attempted in Kenya (see Box 12.1).

To begin, the students learned and repeated a slogan in Swahili: "Kwa afya na elimu bora tuangamize minyoo," which roughly translates to "Fighting worms for better health and education." The head teacher then explained to the class how the next few minutes would unfold. He explained that students were about to be called to the front of room in groups, and each child would be given a tablet. They should take the tablet, chew it—it would be a little sweet—and then show the instructor that they had swallowed it. As each student finished the process, another teacher would mark that they had been treated on a prefilled class roster.

The process unfolded with some hiccups. Some kids tried to duck out of the class before swallowing; others were reluctant to open their mouths to prove that they had taken the tablet. Setbacks aside, in 15 short minutes, all the students in attendance that day were treated for the types of parasitic worms collectively known as soil-transmitted helminths (STHs). This

Deworm the World serves millions of school children every year. Monitoring on such a large scale can amplify the difficulty of developing a right-fit system: How can an organization ensure credible data collection across a wide range of sites and prioritize actionable information that informs implementation? How can such a large-scale system rapidly respond to issues once identified? This case illustrates the challenge of finding credible and actionable activity tracking measures. How does Deworm the World apply the *credible, actionable,* and *responsible* principles to determine the right amount of data to collect and the right time and place at which to collect it?

was the Kenya National School-Based Deworming Program in action, an initiative implemented jointly by the Kenyan Ministry of Education, Science, and Technology and the Ministry of Health. The Deworm the World Initiative of the nonprofit Evidence Action supported the ministries and monitored the implementation of the program.

This deworming day was just one of many in a program that reached 6 million children in Kenya at high risk of worm infection. To implement deworming at this national scale, the program had trained thousands of teachers and government officials on how to properly administer the tablets and the best way to communicate the importance of deworming to the communities in which they worked.

This case focuses on two data collection challenges faced by Deworm the World as they monitored Kenya's national deworming program. First, how could Deworm the World identify the appropriate data to help them learn about the quality of deworming implementation throughout the country? Second, does the way schools conduct their deworming events ultimately influence the number of dewormed students, and, if so, how?

THE POWER OF IMPACT EVALUATION

Health policy-makers have long known that worms have important health effects in children, including stunting, listlessness, and impaired cognitive development. However, for many years, worm infections were not a public health priority for many governments facing massive public health challenges from high-profile diseases like tuberculosis and HIV/AIDS.

An impact evaluation published by economists Michael Kremer and Edward Miguel in 2004, however, redefined the public health understanding of preventative deworming.[1] Their randomized controlled trial evaluated a deworming program run by the Dutch nongovernmental organization (NGO) ICS and found that school-based deworming had strong impact both on treated individuals as well as on those in nearby communities who had not been treated. Since worms spread through soil, deworming a large group of people decreases the overall prevalence of worms in an area, decreasing the risk of infection even for those who were not treated. Kremer and Miguel found that, in treated schools, absenteeism among treated kids decreased by 14.6 days per year on average. And in communities within a three-kilometer radius of a treated school, the prevalence of worms dropped by 26% while school attendance increased by 5.9 days.

Considering that the NGO deworming program cost about 30 cents per child, the evaluation demonstrated that deworming is an extremely cost-effective way to increase school attendance. For every $100 spent on deworming, students collectively gain an extra 13.9 years of schooling. In comparison, other studies have shown that spending $100 to provide free primary school uniforms to students increases attendance by 0.71 years, while giving merit scholarships increases attendance only 0.27 years.[2]

Follow-on studies that tracked dewormed students have discovered that the benefits of deworming persist well beyond school as well. Nearly a decade after the initial study, researchers found that students who had been dewormed were earning 23% more than those who had not been dewormed and were also more likely to be formally employed.[3]

DEWORM THE WORLD

Impact evaluation provided solid evidence that deworming had substantial benefits. Successful implementation of large-scale deworming initiatives, however, would require a public health system that could implement the program at scale. When Kremer and Miguel's research was published, many governments did not have the technical capacity necessary to efficiently deworm on a national scale. So, in 2007, Kremer and economist Esther Duflo created the NGO Deworm the World to help governments surmount the many logistical hurdles. Deworm the World would provide a full set of services to governments looking to implement deworming programs, including prevalence surveys, program planning, training, drug procurement and management, public awareness, participant mobilization, and evaluation.[4]

Deworm the World began working with the Kenyan government in 2009, training 1,000 district-level personnel and 16,000 teachers to administer deworming to 3.6 million students. In 2011, the program began a five-year campaign with the goal of deworming at least 5 million children per year. Deworm the World was tasked with setting up the new monitoring system for this massive effort before the next round of deworming began in 2012.

HOW DEWORMING THE WORLD WORKS

In Kenya, Deworm the World decided on a cascade training system. Under this system, Deworm the World staff train regional county-level personnel within the Ministries of Education and Health, who in turn train district personnel, who then train the teachers who treat their students. Training information flowed down through this cascade, while monitoring and implementation information would flow up from bottom to top, as shown in Figure 12.1.

Each training would cover all the key program elements, including who should get dewormed, how to administer the tablets, and the method for collecting data about who receives treatment. During the training cascade, regional officials would also distribute monitoring forms, deworming tablets, and community sensitization materials to schools.

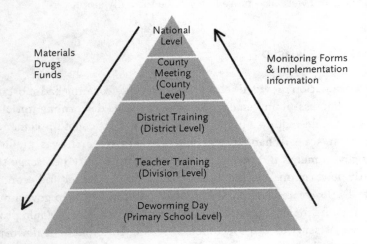

Figure 12.1 The training cascade.

This training design presented a number of advantages. Most importantly, the tiers aligned with the organizational structures of the Ministries of Health and Education, so existing staff within the ministries could administer the program. In addition, distributing medicines and materials through the cascade would dramatically simplify logistics. Rather than transporting the drugs to each of the 1,000 teacher training sessions or to the 10,000 deworming days, the program would distribute the materials to districts and required ministry staff to then pass these materials on to lower levels, at considerable time and logistical savings.

Despite the benefits, the cascade also posed various implementation challenges. Just one error at the top of the cascade could jeopardize the quality of trainings at all descending levels or even keep them from occurring at all. For example, if one head teacher missed their training, several hundred kids would not get dewormed unless the problem was fixed by deworming day. Or, even more drastically, if a teacher training session failed to occur and the government did not reschedule, thousands of kids from dozens of schools would not be dewormed.

Furthermore, since the information contained in the curriculum had to pass through multiple trainings before finally reaching teachers, poor-quality trainings could send garbled implementation instructions to teachers. If procedures were not presented accurately in the beginning, or if a master trainer missed one important piece of information, a whole group of schools might implement the program improperly or fail to implement it at all.

Given these risks, Deworm the World wanted to ensure that the cascade was efficient in delivering information and materials to the teachers running deworming days. But how could Deworm the World monitor a program that involved two government ministries, 1,200 teacher trainings, and 10,000 deworming days spread across half the country? Learning about implementation was just one goal of data collection. Deworm the World also wanted to build a system that provided information about how to make improvements as the program developed.

MONITORING THE IMPLEMENTATION CASCADE

The most important information Deworm the World wanted to know was the number and percentage of students who were dewormed. In developing a monitoring system, though, Deworm the World believed that calculating the number of students dewormed would give the organization only a murky understanding of the overall success of the program.

To focus on learning and improvement, Deworm the World had to go beyond merely calculating the number of students dewormed. It also had to get information about the quality of training events—that they occurred and that they gave teachers the information they needed to deworm children correctly. This information would allow Deworm the World to compare the quality of training events with raw deworming numbers to learn which training components were most correlated with program success.

With this in mind, Deworm the World staff set out to develop a set of measures that would help them understand program implementation. These metrics would cover a range of steps in the process, from the basics of implementation (whether training materials were delivered) all the way to final expected outcomes (reduced parasite prevalence). Key activity tracking measures they needed to understand included:

- The quality and attendance of regional training sessions
- The quality and attendance of teacher training sessions
- The successful delivery of materials and drugs at each cascade level
- The successful delivery of key messages at each cascade level
- The percentage of target schools with appropriate drugs in place prior to deworming day
- The percentage of target schools represented at teacher training sessions
- The percentage of trained schools executing deworming day within two weeks of training

UNDERSTANDING TREATMENT AND UPTAKE

In addition to activity tracking, Deworm the World needed to understand uptake: whether students were being treated as intended. Successful activity tracking of program implementation would help identify whether shortfalls in implementation were causing low treatment rates, but many other factors in student homes and communities might affect these rates as well.

In addition to treating enrolled school-aged children, the deworming program aimed to treat preschool children enrolled in early childhood development (ECD) programs, as well as younger children not yet in school. These additional populations complicated the set of uptake metrics that would need to be collected, which included:

- The number and percent of enrolled children receiving STH and/or schistosomiasis treatment

- The number and percentage of unenrolled school-aged children who came into school to be dewormed for STH and/or schistosomiasis
- The number of children younger than school age dewormed for STH and/or schistosomiasis

The goal of this evaluation would be to ensure that the program continued to reduce worm prevalence. All other factors equal, if the evaluation showed that worm prevalence did not decrease after deworming, that could indicate a decrease in the efficacy of albendazole, the drug that the program used to treat STH. The World Health Organization (WHO) has developed specific guidelines that illustrate what should happen if a decrease in drug prevalence is suspected.[5]

COLLECTING THE ACTIVITY TRACKING AND UPTAKE DATA

With the list of monitoring needs set, Deworm the World staff started figuring out how to define precise indicators, gather information about how the program was implemented, and tally the number of students dewormed. Deworm the World knew that gathering this information would not be easy. There were more than 10,000 schools reporting data from areas all around the country. Simply having schools turn in all of these forms directly to Deworm the World headquarters would be a data entry and reporting nightmare.

The organization's solution was to develop what they called a "reverse cascade" in which forms were collected at the school level and aggregated to produce a single district summary of the number of dewormed students. Since the forms travel in the opposite direction of training and materials (from school to division to district), data would travel the reverse of the implementation cascade.

To design this system, Deworm the World needed to decide what would constitute a successful training. This process would require defining the main elements of each training and the markers for quality in each. First, they determined that trainings in the cascade had four main components:

- The importance of sensitizing communities about worms' effects and how the deworming process worked
- How to correctly mark coverage forms in the cascade
- The explanation of the procedure on deworming day
- The logistics of treating nonenrolled students

The next step would be to define training quality for each topic. That would not be easy. O'Dell noted that many aspects of quality are hard to quantify: Did the trainer present the information in an engaging way? Did the trainer stay on task? Was the trainer able to answer all of trainees' questions?

In the end, the team determined that trying to learn about the more subjective measures of quality would be too difficult to measure accurately. After all, two people could watch the same training and come up with wildly different scores for how engaging it was. So Deworm the World decided to use a simpler and more objective metric. In their view, a training would be considered high quality if all of the materials ended up in the right place and the trainers covered all the material in the curriculum.

WHAT DOES QUALITY TREATMENT LOOK LIKE?

After determining what quality looked like in the training cascade, Deworm the World had to create concrete metrics that would be valid and reliable measures of quality. Considering just one of the many metrics demonstrates the challenges involved: treating nonenrolled students. In the program, children under five in some preschools (referred to by the shorthand term "Early Childhood Development," or ECD students) travel to the primary schools for deworming.

Since ECD students are not enrolled in the schools where they are treated, teachers have to record unfamiliar personal information on each form. In addition, since choking is a hazard for young children, a teacher has to crush the deworming tablet and mix it with water for children younger than three years. A quality training would clearly communicate both of these lessons to teachers, so these would make good indicators for overall training quality.

The trainers at each level of the training cascade focused on three main topics to ensure that teachers got the essential information about working with ECD students:

1. *The importance of treating ECD students*: This element of the training emphasizes that the youngest children are at the greatest risk of contracting worms because they often run around barefoot in infected areas.
2. *Teachers' special roles in incorporating ECD students*: The deworming process may be unfamiliar and intimidating for the younger ECD-aged children. The training should explain how teachers need to plan ahead to prioritize these children on deworming day.

3. *The actual mechanics of treatment on deworming day*: This segment focuses on important process questions such as: What do you do if a child is choking? How do you interact with ECD students? How do you incorporate ECD teachers in the process of treating young kids?

TURNING METRICS INTO DATA

After defining what constituted a successful training, Deworm the World developed a series of metrics, listed on the form in Figure 12.2. The three priorities are covered in questions on the importance of ECD students (3.1), the different roles for teachers (3.2 and 3.6), and the mechanics of treatment (3.3, 3.4, 3.5, 3.7).

To conduct the monitoring, Deworm the World would need to train a set of monitors who would attend various trainings and evaluate their quality using the form. Since a large number of monitors would be collecting data across a wide variety of schools, these forms needed to be clear, easy to follow, and as mistake-proof as possible. For most indicators, monitors evaluate the quality of training using a 0–2 or 0–3 scale as shown in the form. The forms also include yes/no questions about whether a particular training element was covered in training, which serve as proxies for the quality of a training. For example, Deworm the World staff believed that having a teacher play out the role of an ECD student in a mock exercise (3.5) indicated that the trainer was very thorough and managed time well, as this took place at the end of the training curriculum.

The form also includes a section designed to capture the topics about which attendees asked the most questions as an indication of a training's weak points. For example, if Deworm the World found in analyzing the data that participants routinely asked about how to sensitize the community, the organization would know to look deeper into that issue and either to revise the training or better train the trainers.

Analysis Question 1: What challenges of credibility and reliability do you see in measuring the quality of deworming trainings? Do you think the scales used (0–3 or 0–2) are an acceptable method? What other approaches might you recommend?

Analysis Question 2: Do you think that the data collected on the training quality control form will be actionable? What other resources would give a more complete picture of training quality?

3.0 ECD Children

		0 - Never Mentioned	1 - Mentioned, but passed over, not discussed in depth	2 - Discussed and emphasized, the message was clearly and adequately taught.	3 - A repeated message covered thoroughly throughout the day, a key point of emphasis and discussion, and was clearly learned by the participants
3.1	Which statement best describes what was taught regarding the importance of treating ECD children?	**MARK ALL THAT APPLY** **0 – NO MENTION OF ECD CHILDREN AT ALL (do not mark any other boxes)** **1 – ECD CHILDREN ARE A CRUCIAL ELEMENT OF THE PROGRAM** **2 – ECD CHILDREN HAVE A HIGHER WORM BURDEN, & THE BENEFITS OF DEWORMING ARE GREATEST IN ECD CHILDREN** **3 – ECD CHILDREN REQUIRE EXTRA WORK AND TARGETED ACTIVITIES**			[ ] [ ] [ ] [ ]
	Tick in the box that best describes how each message below was taught				
3.2	Head Teacher's role in preparing school for ECD children				
3.3	How to handle a choking child				
3.4	For children under 3, crush the tablet and mix it with water				
3.5	Did somebody act as an ECD aged child during the mock exercise?	1— YES 2 — NO -77: *No mock exercise done*			
3.6	Did the instructors explain the following? On Deworming Day, an ECD teacher should go to the local primary school first to direct children to the local primary school, then the ECD teacher should go to the primary school to assist with ECD children.	**0 – NOT COVERED AT ALL** **1 – PARTIALLY EXPLAINED, NOT EVERY DETAIL COVERED** **2 – FULLY EXPLAINED** **8 – A CONTRADICTORY MESSAGE WAS TAUGHT** (write here):_____			
3.7	Did the instructors explain the following? For children under 3, crush the tablet and mix it with water	**0 – NOT COVERED AT ALL** **1 – PARTIALLY EXPLAINED, NOT EVERY DETAIL COVERED** **2 – FULLY EXPLAINED**			[ ]

Figure 12.2 Form 3.0: Early childhood development (ECD) children.

The preceding example is just a snapshot of one of the forms used to measure the quality of implementation; a total of 32 forms were used to monitor the activities of the National School-Based Deworming Program. The other forms tracked teacher knowledge before and after training, registered the events of deworming day, and monitored other important events in the cascade.

DECIDING HOW MUCH TO MONITOR

After determining how to measure training quality, Deworm the World had to decide how to make this system fit its learning needs when operating at full scale. The first problem was deciding which trainings to monitor. A simple random sample at each stage of the cascade would be insufficient because it would not provide information about whether the training cascade was working as intended. For example, if they only had data about district-level trainings from one district and data about deworming days in another district across the country, they would not be able to draw a clear picture of training quality throughout the cascade.

Another challenge was to figure out how much data to collect. The trainings were spread out across a network of rough roads in rural areas. Therefore, it would take a legion of monitors to reach all events in the cascade. And, even if Deworm the World could find the monitors to keep track of that information, they would then have to enter and process all of those data. However, collecting too little data was also a concern. Since the program was so large, limited regional coverage would give Deworm the World only a spotty understanding of activities around the country. In addition, limited data might not be sufficient to keep those implementing the program accountable for their program responsibilities.

As a solution, Deworm the World decided that the cascade structure would form the basis of the monitoring system. At the district level, they randomly selected 35% of the 111 district trainings to be monitored. Within the districts chosen, 10% of teacher trainings were monitored, giving a total sample of 200 teacher trainings in 45 districts. The overall sampling strategy is shown in Figure 12.3. This strategy gave Deworm the World complete monitoring information at each level of the cascade in a district, data that they could link to the number of students dewormed in these districts.

This relatively compact setup also had a logistical advantage. By monitoring only 35% of districts, monitoring teams stayed in smaller

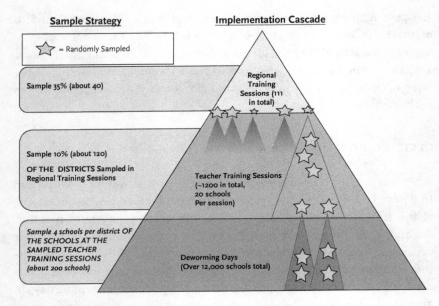

Sample Strategy

☆ = Randomly Sampled

Sample 35% (about 40)

Sample 10% (about 120)
OF THE DISTRICTS Sampled in
Regional Training Sessions

Sample 4 schools per district OF
THE SCHOOLS AT THE
SAMPLED TEACHER
TRAINING SESSIONS
(about 200 schools)

Implementation Cascade

Regional
Training
Sessions (111
in total)

Teacher Training Sessions
(~1200 in total,
20 schools
Per session)

Deworming Days
(Over 12,000 schools total)

Figure 12.3 Sampling within the cascade.

geographic areas, allowing them to visit a greater number of schools than if the sampling had been purely random.

Even after deciding what and who to sample, one issue still remained: when to act on the monitoring data. In any program, it is difficult to know at what point to take action. If monitoring efforts found a single flaw in one training, and that district subsequently dewormed a low number of students, this would not be enough information to make large-scale changes to the program. But what if monitoring revealed 10 such cases, or 20? At what point do the findings warrant changing the program? With the deworming program about to go live, Deworm the World decided to wait to answer that question until it got some results.

> Analysis Question 3: How many instances of poor training should be permitted before prompting Deworm the World to try to fix a given implementation issue?

DEWORMING GOES LIVE

With the monitoring system set, the deworming program went live in July 2012. Results from activities across the region started coming in shortly thereafter, and Deworm the World received data for this first round of deworming in Western Kenya by December 2012.

From the monitoring data, the team gathered a few important lessons that would inform subsequent rounds. Critically, they learned that the most important predictor of the quality of a deworming day was whether the training for teachers happened in the first place. Thirteen percent of schools dewormed without a training; of these, 30% did not have enough tablets, 24% did not deworm the whole class, and 41% of teachers did not fill out the main reverse-cascade form correctly. Their performance was significantly worse than that of schools that did receive training, where 12% did not have enough tablets, 12% did not deworm the whole class, and 34% did not fill out all parts of the cascade reporting form. To address this disparity, Deworm the World tabulated training numbers for each county and encouraged local health and education officials to improve in areas with low treatment numbers.

In addition to this focus on making sure that trainings happened as planned, the program also investigated which elements of training traveled down the cascade poorly and added more emphasis on those subjects in training modules.

These data inspired a few changes to help increase coverage. Deworm the World instituted county-level meetings to train staff on how to effectively roll out the cascade. The organization has also developed Community Health Worker Forums that help these staff effectively support the deworming campaign. In the future, Deworm the World planned to improve community sensitization methods (such as transmitting messages about deworming over radio) to increase coverage.

At the same time, the monitoring team continued to streamline data collection forms to gather the most actionable information. Finding the "right fit" is not easy in a program operating at national scale. By constantly thinking through challenges of size, scope, and quality, Deworm the World built a monitoring system that provides credible, actionable information to improve programs, even as it continued to deworm millions of kids across Kenya.

APPENDIX: WORM PREVALENCE AND TREATMENT MAPS

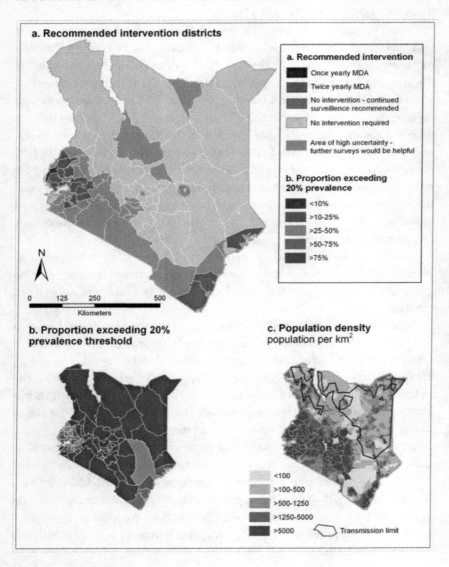

a. Recommended intervention districts

a. Recommended intervention
- Once yearly MDA
- Twice yearly MDA
- No intervention - continued surveillence recommended
- No intervention required
- Area of high uncertainty - further surveys would be helpful

b. Proportion exceeding 20% prevalence
- <10%
- >10-25%
- >25-50%
- >50-75%
- >75%

N

0 125 250 500
Kilometers

b. Proportion exceeding 20% prevalence threshold

c. Population density
population per km²

- <100
- >100-500
- >500-1250
- >1250-5000
- >5000
- Transmission limit

CASE ANALYSIS

Analysis Question 1: What challenges do you see in measuring the quality of deworming trainings? Do you think the scales used (0–3 and 0–2) are an acceptable method? What other approaches might you recommend?

The main issue in measuring quality is the validity of any quality metric. Quality is by nature highly subjective—any of Deworm the World's approaches to measuring quality may be biased by the monitor assigned to "grade" a given teacher.

Commonly, organizations handle this challenge by translating abstract concepts such as "quality" into specific aspects of quality that can be measured on a numeric scale. Deworm the World's scales attempt to include enough information to be actionable but not so much that they weaken credibility. A 10-point scale, for example, would add a lot more subjectivity to data collection (how do you decide between whether the training is a seven or eight?) without providing much more information than the simple 3- and 4-point scales Deworm the World used. In the end, whether the simple scales gave the organization enough actionable information remains to be seen—when this book went to press, the team was still gathering data and analyzing the numbers showing how many children had been dewormed.

Such quality metrics should be coupled with strong training protocols for monitoring staff to be sure that monitors score events of similar quality in the same way. Thorough training could include extensive explanation of different scores and a practice quality score session in which a group of monitors is asked to watch and grade a training, with the "right" answers illustrated and discussed at the end of the session.

Although tracking inputs like this is a common way to assess quality, Deworm the World could also measure outputs by testing trainee knowledge after a training. If the trainees do not score well, the training cannot be considered high quality—this is an example of the shutdown rule we discussed in Chapter 5. This method does come with flaws, though, as one cannot be sure if the results reflect the quality of the training or the characteristics of the cohort being trained. Some people are quicker learners than others.

> Analysis Question 2: Do you think that the data collected on the training quality control form will be actionable? What other resources would give a more complete picture of training quality?

In general, the form tracks whether a training event happened and at what quality, which provides actionable information that can help improve program implementation. For example, if Deworm the World observes that trainers routinely omit a certain component of the training, the organization can emphasize this component more in the master training session so that the message is more likely to spread throughout the rest of the cascade.

As we describe in the case, Deworm the World was able to improve actionability by coupling this information with deworming implementation data. This helps the organization learn whether a correlation exists between the quality of trainings and the number of students dewormed. One caveat: interpreting data in this way requires extreme care to be sure that the data are picking up on an actual connection and not just a spurious correlation, or a correlation driven by alternative explanations. As we demonstrate in the case, the organization has been able to use the data on training quality to make meaningful changes to the program. For example, the program has changed its community sensitization activities based on interviews with community members about how they were informed about deworming day.

> Analysis Question 3: How many instances of poor training should be permitted before prompting Deworm the World to try to fix a given implementation issue?

Assessing when to act on problems does not require technical expertise. Instead, it requires intuition and a deep knowledge of a program and the staff who implement it. Since the structure of the cascade means that small glitches in implementation could drastically affect deworming numbers at the end of the line, Deworm the World could pledge to respond quickly and make changes to the program whenever a problem is found. Or the organization may decide that, because the program operates at national scale, there is a lot of noise and that a few isolated problems do not merit a concerted response. In this case, staff would likely wait for the monitoring data to reveal systematic problems before making changes.

As an example of this dilemma, consider what the organization should do if a representative sample found that districts that did not simulate deworming day in their trainings only dewormed 40% of students, while districts that did practice deworming dewormed 80%. In this case, such a large discrepancy should certainly trigger action—Deworm the World should require districts to practice the deworming process in their trainings. But other results will surely be more nuanced. What if the difference in students dewormed between the two groups was only 5%? In this case, decision-makers would have to come to a consensus about what they deem necessary given their knowledge of the workings of the program.

CHAPTER 13
Un Kilo de Ayuda

Finding the Right Fit in Monitoring and Evaluation

HEALTH THROUGH DATA

At the start of her day, Teresa Lopez, a health promoter working for an organization called Un Kilo De Ayuda (UKA), logged into a system called InfoKilo. The database contained detailed health information about all 50,000 beneficiaries participating in UKA's Programa Integral de Nutrición (PIN) in five states in Mexico. The information gave Teresa critical information for planning her day, helping her decide where to focus her work that day in visits to two communities in rural Estado de México (see Box 13.1).

The InfoKilo system highlighted a few pressing issues that she would have to attend to. First, the record for a child named Juan Carlos was flagged red, indicating that he was malnourished. Since Juan Carlos had been healthy on her last visit, Teresa would make sure to visit his mother to see what was going on. She also noted the records of three anemic children in the communities; Teresa would visit their mothers to see if they were preparing the iron-fortified supplements that UKA distributed in food packets for children.

This preparatory work in InfoKilo was especially important as she had many other tasks to complete in her visits to the towns. In addition to following up with those not making progress in the program, Teresa would have to make sure that each family received food packets, conduct a training for mothers on the importance of breastfeeding, and test some of the pregnant women and children for anemia. It was also time for

This case explores two common challenges facing organizations around the world: how to collect the right amount of data and how to credibly use outcome data collected during program monitoring. Health promoters at Un Kilo de Ayuda in Mexico use regularly collected health data on more than 50,000 children to structure their work, track their progress, and identify at-risk children in time to treat health problems. In this case, you will assess the tradeoffs between actionability and responsibility that Un Kilo de Ayuda faces in determining how much data to collect. You will also examine the challenges of monitoring data on a program's outcomes instead of outputs, particularly when it comes to asserting a program's impact on those outcomes. Finally, you will propose ways to generate credible data on one of the organization's programs when plans for an impact evaluation fall through.

surveilling the overall nutritional status of the community, meaning that she would have to weigh and measure each child enrolled in the program. She would then record the height and weight of each child on paper and enter the information in InfoKilo when she returned to the office at the end of the day; this would give her up-to-date information when she visited again in two weeks.

When Teresa visited Juan Carlos's house that day, she learned that the child had been very sick with diarrhea. His mother was worried because he was much thinner than he had been just a couple of weeks ago. To explore possible causes, Teresa asked her about water and sanitation in the home. Did she use two separate buckets for washing and cooking? Did she and others in the family wash their hands regularly? The mother agreed that the family could adopt better water practices to try to prevent future issues and promised that she would give John Carlos more fortified and high-calorie foods while he was recovering.

Teresa then visited the three families with children flagged in her database as anemic. The mothers of these children knew that UKA's supplements were important but wanted to know how to make them taste better. They said their kids refused to take them because they tasted terrible. Teresa suggested adding some sugar to help make the supplements more appealing.

With her work with these four families finished, Teresa hopped in her car to travel to the next field site. Throughout the day, information from the InfoKilo system was a constant companion, helping her decide how to best help each beneficiary of the program. InfoKilo was not only a tool for managing day-to-day operations, though; it also formed the backbone of UKA's evaluation efforts. UKA and other governmental agencies used the height, weight, and nutrition data stored in InfoKilo to monitor trends, focus UKA efforts, and report on beneficiary progress.

Although the system had many uses at UKA, InfoKilo also came with a distinct challenge. First, keeping the system up to date could be a burden to health promoters who had to regularly measure the weight, height, and hemoglobin of all 50,000-plus children in the program, in addition to their regular duties. Teresa sometimes found herself wondering whether the benefits of the system were worth the cost. Second, program managers wondered whether the information collected through the system could deliver clear estimates of program impact, given that there was no comparison group. A great deal of time and effort was being expended, yet the program still didn't have clear impact data.

UN KILO DE AYUDA

Although Mexico has the highest obesity rate in the world, many children—particularly in rural areas—do not get enough food. Seventy percent of rural families are food insecure, with limited access to fresh fruits and vegetables. This insecurity leads to persistent malnutrition. Nationwide, 14% of children under age five are stunted and 26% are anemic.[1,2] Over time, poor nutrition causes stunting and damages neurodevelopment, increases risk of mortality, and causes long-term adverse effects like reduced capacity for physical labor and lower performance in school.

UKA originally started in 1986 as a nonprofit food assistance program in the Mexican states of Chiapas, Yucatán, Oaxaca, and Estado de México. The original goal of the organization was to leverage connections with companies and state governments to increase food security in rural areas and fight malnutrition.

Yet as UKA worked in these regions in the years that followed, the organization found that simply providing food did not address the more systemic causes of malnutrition. The food might sit unused at home because mothers did not know how to prepare it or because their kids thought that the foods did not taste good. There were external factors as well—one bout of diarrhea from unsafe water could undo much of the progress achieved through food assistance.

UKA resolved to take a more holistic approach and tackle the diverse causes of malnutrition through a single program. In 2000, UKA (with support of the Salvador Zubirán National Institute of Medical Sciences and Nutrition) launched PIN, with the goal of eradicating malnutrition in children under five by 2024. The first step in building a more comprehensive program was adding a nutrition education initiative, which focused on supporting the healthy development of children under five through breastfeeding and proper food choices. Shortly after, UKA piloted an initiative that tested and treated kids for anemia.

Yet as the organization expanded over the next decade, it found that nutrition was only one factor influencing the overall development of young children. Many children faced developmental deficits, and improving nutritional status was threatened by unreliable and unclean water sources. To address these additional challenges, UKA added training for mothers on how to promote the mental stimulation of their children and delivered toys to help young children build motor skills. To address the health threats posed to children by water-borne disease, UKA also added a safe water program that taught the importance of handwashing and provided water filters and other purification products to households.

The program grew steadily. By 2013, UKA served more than 50,000 children per year in about 800 communities in five states in Estado Mexico, Chiapas, Oaxaca, Sinaloa, and Yucatan through the PIN program.

A COMPREHENSIVE NUTRITION PROGRAM

Although it is not the only nutritional support program in Mexico, UKA's PIN is unique in that it takes a holistic approach to supporting child nutrition by combining a diverse range of programs, including nutrition surveillance, anemia detection, nutrition education, food packages, neurodevelopment surveillance, and safe water provision. Throughout the program's development, UKA consulted with experts to ensure that the program's design reflected the best available evidence on early childhood development.

Fighting malnutrition has been the primary goal of the PIN program since the organization's founding. The nutrition component of the program consists of nutrition surveillance, nutrition education, and food package delivery.

Nutritional surveillance consists of UKA field workers measuring the weight of each child in the program every two months and height every six months. These height and weight measurements are then plotted on charts that benchmark these indicators against what should be expected at a given age. This allows UKA to identify varying degrees of nutrition and malnutrition in children.

UKA field officers also conduct educational sessions for mothers during biweekly visits. During these sessions, mothers are encouraged to analyze, discuss, and reflect on a given topic of child health and nutrition. The sessions cover many different themes ranging from recognizing the effects of anemia to neurodevelopmental assessment of young kids.

The goal of the sessions is to promote behavior change, build skills, and thereby minimize malnutrition risk and shorten recovery time for sick children. To reinforce the lessons in the trainings, UKA encourages mothers to track their children's growth on a color-coded weight-for-age chart, a simple tool for diagnosing malnutrition and a visual reminder of children's nutritional needs.

To complement these efforts, UKA offers a subsidized package of foodstuffs that families can purchase every 14 days. Some of the products provide nutrients important for developing children and are intended exclusively for children five years old or younger. Even though the food package delivers a wide range of staple goods, it is intended only to supplement diets, contributing between 20% and 25% of the daily caloric and protein requirements of a family of five. In 2013, UKA distributed 523,689 packets to more than 20,000 families.

All children in the program are tested for anemia through a finger-prick hemoglobin test every six months. Results take one minute; if the test comes back positive for anemia based on World Health Organization thresholds, UKA will administer a liquid iron treatment to the child. In addition, the field officer will discuss the diagnosis with the child's mother, explain how to treat anemia through proper nutrition, and underscore the importance of using the food in the nutritional package to help combat anemia in the future.

UKA evaluates the neurodevelopment of children at 12 and 24 months of age. A field officer conducts a standardized assessment that UKA developed in consultation with a panel of early childhood development experts. It measures cognitive development, fine and gross motor skills, and social and emotional development against age-specific benchmarks. If the child is not developing as expected, the field officer will recommend early-life stimulation techniques and games that his or her mother can use to help. UKA also encourages mothers to have their children play with stimulating toys from a very young age.

A safe water and handwashing campaign is the newest component of PIN. It aims to combat an important threat to child nutrition: without sanitation infrastructure, progress achieved in other areas of child development can be undone by sickness and regular bouts of diarrhea. To decrease risk, UKA distributes purification tablets and filters. Staff also train mothers in proper sanitation and hygiene, including the importance of keeping clean and dirty water separate in the home.

DATA COLLECTION AT UKA

In addition to monitoring height, weight, hemoglobin, and neurological development, UKA conducts a survey of every family when they start the program to gather basic demographic information. These include household size, type of ceiling and flooring, type of stove, method of garbage disposal, source of drinking water, typical diet, and membership in the national social assistance program Oportunidades. Families in the Oportunidades program receive cash payments if they satisfy certain program requirements, such as regularly attending school or visiting a health clinic. These data help UKA ensure that it is reaching the populations who most need assistance.

The information gathered through nutrition surveillance, anemia detection, neurodevelopment monitoring, and the entry-level survey is entered into the InfoKilo database we introduced at the start of the chapter.

InfoKilo is a monitoring, reporting, and real-time processing system that receives and sends data through local UKA service centers. The system is vital to the goals of the PIN program: measurement, intervention, and behavior change. In addition to supporting the day-to-day operation of the program, InfoKilo helps UKA evaluate if the program is working as planned.

Monitoring

Field officers use InfoKilo to monitor the health of individual children and prioritize their fieldwork. If a mother has a malnourished or anemic child, the system highlights her record in red or yellow, a signal meant to prompt health promoters to investigate the cause. Since the biweekly food packet should meet a significant portion of the nutritional needs of children in the program, field officers do not distribute extra packets to families with a malnourished child. They reason instead that, if food provision does not fix the problem, some other factor must be causing the malnutrition. These factors could include sickness, anemia, or others.

Before beginning each day, field officers use InfoKilo to decide how to allocate their time between group and individual interactions with mothers and also to determine the best way to help each ailing child. Once a field officer identifies families with the clearest need, he or she can then intervene and provide the training that mothers need to best support the development of their children.

To ensure that this extra attention translates into improved health outcomes, malnourished children are weighed once every two weeks instead of once every two months. This information is entered back into InfoKilo so that field officers can monitor progress.

Evaluation and Reporting Results

In addition to its role in guiding operations, InfoKilo supports UKA's efforts to evaluate their program. UKA partners with the Salvador Zubirán National Institute of Health Sciences and Nutrition to analyze the data in InfoKilo. Every two months, the Institute analyzes the most recent data to identify individual- and aggregate-level trends in the nutrition outcomes just described (such as weight-for-age), as well as information on overall program coverage for communities where UKA works.

In reports to donors, UKA cites these trends as evidence of the impact of its multidimensional approach. Usually, the results have pointed toward before-and-after evidence of program success: for example, the report might note that two-thirds of children in the PIN program experienced improved nutritional status after six months in the program. These outcomes are often compared to national averages as a way of benchmarking progress. UKA also includes vignettes of individual children in reports, drawing on InfoKilo records to describe the child's household characteristics and family diet, as well as their nutritional status before, during, and after participating in program. (See Appendix A for a sample of one of these reports.)

Reports may be tailored to the geographic or programmatic interests of specific donors, containing simple statistics about the beneficiary population and PIN action over a particular period and location of interest.

Analysis Question 1: Considering the types of monitoring data discussed in Chapter 5, do you think UKA has the right balance of activity tracking, targeting, engagement, and feedback data? What are the tradeoffs between actionability and responsibility that the organization must make?

> Analysis Question 2: UKA donor reports use before–after outcome comparisons, comparisons with national averages, and anecdotes about children to demonstrate the program's impact. Is this approach credible? How might UKA more credibly demonstrate accountability to donors?

AT THE IMPACT EVALUATION DRAWING BOARD

UKA originally designed the PIN program's six activities based on recommendations and evidence from nutritionists and public health officials. InfoKilo's monitoring system helped ensure that UKA implemented the PIN program as designed. However, sound science alone could not demonstrate that PIN functioned as theorized—that it actually *caused* improvement in child nutrition. UKA could use data in InfoKilo to identify changes in important outcomes among its beneficiary population, but how could the organization learn how much PIN was contributing to these changes?

Originally, UKA focused on using the statistics in InfoKilo to report on changes in beneficiaries' rates of malnutrition and anemia. As the PIN program expanded, though, internal discussions noted the shortcomings of using before–after statements of program impact. UKA started to focus on learning about how to conduct a more rigorous evaluation of their program.

In 2011, UKA started a consultancy with Innovations for Poverty Action (IPA), an organization that designs and conducts randomized controlled trials (RCTs), founded by this book's co-author, Dean Karlan. Together, they began thinking through how to evaluate the impact of the PIN program.

On the surface, evaluating the PIN program would be simple: identify a set of communities that would be appropriate for the program and randomly assign some communities to participate in the program (the treatment group) and others not to (the control group). Such an evaluation would focus on a narrow question: Is the PIN, as designed and implemented, an effective way to promote the healthy development of children under five?

Yet IPA and UKA agreed that this type of evaluation would not yield much insight. The PIN program is complex, with many components potentially responsible for any observed changes, including supplements, education, improved water, and so forth. For better insight into *why* the program was or was not improving child development, they would need to test individual program components to learn which were delivering the most impact.

According to UKA's theory of change, the program worked because of its multifaceted approach addressing all of the barriers to childhood development. But what if that were not true? What if the organization could generate similar impact on childhood development by only delivering food? Or by only providing safe water? Learning about the relative effectiveness of various elements of the program (or whether they added up to more than the sum of their parts) would help UKA validate and refine its theory of change. But it would also have a more practical advantage—by focusing on the activities that delivered the largest impact, UKA could make the program more efficient and expand its reach.

Here, the evaluation ran into a challenge: this type of evaluation would require expanding services to hundreds of new communities in order to create treatment and control groups that had not previously received services. Additionally, to evaluate the relative impact of different program elements, the evaluation would require an even larger sample since there would be several treatment groups, each receiving a particular combination of program elements. New field and analysis staff would have to be hired and trained to collect and process all the data.

UKA had no immediate plans to expand the program to new areas. Without a clear opportunity to slot evaluation into current organizational plans, the impact evaluation would be difficult for UKA to implement.

So UKA and IPA considered narrowing the focus to one element of the PIN program. UKA staff thought the area with the greatest potential for program learning was nutrition programming. Were both the food packet and nutrition education interventions necessary to reduce malnutrition, or would one intervention alone be sufficient? An RCT testing the relative effectiveness of these two program components would compare four groups: one that received only the nutritional training, one that received only the food packets, one that received both packets and training, and a control group that did not receive either.

Yet even this narrower plan faced the same implementation challenges as a broader evaluation: an evaluation of nutrition programming would still require rolling out to new areas. If UKA was to learn from impact evaluation, it would have to find a design that would deliver clear information within resource and logistical constraints.

The Handwashing Proposal

Given the difficulty of evaluating the impact of existing program components, UKA looked for other research questions that would provide useful information without requiring an expansion to new beneficiary populations.

At the time, UKA was piloting a handwashing campaign that offered mothers soap, reminders, and training in proper handwashing techniques. Though handwashing education was not yet part of normal PIN activities, UKA was sure it was needed: the benefits of food supplements or nutrition education could be negated by diseases spread through poor hygiene. Before scaling up the project, UKA wanted to determine whether it was effective at changing handwashing behavior. The organization decided to work with IPA on the evaluation.

Evaluating the handwashing campaign had three clear benefits. First, the new intervention could take place within existing UKA service areas, sharply reducing the cost of running the RCT. Second, evaluating an experimental program component would provide important information about its impact before the organization decided to scale it up. Finally, the research would fill a gap in the evidence about handwashing interventions since UKA and IPA would design the evaluation to generate information not just on the handwashing intervention's impact, but also on how to best run it. To do that, they would investigate several variations of the handwashing program.

First, UKA divided its research participants into a group that would receive handwashing training and a group that would not. Of those who would not, some would receive soap but no training, while the rest would serve as the control, receiving neither soap nor training. The handwashing training group would be divided into four groups: one receiving reminders about handwashing from UKA staff and a bar of soap, another receiving just the reminders, a third receiving only the soap, and a final group receiving only the training. This design would allow UKA to compare the outcomes of each configuration and identify which best fit the program's needs. (Figure 13.1)

The training sessions would promote handwashing by linking it to participating mothers' desires to nurture their children and their expectations that their children would succeed in life. These messages would be delivered through an intensive promotional campaign and stressed in follow-up visits conducted by UKA staff. The evaluation would take a long-term view, measuring impact by observing handwashing behavior after one year and malnutrition after two to three years.

FAST FORWARD

UKA went through the evaluation design process in 2011, hoping to receive a grant to carry out the evaluation, but the funding did not come

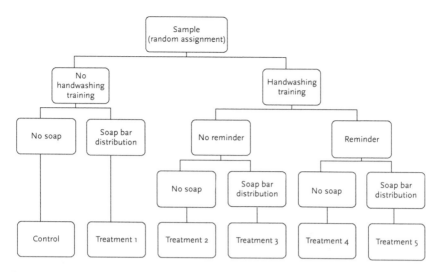

Figure 13.1 Potential handwashing experimental design

through. Without outside funding, UKA put the RCT on hold. The planning effort still paid off, though. Working through the handwashing evaluation proposal stimulated useful discussions about data at UKA. The organization had a better understanding about how to credibly measure changes in outcomes and assess the organization's impact. Through that discussion, UKA developed some creative ways to test improvements to their current programs.

While impact evaluation plans are on hold, UKA is taking steps to improve its monitoring system. UKA is refining the InfoKilo system to include geotagged information on each family, with maps displaying key information about nutrition and pictures of children in the program attached. This will allow the system to better support field officers by providing a wider view of overall nutritional status of beneficiaries in the region in real time.

Together, this work will help UKA build a data collection system that drives operational decision-making and fits current capacity.

Analysis Question 3: The proposed RCT would have generated credible evidence on handwashing interventions that UKA and others could have used to inform programming. Unfortunately, the organization was unable to secure funding for the evaluation. How else could UKA consider evaluating the merits of the handwashing interventions?

APPENDIX A EXCERPT FROM A PRESENTATION OF RESULTS

EXAMPLE OF RECOVERED CHILD: ERNESTO

- Oaxaca, Municipio de San Miguel Peras
- Current age: 4.4 years, date of birth: December 21, 2004
- Ernesto entered PIN on September 28, 2005, when he was 10 months old, weighing 6.2 kg and measuring 62 cm. His malnutrition was SEVERE.

Home

- The ceiling of Ernesto's house is made of tile and the ground is dirt. They have piped water service.
- They go to the bathroom outside and cook on a standing stove, they have electricity and a television.
- Nine people live in the same house and share one room for sleeping.
- Ernesto's family receives assistance from the program Oportunidades.

Anemia

Ernesto was tested for anemia every six months, and only in November 2007 was light anemia detected, for which he was given an iron treatment over six months. [See Figure 13.2]

Date of test	Hemoglobin Level	Diagnosis
May 24, 2006	12	No anemia
November 22, 2006	11.3	No anemia
May 23, 2007	11	No anemia
November 21, 2007	10.6	Light anemia
May 6, 2008	12.4	No anemia
November 19, 2008	11.6	No anemia

Figure 13.2 Sample results of hemoglobin monitoring for UKA Recipient

CASE ANALYSIS

> Analysis Question 1: Considering the types of monitoring data discussed in Chapter 5, do you think UKA has the right balance of activity tracking, targeting, engagement, and feedback? What are the tradeoffs between actionability and responsibility that the organization must make?

The way UKA uses outcome-level nutrition data for targeting—in this case, targeting specific households for additional treatment—is credible. Tracking and analyzing detailed outcome information enables program staff to identify problems early and act quickly to address them. Once InfoKilo flags a breakdown in the theory of change (for example, that children are not getting healthier despite receiving program services), staff visit families to determine the cause. From there, the field officer can use his or her judgment to find the necessary program services to get families back on track.

The organization's activity tracking and targeting efforts are credible and actionable. The data allow the organization to carefully target its program and identify families for whom the program isn't working as intended and who might need extra help. Immediate data entry by field workers means data are available to influence programmatic decisions in a timely manner.

The organization might want to consider collecting additional feedback and engagement data. This could be collected on a regular basis from all participants, or families could be randomly selected to answer additional questions. Feedback and engagement data could help UKA understand when and why families are not following recommended practices, such as handwashing, or why children aren't being fed supplements, as we saw in the case. Such data could help UKA improve its training programs.

The large amount of information already collected, however, also raises concerns about the responsibility of the system. Getting statistics into the system is certainly time-consuming—collecting and entering data for a single community can require an entire day of a field officer's time, considering the time it takes to travel to the community and weigh and measure all children in the program. And that is just one community. Since the system requires bimonthly visits to every community, gathering these data adds up to a huge expenditure of money and time—resources that could be used to deliver more of the program. So UKA will have to seriously consider the tradeoffs involved in additional data collection.

In sum, the InfoKilo system delivers a large amount of actionable data. But, in doing so, it incurs significant costs in money and time that could be spent on program delivery. If UKA decides there is an imbalance between actionability and responsibility, one way to address it would be to pare down the amount of data collected and adopt mobile data collection. The organization could then decrease the number of indicators it measures and increase the efficiency of data collection and entry.

> Analysis Question 2: UKA donor reports use before–after outcome comparisons, comparisons with national averages, and anecdotes about children to demonstrate the program's impact. Is this approach credible? How might UKA more credibly demonstrate accountability to donors?

Although tracking these outcomes is important for targeting, UKA shouldn't use them in donor reports to suggest that changes in beneficiaries' lives were caused by the program. Nutrition could improve or worsen for participating families for many reasons that have nothing to do with the services UKA provides. For example, it may be that household incomes rose because remittances from relatives abroad increased or families joined the national Oportunidades program, which offers cash payments to buy food. If UKA finds that nutrition outcomes improved, how does the organization know that PIN caused the improvement instead of one of these other possibilities? Without a good measure of the counterfactual, UKA cannot credibly claim attribution for these results.

UKA can credibly demonstrate accountability to donors in a number of ways without purporting to measure impact. By tying activities and outputs to a strong theory of change supported by the best available literature, UKA can demonstrate that it is doing what it said it would do to improve childhood nutrition. By summarizing the demographic information it collects about program beneficiaries, the organization can show that it reaches its target population. And by highlighting any programmatic or management changes made in light of tracking or outcome data, UKA will demonstrate that it is continually learning and improving program operations.

> Analysis Question 3: The proposed RCT would have generated credible evidence on handwashing interventions that UKA and others could use to inform programming. Unfortunately, the organization was unable to secure funding for the evaluation. How else could UKA consider evaluating the merits of the handwashing interventions?

While the full RCT would have delivered rigorous evidence of the program's impact, UKA could consider some alternate methods to test the program's theory and determine if a wide-scale rollout is a good idea. Recall the shutdown rule from Chapter 6: with a newly available program, if a single round of data collection fails to detect the desired changes in the short-term outcome, the program is not working and should be redesigned or scrapped. (Remember that detecting the desired change does not necessarily mean success but simply the absence of failure.) The shutdown rule could be a good fit for the handwashing program. Suppose handwashing behaviors are unchanged after UKA's intervention. It seems very improbable that, if not for UKA, handwashing otherwise would have *declined*. So a finding of no impact is likely to be a sign that the program is not working as intended.

UKA could consider piloting each component of its handwashing program—training and soap distribution—in different communities and immediately collect data on whether individuals changed their handwashing practices or used the soap. If the data show behavior change or soap usage, UKA can rule out program failure. While less satisfying than proving impact, it would provide some reassurance that it would be responsible to implement the handwashing program.

PART III

The Funder Perspective and Concluding Thoughts

CHAPTER 14

The Institutional Donor Perspective

So far, we have discussed monitoring and evaluation from the implementing organization's perspective. We have focused on what data and analysis organizations ought to make available to their stakeholders and what data they should collect and analyze for their own management purposes.

We now consider the perspective of the institutional donor. By "institutional" donor, we mean foundations and government or any entity with enough resources to have a "strategy" across grants and staff employed for the purpose of implementing this strategy.

The informational needs of institutional donors may differ from the needs of the organizations they fund. If donor needs are always a subset of what an organization needs, this is not a problem, but what if a donor needs data that an organization's management does not? Unfortunately, everyone's interests are not always fully aligned. We can think of a number of reasons why a donor may want some data that would not be collected under an implementing organization's "right-fit" monitoring and evaluation strategy.

First, a donor, such as a foundation, may want to use the same metrics across its entire portfolio of grants and contracts. To do so, donors may require data that are not optimal from an implementer's perspective. Perhaps the primary outcome that the donor is seeking to change is not the same as the organization's primary aim. From the perspective of the organization, the cost of measuring a secondary outcome (the donor's primary outcome) is not worth the benefit. The donor may also want to invest in developing good metrics, both for comparability across their portfolio and so the organizations they support do not have to use resources coming up with their own. In some cases, such metrics may align perfectly with organizations' needs, but in others they may be a bit off. This will likely be the case if the funder supports a portfolio of widely varying organizations.

Second, a donor may be trying to address a broad social problem, but each organization they support works on only one aspect of the problem. The donor needs data to measure how well they are doing at addressing the problem as a whole, whereas each individual organization may have no internal need for such data. For example, suppose a donor wants to improve literacy rates for all children in a country living below the poverty line. To do so, they are supporting many different local education organizations that work in schools with different types of students. The donor wants to know the poverty rates of the children being served in each school compared to those not served. The organization may have a slightly different goal—say, increasing educational achievement for girls—and may not have any internal use for poverty data. Nonetheless, such data are crucial for donors to assess how well they are achieving their broader goal of improving nationwide literacy.

Third, trust and information gaps may lead to different data needs. This is natural and not intended to sound pejorative. In a small organization, for example, managers with strong personal relationships with staff may not need as much accountability data to protect against incompetence or corruption. Daily observation and interaction provide a flow of information on staff activity. But a donor rarely has that relational proximity and so may demand more accountability data (e.g., activity data, with some form of verification) than the organization feels is necessary to demonstrate it is doing what it promised.

Fourth, an organization's management and a donor may have different judgments regarding how to apply the CART principles (Credible, Actionable, Responsible, and Transportable). We have set out a framework in this book, but even we, the coauthors of this book and the staff at Innovations for Poverty Action that have worked with us, have had extensive debates about how to apply the CART principles in specific situations in this book and in our work more generally. Our views usually converge, but that end point is not always immediately clear even to seasoned practitioners in the field.

Fifth, donors and organizations may have different preferences. Some organizations can tolerate a lot of risk, others are more risk-averse. One may hear arguments that some preferences are better than others, but if we use the term "preferences" in the way that economists do, then there is no such thing as "better" preferences. Preferences are a personal matter, and saying someone's preferences are better than someone else's is akin to saying that vanilla is better than chocolate. Some just prefer one over the other, and others the reverse, all else equal. (If you are arguing with an economist about whose preferences are "better," we suggest invoking the *Animal Farm* rule of preferences: all preferences are equal, but some preferences are more equal than others. (Although it helps to add afterwards that this is a joke.) In the case of data requirements, for example, if a donor has more risk-averse preferences than an organization, the donor may be more cautious about relying on existing evidence from other settings to demonstrate the efficacy of an approach. The donor may insist that the organization conduct a new counterfactual impact evaluation for their new setting. A funder or organization with more tolerance for risk may feel that the money spent on such a study would be better spent delivering more services.

We should also note that the principle of risk diversification must be applied differently to implementing organizations and donors. Not all organizations can afford to take significant risks—or survive the failures that may result. This is particularly true of implementing organizations. But foundations should have some failures. If they do not, they have almost surely taken on too little risk. The complex problems that large donors often address will not be solved without some failures. This is yet another reason why conducting high-quality monitoring and evaluation and sharing those results is important, so that the rest of the world can learn from the failures.

The points about judgment and risk tolerance also apply to debates *within* an organization: an organization is not a monolithic beast, and no doubt staff opinions will differ when it comes to how to structure monitoring and evaluation. And the data needs of line staff and managers may differ. As we discussed in Chapter 5, determining right-fit will require consensus building that is part of the management challenge of putting together a right-fit monitoring and evaluation system that management and staff will actually use.

Sixth, a donor may care about generating knowledge that others can use elsewhere to solve their problems. An organization, on the other hand, may appreciate the value of transportable knowledge but may not be able to prioritize it enough to bear its full cost. Thus, if with each grant a donor hopes to not only address a specific problem in a specific location, but also to generate knowledge that can help shape policy elsewhere, they may push an organization to collect more data than the organization normally would. Naturally, it also makes sense for the donor to pay for that knowledge generation.

Seventh, donor data requirements can exacerbate natural tensions within funded organizations. What if the tension over data analysis is within an organization, such as between an organization's board and management? For fundraising purposes, a board often wants to advertise outcomes achieved. Lacking a counterfactual, they may not be credible in making those claims. If a donor does not recognize that there are no appropriate data to make a certain claim, an organization may find itself collecting bad data or performing poor data analysis to satisfy this donor. We discourage this practice, but we also recognize that it is a reality that plenty of organizations are going to face.

Seven may seem like a lot of reasons, but only a few, if any, of these reasons will apply in most cases. Where these reasons apply, there are good reasons for a foundation to ask for more data but also to offer to the implementing organization additional funds to cover the costs. The bottom line is that donors need to be careful about the data and analysis they require of the organizations they fund and to recognize that aligning those potentially divergent aims may require a willingness to pay for additional data collection. After all, both entities have to ensure they are following the "R" in CART for their own objectives. What is not "responsible" for the organization may indeed be "responsible" for the donor. By providing a framework for thinking about appropriate data collection, it is our hope that this book will provide tools to help address these challenging situations.

The responsible principle also implies that funders should take care not to constantly change the data they require of organizations they fund. Foundations typically have more flexibility than governments to make changes to the data they require from grantees. Governments and social sector organizations are often enmeshed in complex contracting agreements, sometimes with the contract provisions codified in legislation. In such cases, changing data requirements will take time. Often governments have larger policy considerations in mind, a point we return to later.

We predict that the biggest struggle organizations will face in working with donors to implement the CART principles is convincing donors to walk away from asking for outcomes (in other words, giving up on demands to know an organizations' "impact") when the counterfactual is not credible. People have a natural desire to know "did the outcome go up?" even if a good counterfactual is not possible. If seeing malnourished children inspired donors to act, the natural next question to ask is, "After I gave my money, are the children still malnourished?" Alas, as we have discussed, correlation is not causation. In many cases, donors will have to be satisfied with outputs. Fortunately, the CART principles help organizations develop reporting systems that deliver credible, actionable information on how program delivery is faring; whether organizations are reaching their intended clients; and how those individuals feel about the program. All of which is much more than many funders know today!

PAYING FOR SUCCESS?

We have looked at reasons why the data needs of donors and implementers may diverge, but one way of aligning their aims and activities is paying for outcomes rather than paying for services delivered. "Pay for Success" (PFS) is an emerging approach to structuring the relationship between donors and implementers. Such programs are sometimes called "performance-based contracts," "pay for performance," or "social impact bonds." This set of approaches has a common goal: funders pay for social results (outcomes) rather than service delivery (outputs).

A critical aspect of PFS programs is the decision about the output or outcome on which the payment is conditioned. At the simplest end of the spectrum are traditional government contracts, where the funder asks for output data and pays per output (service delivered) rather than paying for costs (or procurement). Such delivery-based contracts are in common use. In these output-based contracts, if the implementing organization figures out how to deliver goods or services more cheaply, they benefit because they get paid for their output irrespective of their costs. Of course, a hybrid model is viable as well, where the implementer is reimbursed for costs, with a second payment conditional on achieving certain outputs.

In many cases, the financing of PFS programs involves raising funds from financial intermediaries who back the programs, often called *social impact bonds*. Two well-known programs illustrate how this works (Rikers in the United States and Petersborough in the United Kingdom). These programs seek to reduce prison recidivism, or the rate at which parolees are reimprisoned after release. Prisons are costly in financial and social terms, and preventing these prison returns could save governments a great deal of money. These programs first establish a clear project goal: reducing reincarceration to a set percentage of those released. Investors provide the money to bankroll the organizations that provide education and training programs to prison inmates and parolees. If the program hits the target, the government pays back the investors. The government ultimately saves money because fewer parolees are reincarcerated. A critical aspect of these programs is *conditionality*. This means government does not simply sign a contract with an organization and then reimburse its expenses after receiving a financial report showing that the organization spent the money how it said it would. Instead, payments are conditional on achieving the preestablished outcome targets.

When PFS conditions payment on achieving actual outcomes, this raises a critical and much-debated question: Must the outcome come with a counterfactual? Should the donor pay merely based on whether the measurable outcome improves? Or based on whether it goes up relative to a comparison group? Hopefully, by now you know where we stand on this: there is not much point to paying based merely on an outcome without a comparison group. A funder could end up paying for dumb luck (because outcomes improved for reasons that had nothing to do with anything the organization did), or refusing to pay even though the organization was quite successful (outcomes did not improve, but they would have gotten worse if not for the intervention of the organization).

PFS and related programs are an important part of a contemporary movement[1] focused more generally on achieving clearly defined measurable social outcomes for beneficiaries in the provision of social services. One strength of PFS programs is that donors pay only when organizations achieve their desired outcomes. As a result, PFS programs align the incentives of funders and fundees in a way that traditional funding schemes do not. Contracting on outcomes also leaves decisions about how to deliver programs to the implementing organizations who are arguably best positioned to make these decisions.

But PFS programs also have potential drawbacks. When organizations are paid for delivery, a donor could potentially cherry-pick the cheapest outcomes for which to pay. In this case, the donor only addresses the low-hanging fruit of social change and ignores the hard cases that may be the most important societal problems to address. Just because an outcome cannot be inexpensively "purchased" does not mean it should fall off the priority list.

There are other risks to the PFS model. For starters, while donors can mitigate their own risk via diversification in investments, participating organizations are often risk-constrained. The high cost of failure may create a disincentive for government or organizations to try innovative new ideas. Whether organizations innovate as much as they would in another setting depends largely on how their contract is written. Clearly, some programs, such as challenge or "prize" projects that award money to the first to solve a scientific or technological problem, are designed directly for innovation. But for more results-oriented implementation PFS projects, such as homelessness services or parolee rehabilitation, PFS may result in lower levels of innovation than is socially desirable.

Another drawback to the PFS model is that it is hard to alter compensation for particularly tough (and costly to the implementer) cases that generate excess social benefit. For example, suppose that a donor government pays $1,000 per additional success case in parolee rehabilitation treatment relative to a control group. The contracted organization will have an incentive to take on all cases they can successfully treat for $1,000 or less. But what if the cases that are more costly to treat are the ones that also are doing the most harm to society? Unless the payment scheme is somehow adjusted for tougher cases, the implementing organization will not attempt the most important cases, and those foregone cases will continue causing social harm. This is exactly one of the arguments for paying for outcomes (with a counterfactual). Compensate an organization for the good that they do for society as a whole—yet that compensation requires a ton of measurement, constantly. Perhaps too much.

If we already know the efficacy of an idea, requiring counterfactual evidence on an ongoing basis creates no additional knowledge for the world. The *only* reason to do it is to figure out how much to compensate the implementing organization. That money could (and we believe usually should) instead be put toward helping more people—this is the "responsible" CART principle. But if an implementer is not doing a randomized controlled trial (RCT), we are back to either using before–after comparisons, which could produce very wrong estimates of impact, or using outputs to measure success, which is exactly the structure PFS programs are meant to correct.

PFS can be very helpful in aligning the goals of donors and implementers in a particular project, but there are limits to the ways this mechanism can be employed to solve wider social challenges. Take a theoretical job training program. If the program works for participants, it helps them individually remain employed. But does it actually make labor markets work better and more efficiently, with more people successfully "matched," or are other people now out of jobs while the people who received extra training are employed? Answering that question is more complicated than just tracking the outcomes of a simple job training program. In this example and in many others, different techniques are needed, both theoretical and empirical, to assess the actual impact of a program. Building such issues into a PFS scheme is extremely challenging.

IMPLEMENTING PAY FOR SUCCESS

Given both the benefits and drawbacks of outcome-based payment programs, how should foundation and government agency funders think about contracting for outcomes versus outputs? As our discussion shows, there are essentially three different models for contracts: (1) paying when the implementer has spent money or done work, (2) paying for outputs, and (3) paying for outcomes. Each has different requirements for both contracts and metrics. In each case, the first question to ask is "who has the comparative advantage to be managing the project?"

In all three models, it is important to identify which implementing organizations have incentives to participate and how well they will execute. Much of these projects' success is driven by the project choice and the quality of implementation. Considering the spectrum of project difficulty aids the decision-making process. On the easy-implementation end of the spectrum, the organization merely has to choose a good idea, and the government merely has to cover costs or pay for outputs. No need to track outcomes because there is little to no potential for poor or inappropriate implementation (by assumption, as we said, this is one end of the spectrum). On the other end, though, the project idea is merely a starting point, and implementation can differ wildly. Here, if you want to know if the program achieved its goals, you will need to track outcomes and incorporate a counterfactual into the analysis. Some donors have an instinctive desire to always want to pay for outcomes, but a realistic look at what can be monitored and what cannot should guide the decision. It simply may not be possible to measure the counterfactual credibly in a given project.

One of the issues that government agencies have to consider in outcome-based contracts is that innovation can be discouraged if they are only paying for success. Governments should want to take the risk inherent in diversifying in order to produce learning, but implementing organizations are not able to diversify in an outcome-based contract. Organizations will not take any risk because they cannot afford to suffer the loss that comes from not achieving the outcome. Or, they will do the least risky thing that gets to the point of payout because they cannot afford mediocre outcomes that will get $0 back. The implementers will be risk-averse when the donor wants them to be risk-neutral. If the agency is trying to create true innovation, it should want the implementers to be aggressive and try new things, so it should pay for outputs rather than outcomes.

Implementing PFS programs may require certain conditions. PFS programs put a premium on credible evidence that a program is likely to work based on prior evaluation of a program or others similar to it. Such programs also need actionable, contemporaneous (rather than retrospective) monitoring and evaluation to ensure that the program is on course and achieving its intended outcomes. The ability of implementers and funders to establish robust monitoring systems is critical to reducing risk and providing incentives for investors to participate.

PFS programs also require governments and investors to shift their funding and investing orientation. Governments need to develop the motivation and capacity to design and manage contracts to achieve social outcomes rather than just agreeing to pay for services rendered. Philanthropies and commercial investors must be willing to shoulder the risk of financing social service providers between the time that a program starts and when it achieves the agreed-upon social outcomes. As Suzanne Adatto and Paul Brest note, PFS programs aim to "transform the way foundations and governments and service providers think about and contract for social services—connecting performance, costs, and evaluable outcomes in ways that ultimately benefit taxpayers, intended beneficiaries, and other stakeholders."[2] PFS is one option that donors can use to help align incentives with organizations, but they should consider its drawbacks carefully as well.

DONORS AND THE CART PRINCIPLES

The CART principles and the Goldilocks approach to evidence provide a common language and framework that organizations and donors can use for productive conversations about what to measure and when. The CART principles prioritize credible information, giving both sets of organizations a way to avoid collecting poor-quality data that will not inform decisions. The actionable principle reminds implementers and funders that all data should be put to use, which typically means prioritizing organizational data needs.

The bottom line is that donors need to be careful about the data and analysis they require of their implementing organizations and recognize that aligning potentially divergent aims may require a willingness to pay for additional data collection. After all, both entities have to ensure they are following the "R" in CART for their own objectives. What is not "responsible" for the organization may indeed be "responsible" for the donor. By providing a framework for thinking about appropriate data collection, it is our hope that this book provides tools to help address these challenging situations.

CHAPTER 15

The Retail Donor Perspective

Most individual donors lack full-time advisors to help them give effectively, i.e., advisors who can steer them to organizations with credible monitoring systems and evidence of impact, and who can help negotiate funding to specific projects. These are luxuries of institutional donors. Instead, most individual donors must rely on publicly available information or no information at all. We refer to such donors as "retail donors." In the absence of rigorous information, they must base decisions largely on anecdotes, personal connections, or happenstance. That wastes philanthropic dollars.

This chapter teases apart the information shortfalls that define the predicament of such retail donors, donors that may want to use the CART principles of credible, actionable, responsible, and transportable data in choosing charities, but have little way to actually do so. We then outline a potential solution to these information shortfalls, an "impact audit."

THE INFORMATION CHALLENGE

The task facing retail (and institutional) donors keen to maximize the impact of their donations is technically challenging. Isolating the impact of tutoring programs on high school graduation rates, the impact of public health initiatives on the spread of sexually transmitted diseases, or the impact of skill-based job training on employment rates of chronically unemployed workers is difficult even for sophisticated academics and policy analysts.

Making matters worse, organizations have little incentive to generate data for the simple reason that funders often do not demand such data. In the current world of philanthropy, organizations which elide rigorous assessment suffer little penalty.

Naturally no (non-fraudulent) organization sets out to waste donor dollars. But some do. No organization denies the centrality of impact. But few measure it. Without clean evidence of impact, even donors keen to maximize their philanthropic impact instead may base their decisions on happenstance.

Of course, impact is not the only reason people give to nonprofit organizations. Donors may give due to *social reciprocity* (I gave because my friend asked me to donate); *reputational boost* (I gave to look good in front of others); *personal consumption* (I gave to something that I use myself, such as a specific museum, opera, community organization); *ethical duty* (I believe I have an ethical duty to contribute to a set of people or cause); or *political beliefs and group association* (I want to be a member of the set of people fighting for a specific cause). Such concerns may (or may not, depending on your perspective) be admirable reasons for giving. And people will always give for those reasons and no doubt many more. And people give for multiple reasons at the same time. But we believe it would be nice if, for those who do want give to maximize their impact on society, they had better tools to do so. So how can a donor find the best organizations working in a given area, say education or poverty alleviation? How are they to choose?

The lack of a broad based, impact-focused rating system leaves nonprofits unaccountable for outcomes. Retail donors hear nonprofits laying claim to large outcomes, but only a handful of nonprofits prove the point—prove that interventions raise outcomes above what would occur in the absence of intervention. In other words, few nonprofits marshal data to prove that outcomes post intervention exceed counterfactual outcomes. Therefore, retail donors are left to sway back and forth in the wake of informal impressions, nonprofit-driven public relations, isolated tales of success, and fortuitous personal connections.

In essence, too many nonprofits survive despite mediocrity or worse.

CHALLENGE OF RATINGS IN THE SOCIAL SECTOR

At the risk of oversimplification, consider the difference between for-profit and mission-based social organizations. Corporations vary widely in what they do but ultimately share a single mission: maximize profits. It follows that investors can judge performance with a single metric: risk-adjusted rate of return. Financial analysis and audits provide investors with credible, public information about this metric.

Most mission-based social organizations, by contrast, share no single mission. Each adopts its own. Some educate learning-disabled students, fight bullying, or staunch political corruption. Some address issues for those in extreme poverty. Still others seek to nourish marriage or love of baroque music. And so on. In a world of idiosyncratic missions, there can be no single metric by which to measure success. The tools of a financial analyst or auditor do not capture whether a nonprofit succeeds at its mission.

For a rating system to serve the needs of retail donors, it needs to provide recommendations that assess impact credibly and cover a wide variety of organization types, addressing many different causes with different strategies.

Two issues here demand scale.

First, few donors will simply cede all decision-making to a third party and ask "what organization is doing the most good per dollar donated?" Instead, a donor may have a charity in mind and want to know if it is doing reasonable work. Or, they may have a cause in mind and want to find a set of noble charities working in that cause. For a rating system to find traction, individuals must have a good chance of finding the information they seek. They will not keep coming back if the rated charities never line up with their interests.

Second, a good nonprofit rating system not only helps donors find effective organizations, but it also imposes discipline on the organizations themselves, driving them to operate more efficiently and choose the best ideas to implement. To see why, let's return to the example of for-profit corporations. Financial information on for-profit firms drives investors to productive firms and away from bad ones. And that process also nudges the bad ones to improve, learn, and innovate.

Unfortunately, there is a clear tradeoff between scale and accuracy, particularly when it comes to applying the CART principles to the rating of nonprofits. While there are a handful of metric-providing systems in place, they tend to fall short either on metrics or on reach. This is why we predict the most useful innovation will not be a single rating organization that figures out how to be rigorous at scale, but rather an institutional shift to create and embrace industry standards that many raters can use, perhaps even competing to conduct the most reliable ratings.

What institutionally is needed? As Gugerty argues,[1] the social sector needs a set of institutions that can fill this information gap and provide a credible signal of organizational quality. What creates a credible signal? Ratings standards must be relatively stringent, otherwise they provide little additional information and potential donors cannot distinguish high-quality organizations from poor ones. Ratings information must also be relevant, assessing organizations based on their missions and intended outcomes. The information must also be reliable, which typically means it is verified by a third party. Finally, the ratings system must achieve scale. Organizations often must incur costs (such as documentation preparation and audit) to participate in a rating system, so they need an incentive to participate. If standards and ratings are widely accepted, donors are likely to reward those organizations that participate and avoid those that do not. Naturally, this will lead to most organizations participating.

THE LANDSCAPE OF NONPROFIT RATING SYSTEMS

A quick tour of the current rating landscape illustrates the challenges raters face. Charity Navigator is easily the largest nonprofit evaluator, measured either by the number of charities reviewed or public awareness and number of users. But Charity Navigator's metrics focus largely on revenues and costs and evaluating quantifiable and easily observable management and governance aspects. This system reveals nothing about whether the organization is achieving its desired impact. Some programs simply cost more money to administer than others. When you choose a new cell phone, do you care how much of the price covers the materials inside the phone versus the labor? No. So why care about the operational details of nonprofits? We need to know: For each dollar you put in, what do you buy in impact? And, unfortunately, overhead ratios do not give information on what matters.[2]

A number of other ratings agencies evaluate similar accounting and governance metrics but with smaller reach, including BBB Wise Giving Alliance, Charity Intelligence Canada, Charity Watch, Intelligent Philanthropy, Ministry Watch, Serious Givers, and Smart Givers Network, among many others. Only Charity Intelligence Canada, Wise Giving Alliance, and Charity Watch have achieved significant scale, and they still cover only a small portion of the market. Although several mention the importance of impact, none of these ratings agencies rigorously assesses organizations based on their social impact.

Two organizations compose rankings based on aggregating reviews done by others. Philanthropedia (recently acquired by GuideStar) aggregates expert reviews to rank charities by philanthropic cause. GreatNonprofits aggregates user and client reviews, much like Yelp. However, just like Yelp, individuals who are either extremely happy or unhappy with the organization are most likely to provide rankings, leading to real bias in the reviews. And these reviewers often have limited interaction with the organization and lack "credible" information or analysis to assess impact. As a result, there is little reason to think the aggregation of such opinions will yield wisdom.

GuideStar is the largest source of information about charities. But it does not rate or rank their impact. Rather, GuideStar combines information provided by charities with information charities file with the Internal Revenue Service and makes these data available to the public. GuideStar rewards charities that provide voluminous data by giving them higher levels of certification. This is a critical role for the philanthropic market. But GuideStar neither verifies the accuracy of the self-reported information nor assesses whether this information is actually helpful, i.e. actually informs the donor about the effectiveness of the organization. We agree with GuideStar that transparency is a virtue (it is part of the "transportable" concept in CART). However, donors may well want to avoid a charity that, however transparent, operates ineffectively.

GiveWell provides, to our knowledge, the most rigorous publicly available assessment of cost-effectiveness. But we are back to the tradeoff we discussed earlier: GiveWell reports on only a handful of nonprofits. Their high-quality reviews are useful to donors interested in the single cause that GiveWell examines (international poverty and health) and to donors singularly focused on cost-effectiveness. But GiveWell provides no useful guidance to donors who have chosen a cause because of some passion and want to know which, among organizations working on that cause, are the most effective ones. We fear this is the vast majority of donors. And by "cause" here we mean both the sector of engagement (education, environment, human rights, etc.) and geography (United States, United Kingdom, Latin America, Africa, etc.). Even donors interested in international poverty and health often start with a specific nonprofit in mind and ask "is this charity a good one?"

For the typical donor, odds are low that the charity they are interested in will be mentioned on GiveWell's website. Thus, retail donors must fully embrace GiveWell's selection of cause, philosophy, and analysis and be willing to donate to charities they may never have heard of before. For the record, we admire their analytics and attention to detail. And we believe they are providing an absolutely critical and useful role in the philanthropic sector. We note that GiveWell reports more than $110 million moved towards organizations they recommended in 2015; this is impressive, and, given their modest budget, Givewell is likely a high return on investment themselves for a donor.

But far bigger mounds of money remain unmoved, especially among donors that may not be willing to switch to GiveWell's causes, but instead, want to know the best organizations operating in their sector of interest.

And so we need approaches that fill in the gaps.

ONE OPTION: IMPACT AUDITING

As you can see, there is a big gap here for the retail donor. No rating system is based on evidence of impact and covers many nonprofits and causes. To solve the problem, this book's co-author, Dean Karlan, co-founded a nonprofit organization in 2015 called ImpactMatters.

ImpactMatters conducts what it calls "impact audits." These audits certify whether the claims made by nonprofits about their impact are supported by professional assessment of data and evidence systems. Its vision is ambitious, seeking to reshape philanthropy by creating an industry standard for assessment. Down the proverbial road, we see funders requiring applicants to undergo our impact audit (or someone else's equally rigorous audit). Once that happens, we see nonprofits flocking to undergo impact audits to demonstrate their effectiveness and maintain their external support.

BENEFITS OF IMPACT AUDITING

For nonprofits, impact audits offer two tangible benefits. First, they provide donors and other stakeholders a credible estimate of impact and a rigorous assessment of an organization's evidence systems. This may be based on the organization's data or may be based on mapping the organization's management data and design to appropriate data from elsewhere. These data are then used to make (hopefully confident) predictions about likely impacts. By creating a recognizable, trusted independent rating system, ImpactMatters provides a way for high-quality nonprofits to visibly display a measure of their quality to funders.

Second, the ImpactMatters team accompanies each audit with a private management letter that sets forth recommendations for improving data analysis and performance. Nonprofits emerge from the audit process with detailed information about strengths and weaknesses, a roadmap toward improved performance, and resources and materials to help them improve.

HOW IMPACT AUDITS WORK

Impact audits help resolve the information challenge in the social sector in several ways. Audits assess whether the organization has set forth a clear, achievable mission and identified outcomes that tightly reflect its mission. Next, the audit examines whether the organization analyzes data according to the best social science practices (i.e., credible data and analysis). Specifically, does the nonprofit set forth smart counterfactual estimates for the progress that populations would enjoy even in the absence of the nonprofit's intervention? If they do not produce impact analysis themselves, is there a clear alternative setting that has demonstrated the reliability of their theory of change, and do they have strong management data that allows a third party to have confidence that the nonprofit is implementing its program as designed? The analysis also includes estimating unintended harm caused by the nonprofit's interventions. For example, displacement effects: If the nonprofit subsidizes one entrepreneur to help her grow her business, does this hurt other entrepreneurs in the area?

Finally, the audit looks at how the organization uses data to continuously improve delivery of its services.

Impact audits built on these elements tell donors whether the nonprofit's claims of impact are tethered to credible evidence and a commitment to learning and improvement. This helps donors decide how to spend their money wisely while also helping nonprofits identify what they are doing well and, yes, not-so-well.

COMPONENTS OF AN IMPACT AUDIT

Impact audits are short-term engagements (about three months). An audit team collects information about the organization's intervention and operations and reviews available internal and external evidence on the organization's impact. The audit assesses organizations on four dimensions:

1. *Impact and Cost Calculation*: What is the best estimate of the impact of the nonprofit, and the costs required to generate that impact?
2. *Quality of Evidence*: Are there credible data and analysis of impact, appropriate for the organization's activities? An organization providing delivery of a service may need to show solid counterfactual evidence (or have a design based on someone else's strong counterfactual evidence with a strong ability to argue that their operations and setting match the operations and setting where the counterfactual evidence was

generated). An organization working to advocate for systemic change, however, may be outside of what is possible for such counterfactual rigor. The rating rubric meets the organization where they are and does not demand more rigor than is viable. This score depends heavily on the "credible" and "responsible" CART principles.

3. *Quality of Monitoring Systems*: Does the organization collect and review relevant data for management purposes? Are the data collected credible and actionable for the organization? Does the organization go beyond the finance and tracking data often required by donors to collect data on take-up, engagement, and feedback?

4. *Learning and Iteration*: Does the nonprofit use the data it collects to continuously improve the quality of its operations? Do they have clear internal processes for sharing and learning from data? We believe iterative learning predicts future success. Few things work forever. Thus, we want to see organizations develop data systems that support learning and iterating, adapting as times and markets change, but doing so with good evidence and reasoning, not merely because moods or leadership changed.

If the organization agrees to publication, it is issued an impact audit report, which includes a rating along with detailed analysis and supporting information. The cost of the impact ratio is calculated separately for each outcome under review. In other words, no attempt is made to add up the benefit of different outcomes into an estimate of overall benefit. In contrast to evaluations conducted by firms or non-profits like MDRC, Mathematica, MIT J-PAL, or IPA impact audits assess the quality and meaning of data already collected. ImpactMatters does not collect additional primary data.

Here's a key point. Other ratings systems serve the funder only. By contrast, impact audits feed findings back to the organization under review, giving it a clear road to improvement.

CREATING AN INDUSTRY STANDARD

The information challenge in mission-based work creates a real dilemma for donors. Quality is hard to measure, and donors are often "flying blind," supporting organizations with little information on their activities or impact. This information challenge likely limits the total amount of giving.

Impact audits represent one possible solution. If impact audits are widely adopted, we expect to see three things. First, organizations will shift toward interventions with greater impact and evidence, as appropriate. Next, donations will follow, shifting to nonprofits that generate greater impact. Finally, impact audit standards will be adopted by others, creating a market for high-quality monitoring, learning and impact.

ImpactMatters hopes that other firms will follow its lead, with impact audits becoming a de facto requirement for social sector organizations. In addition, just as generally accepted accounting principles have improved practice over time, the impact audit standard could improve practice across the sector by creating new norms for effectiveness.

CHAPTER 16

Concluding Thoughts and (Hopefully) Helpful Resources

We hope that after reading *The Goldilocks Challenge*, you can confidently answer the question: "What data should I be collecting to improve my program and learn whether or not I am achieving my goals?" The first epiphany we hope readers have is that they should *not* always collect data on the "big" impact question. When you can do impact evaluation well, it generates important benefits for stakeholders and for people who may benefit from your programs in the future. But collecting bad data or analyzing data badly can be a costly waste of social and organizational resources. Sometimes it is better to just say no. We have presented concepts and tools that will help you know when to say yes and when to say no to impact—and how to build right-fit monitoring and evaluation systems, collect credible data, and conduct credible analyses.

The second epiphany we hope readers have is that a great deal of good can be done by collecting high-quality monitoring data. These data are often less costly to collect than impact data and can provide needed accountability to stakeholders along with opportunities for programmatic learning and improvement. We believe that better monitoring for learning and improvement is the single most important change most organizations can make.

THE GOLDILOCKS RIGHT-FIT EVIDENCE INITIATIVE

Making the changes we suggest in this book will take time, capacity, and commitment. We have developed several ongoing resources and initiatives to support organizations in this journey.

The Goldilocks Right-Fit Evidence Initiative, housed at Innovations for Poverty Action (IPA), https://www.poverty-action.org/goldilocks, is a new effort by IPA to work with donors and implementing organizations to help them figure out what would constitute a "right-fit" monitoring and evaluation system for them. Thus, the Goldilocks Right-Fit Evidence Initiative complements IPA's traditional randomized evaluation work and helps organizations find the right-fit in their monitoring and evaluation systems. The initiative provides resources and consulting services for organizations, donors, and governments seeking to design and support the implementation of cost-effective, appropriately sized monitoring and evaluation systems.

Next, the online Goldilocks Toolkit provides deep dives into topics we could not fit into this book, a growing body of supplemental case studies, and additional resources on topics ranging from developing a theory of change, to where to look for evidence, to the nitty gritty of how to collect data, and more. The toolkit provides a platform where we can share ongoing resources and experiences as we move from Goldilocks 1.0 to Goldilocks 2.0. The toolkit also houses the Goldilocks "cheat sheet," designed to help organizations get started on their journey to "right-sized" (see Box 16.1).

NEXT STEPS

We look forward to hearing feedback on this book and the online Toolkit for future editions and extensions. We have already identified a number of areas for future work:

First: social enterprises. We have written generally about mission-based organizations, but our analysis applies most directly to nonprofit organizations. Many new forms of for-profit, mission-based firms are emerging ("social enterprises"). For these organizations, social impact is only one of the primary concerns of stakeholders. How does that influence what it means to collect data responsibility?

Second: organizational behavior and operating at scale. The past 20 years have seen a huge increase in the number of development researchers engaged in evaluation projects with nonprofit organizations and governments. While this has led to tremendous insights on underlying theories of development and knowledge on the impact of specific

Box 16.1 GOLDILOCKS CHEAT SHEET 1.0

PLANNING

1. Create a theory of change:
   a. Write it out.
   b. Identify steps that are critical and poorly understood or potentially flawed. Focus evidence gathering there.
2. Develop a monitoring plan:
   a. Consider how (and whether) to collect each type of monitoring data:
      i. Financial
      ii. Activity tracking
      iii. Targeting
      iv. Engagement
      v. Feedback
   b. Can you use the data? Will you? Is the intended use worth the cost of (credible) collection?
3. Develop an impact plan: Consider the *credible* criteria. Can you measure impact credibly (consider data quality and the need for a counterfactual) and responsibly (consider cost)? If not, don't measure.
4. Action plan: Specify the actions you will take depending on the evidence gathered from the monitoring plan and from the impact measurement plan.

USING

5. Collect data. Use the CART principles to prioritize those data that can be collected credibly, have a clear use, and are a responsible use of resources.
6. Analyze data. Ideally in easily automatable ways (particularly for monitoring data, which will come in frequently). Share internally in a learning venue. Involve staff, learn collectively, articulate improvements.
   a. Look for surprises. Challenge yourself.
   b. Any gaps from the planning phase now glaring at you?
   c. Are the data high quality?
7. Share externally. Get feedback.
8. Improve. If analysis yields surprises, either (a) examine action plan and take planned action, or (b) revisit data collection and analysis; if the results are doubtful, consider collecting more to confirm the surprise before making costly changes.

Repeat. Continue learning and iterating and improving.

programs, less attention has been paid to the organizational behavior of large operations. Specifically, we may now know that "A causes B" when A is implemented by specific organizations, but we do not always know whether A can be delivered at the same quality by another organization, one that is perhaps managed differently, operating at a different scale. What broad lessons can be learned about performance management for large-scale organizations? This book is a starting point for the discussion on how the use of data, incentives within organizations, and training are all critical for improving the quality of service delivery. We look forward to continuing that conversation.

Third and relatedly: government contracting. In the United States and elsewhere, social organizations often receive large portions of their funding through contracts with governments for the delivery of services. We discussed the implications of moving toward performance-based contracting in Chapter 14. Even in the interim, however, there is great scope for moving toward "right-fit" data collection systems in the contracting ecosystem. Such systems are critical for moving to scale, and improvements in system compatibility and the promise of "big data" offer opportunities to create large-scale measurement systems at relatively low cost.

As "big data" get bigger, however, issues of privacy that are often high on the mind of people in wealthy countries are going to be of greater importance. Informed consent processes for surveys address such issues during primary data collection. But while administrative data from mobile operators and financial institutions create tremendous opportunities for improved monitoring and evaluation, they require close attention to privacy concerns. The *responsible* principle will likely require growing emphasis on the privacy issue: it may make total sense for an organization to collect administrative data to improve its programs and track its performance. But without sufficient protocols in place to protect individuals' privacy, it may be socially irresponsible to collect and store the data.

We plan to return to these issues in Goldilocks 2.0. But for now we leave you with one final parting summative thought: if you cannot collect and analyze credible and actionable data, at a responsible cost relative to the benefit, then do not bother collecting the data. Use that money to help more people instead.

ACKNOWLEDGMENTS

This book benefited from contributions from many individuals.

Tania Alfonso and Kelly Bidwell helped get the project off the ground. Brian Swartz helped launch the project in Uganda, recruiting the first set of organizations that served as case studies and laboratories for our ideas. Libby Abbott took up the mantle, refining the cases and testing out our ideas. Ted Barnett expanded our work to Kenya, Mexico, and Nepal and worked closely with us to draft the first version of *Goldilocks*. Without him, the journey would have been so much longer.

Delia Welsh and Tetyana Zelenska developed the Goldilocks Toolkit for the Innovations for Poverty Action website (under the "Right-Fit Evidence Initiative"), adding new cases and important guidance on putting the principles into practice. We thank Google.org for funding the work to produce the Toolkit.

Trina Gorman provided organization, editing, and invaluable structure. Both Laura Burke and Megan McGuire got us over a number of humps and on the way to publication. Finally, Chris Lewis helped smooth out the rough patches and pull it all together.

At Oxford University Press, we thank David Pervin, Scott Parris, and, in particular, Terry Vaughn for helping to make this book idea come to reality. We wish you were here to see the fruits of the labor. At Levine & Greenberg Literary Agency, we thank Jim Levine and Kerry Sparks.

Along the way, so many others attended presentations, read drafts, and gave us invaluable feedback. We thank in particular Kathleen W. Apltauer, Trey Beck, Paul Brest, Lilly Chang, Shannon Coyne, Elijah Goldberg, Trina Gorman, Jessica Kiessel, Ben Mazzotta, Cindy Perry, Steven Rathgeb Smith, Sneha Stephen, Michael Weinstein, and an anonymous reviewer for their time, energy, and enthusiasm about these ideas.

ACRONYMS

CART	Credible, Actionable, Responsible and Transportable
CHW	Community health worker
ICS	International Child Support
IPA	Innovations for Poverty Action
J-PAL	Jameel Poverty Action Lab (the full name is the Massachusetts Institute of Technology Abdul Latif Jameel Poverty Action Lab)
NFA	Nutrition for All (a fictitious nonprofit organization)
NGO	Nongovernmental organization
PFS	Pay for Success
RCT	Randomized controlled trial (also randomized control trial)
SIF	Social Impact Fund
SNV	Stichting Nederlandse Vrijwilligers
TCAI	Teacher Community Assistant Initiative
UKA	Un Kilo de Ayuda
WASH	Water, sanitation, and hygiene

NOTES

CHAPTER 1

1. Podcasts and Africa (2016).
2. "United Nations Millennium Development Goals" (2016).
3. The Paris Declaration on Aid Effectiveness and the Accra Agenda, accessed April 16, 2016, http://www.oecd.org/dac/effectiveness/34428351.pdf.
4. For recent books on RCTs in developing countries, see Banerjee and Duflo (2011); Karlan and Appel (2011); Glennerster and Takavarasha (2013); Ogden (2016).
5. Haskins and Baron (2011).
6. Social Innovations Fund website, accessed April 16, 2016, https://data.gov.uk/sib_knowledge_box/home.
7. Centre for Social Impact Bonds, accessed April 16, 2016, https://data.gov.uk/sib_knowledge_box/home.
8. "NextGenDonors" (2013).
9. Karlan and Appel (2011).

CHAPTER 2

1. J-PAL and IPA (2015).
2. "Mali Celebrates Global Handwashing Day with Live Performances and Hygiene Events," UNICEF, accessed April 16, 2016, http://www.unicef.org/infobycountry/mali_51551.html.
3. World Development Indicators | Ghana | Data, World Bank, accessed April 16, 2016, http://data.worldbank.org/country/ghana; "Ghana Looks to Retool Its Economy as It Reaches Middle-Income Status," Text/HTML, World Bank, accessed April 16, 2016, http://www.worldbank.org/en/news/feature/2011/07/18/ghana-looks-to-retool-its-economy-as-it-reaches-middle-income-status.
4. Hannah, Duflo, and Greenstone (2016).
5. Glennerster and Takavarasha (2013).
6. Iyengar and Lepper (2000).

CHAPTER 3

1. Weiss (1998).
2. Van den Steen (2004).
3. Russo and Schoemaker (1992).
4. A number of resources exist for outcome mapping, such as Backwards Mapping and Connecting Outcomes, http://www.theoryofchange.org/what-is-theory-of-change/how-does-theory-of-change-work/example/backwards-mapping/. Links

to additional resources can also be found the Goldilocks Toolkit at http://www.poverty-action.org/goldilocks/toolkit.

CHAPTER 4
1. http://feedbacklabs.org/.
2. "Vaccines Are Effective | Vaccines.gov" (2016).
3. Jessica Cohen and Pascaline Dupas (2010).
4. Cohen and Dupas (2010).
5. "The Price Is Wrong" (2011).
6. Bandiera et al. (2013).
7. Banerjee et al. (2015).
8. "Building Stable Livelihoods for the Ultra Poor | Innovations for Poverty Action" (2016)

CHAPTER 5
1. "The Overhead Myth" (2017).
2. Karlan (2014).
3. Bertrand et al. (2010).
4. Karlan (2014).
5. "WHO | Moderate Malnutrition" 2016.
6. Levine, Bruno van Vijfeijken and Jayawickrama (2016).

CHAPTER 6
1. "History | Pratham" (2016).
2. Banerjee et al. (2005).
3. Glewwe, Kremer, and Moulin (2009).
4. Glewwe et al. (2004).
5. Merriam Webster online, http://www.merriam-webster.com/dictionary/bias.
6. The Institute of Education Sciences and National Science Foundation, National Academy of Sciences, Congressional Budget Office, US Preventive Services Task Force, Food and Drug Administration, and other respected scientific bodies consider RCTs the strongest method of evaluating the effectiveness of programs, practices, and treatments (see "Demonstrating How Low-Cost Randomized Controlled Trials Can Drive Effective Social Spending," 2015).
7. Miguel and Kremer (2004).
8. This is the motivation behind "credit scoring experiments" done for microcredit (for example, see Karlan and Zinman 2010, 2011; Augsburg et al. 2015).
9. Gugerty and Kremer (2008).
10. Angrist et al. (2001).
11. "Demonstrating How Low-Cost Randomized Controlled Trials Can Drive Effective Social Spending," 2015.
12. Evaluating the Teacher Community Assistant Initiative in Ghana | Innovations for Poverty Action (2016).
13. Banerjee et al. (2015).
14. Bandiera et al. (2013).

CHAPTER 7
1. The General Social Survey has been used for more than 40 years to measure social characteristics and attitudes in the United States, see http://gss.norc.org/About-The-GSS, accessed April 15, 2016.

2. In 2005.
3. Types of Malnutrition | WFP | United Nations World Food Programme - Fighting Hunger Worldwide (2016).
4. Karlan and Zinman (2011).
5. Goldacre, Ben. 2010. *Bad Science: Quacks, Hacks, and Big Pharma Flacks.* 1st American ed. New York: Faber and Faber.
6. Innovations for Poverty Action, "Using Administrative Data for Monitoring and Evaluation," *Goldilocks Toolkit,* February 2016.
7. Morten (2013).
8. Sandefur and Glassman (2015).
9. For more information on assessing the quality of administrative data, see the Goldilocks Toolkit and "Using Administrative Data for Randomized Evaluations," Abdul Latif Jameel Poverty Action Lab, December 2015.
10. World Health Organization, "Moderate Malnutrition," accessed April 15, 2016, http://www.who.int/nutrition/topics/moderate_malnutrition/en/.
11. Harris, Harris, and Smith (2012).
12. Osunami and Forer (2016).
13. Gertler et al. (2011).
14. For more details on what this process looks like, see the Ethics section of J-PAL's guide, "Using Administrative Data for Randomized Evaluations," https://www.povertyactionlab.org/sites/default/files/documents/AdminDataGuide.pdf.

CHAPTER 9
1. "BRAC Uganda Annual Report 2010" (2016).

CHAPTER 10
1. Karlan, Morten, and Zinman (2015).
2. A complete description of how to construct a full monitoring and evaluation system for a microfinance program is well outside the scope of this book; for more information about the key indicators to track, read a primer from Consultative Group to Assist the Poor (CGAP) called "Measuring Result of Microfinance Institutions: Minimum Indicators" at http://www.cgap.org/publications/measuring-results-microfinance-institutions-minimum-indicators.

CHAPTER 11
1. "Joseph Kony Captures Congress' Attention—Scott Wong—POLITICO.com" (2016).

CHAPTER 12
1. Miguel and Kremer (2004).
2. "Deworming: A Best Buy for Development" (2012).
3. Baird et al. (2011).
4. "What We Do" (2016).
5. Montresor et al. (2002).

CHAPTER 13
1. "Mexico: WHO Statistical Profile" (2015).
2. "World Development Indicators | World DataBank" (2016).

CHAPTER 14

1. Paul Brest and Susan Adatto discuss these programs in "The Promise of Pay-for-Success Programs and Barriers to Their Adoption" (Adatto and Brest, 2018).
2. Adatto and Brest (2018).

CHAPTER 15

1. Gugerty (2009); Prakash and Gugerty (2010).
2. See Karlan's 2011 Freakonomics blog post: http://freakonomics.com/2011/06/09/why-ranking-charities-by-administrative-expenses-is-a-bad-idea/. An important exception to ignoring overhead ratios: there are some, very few, organizations that are fraudulent, that spend over half of their money paying senior management, sometimes even as high as 95%. These are basically scams, and overhead ratios do inform the public about such charities. Unfortunately, there is likely no overlap between the set of people these charities market to (via door-to-door or phone banking) and the set of people who know how to look up the overhead ratios of a charity on a site like Charity Navigator.

GLOSSARY

Activities: the essential program elements needed to provide a product or service

Anchoring: a source of bias in data collection that occurs when a person's answer is influenced by some concept accidentally or purposefully put in the mind of the respondent

Assumptions: the conditions that have to hold for a certain part of a program or policy to work as expected

Bias: (in the context of data collection) the systematic difference between how someone responds to a question and the true answer to that question

Concurrent validity: when an indicator produces data consistent with closely related indicators

Construct validity: how well an indicator captures the essence of the concept it seeks to measure

Counterfactual: (in the context of impact evaluation) how individuals or communities would have fared had a program or policy not occurred (or occurred differently)

Criterion validity: how well an indicator predicts another outcome (two types of criterion validity are *concurrent validity* and *predictive validity*)

Engagement data: Data on who participates in programs, policies, or products, as well as data on how extensively individuals or firms participate

Experimenter demand effects: occurs in the context of an experiment in which individuals, aware of their treatment assignment, answer in specific ways in order to please the experimenter (note that this is distinct from *Hawthorne* or *John Henry effects,* in which people behave differently because of their awareness of their treatment status)

Hawthorne effect: when an individual's awareness of being in a treatment group as part of a research study leads them to change behavior

Impact: the change in outcomes for those affected by a program compared to the alternative outcomes had the program not existed

Impact evaluation: an analysis that estimates the impact of a program

Indicator: a metric used to measure a concept

John Henry effect: when an individual's awareness of being in a control group as part of a research study leads them to change behavior

Mere measurement effect: when merely measuring somebody causes them to change their later behavior

Observer bias: when a surveyor's knowledge of the study or the treatment/control assignment influences how they behave toward respondents (i.e., the surveyor consciously or subconsciously nudges respondents to answer or behave in a certain way)

Organization: nonprofits, government, and social enterprises

Outcomes: the intended (and unintended) results of program or policy outputs

Outputs: the products or services generated by program activities; deliverables

Predictive validity: when an indicator is a good predictor of a different, future indicator

Reliable: data are consistently generated; the data collection procedure does not introduce randomness or bias into the process

Social desirability bias: the tendency of individuals to answer questions in what they perceive to be the socially desirable way (*see also* Experimenter demand effects)

Social enterprise: a for-profit firm that has a positive impact on society, over and beyond that accruing to the owners of the firm and their clients or consumers. Note that many stop the definition at merely "a positive impact on society." We believe this is too broad of a definition, as any firm which honestly sells a product makes its owners and consumers better off. So without the "over and beyond" part of the definition, just about all firms would be deemed "social enterprises," and then the jargon loses any real meaning. To the wonkier economist reader, "over and beyond" refers to "externalities."

Take-up: the binary categorization of someone's participation (or not) in a program, policy, or product.

FURTHER RESOURCES

CREATING A THEORY OF CHANGE

- Guiding Your Program to Build a Theory of Change, Goldilocks Toolkit, https://www.poverty-action.org/publication/goldilocks-deep-dive-guiding-your-program-build-theory-change
- Nothing as Practical as Good Theory: Exploring Theory-Based Evaluation for Comprehensive Community Initiatives for Children and Families, by Carol Weiss. In New Approaches to Evaluating Community Initiatives: Concepts, Methods, and Contexts, by James P. Connell (Editor), Anne C. Kubisch (Editor), Lisbeth B. Schorr (Editor), Carol H. Weiss (Editor) Aspen Institute, 1999.
- Organizational Research Services (2004). Theory of Change: A Practical Tool For Action, Results and Learning Prepared for the Annie Casey Foundation. http://www.aecf.org/upload/publicationfiles/cc2977k440.pdf

MONITORING AND ADMINISTRATIVE DATA

- *Using Administrative Data for Monitoring and Evaluation* in the Goldilocks Toolkit (www.poverty-action.org/goldilocks/toolkit). The Goldilocks Toolkit is a living set of documents, some deep-dives on issues discussed here, new content beyond what the book covers, and additional short cases that illustrate how organizatios have wrestled with these issues.
- *Assessing and Monitoring Program Progress* by Peter H. Rossi, Mark W. Lipsey, and Howard E. Freeman.
- Evaluation: A Systematic Approach by Peter H. Rossi, Mark W. Lipsey, and Howard E. Freeman. Sage Publications, 2003.
- *Developing a Process-Evaluation Plan for Assessing Health Promotion Program Implementation: A How-To Guide* by Ruth P. Saunders, Martin H. Evans, and Praphul Joshi., Health Promotion Practices,. 2005. 6(2):134–47.

IMPACT EVALUATIONS

- *Running Randomized Evaluations*, by Rachel Glennerster and Kudzai Takavarasha. Princeton University Press, 2013.
- *Impact Evaluation in Practice*, by Paul Gertler, Sebastian Martinez, Patrick Premand, Laura B. Rawlings, and Christel M.J. Vermeersch. World Bank, 2016.
- *Introduction to Rapid-Fire Operational Testing for Social Programs, Organizational Challenges of Impact Evaluation,* and *Measuring the Impact of Technology-Based Programs* in the Goldilocks Toolkit (www.poverty-action.org/goldilocks/toolkit).

HIGH-QUALITY DATA COLLECTION

- *Designing Household Survey Questionnaires for Developing Countries: Lessons from 15 Years of the Living Standards Measurement Study*, by Margaret Grosh and Paul Glewwe. World Bank, 2000.
- *Using Administrative Data for Randomized Evaluations*, by Laura Feeney, Jason Bauman, Julia Chabrier, Geeti Mehra, and Michelle Woodford. Jamee Latif Povery Action Lab (J-PAL), 2015 (https://www.povertyactionlab.org/sites/default/files/resources/2017.02.07-Admin-Data-Guide.pdf)
- *Resources for Data Collection and Storage*, in the Goldilocks Toolkit (www.poverty-action.org/goldilocks/toolkit).

WORKS CITED

Adatto, Suzanne and Paul Brest. 2018. "The Promise of Pay-for-Success Programs and Barriers to Their Adoption." Working paper.

Angrist, Joshua, Eric Bettinger, Erik Bloom, Elizabeth King, and Michael Kremer. 2001. "Vouchers for Private Schooling in Colombia: Evidence from a Randomized Natural Experiment." Working Paper 8343. National Bureau of Economic Research. http://www.nber.org/papers/w8343.

Augsburg, Britta, Ralph De Haas, Heike Harmgart, and Costas Meghir. 2015. "The Impacts of Microcredit: Evidence from Bosnia and Herzegovina." *American Economic Journal: Applied Economics* 7 (1): 183–203. doi:10.1257/app.20130272.

Baird, Sarah, Joan Hamory Hicks, Michael Kremer, and Edward Miguel. 2011. *Worms at Work: Long-Run Impacts of Child Health Gains*. Berkeley: University of California at Berkeley. https://kogod.american.edu/cas/economics/pdf/upload/Baird-paper.pdf.

Bandiera, Oriana, Robin Burgess, Narayan Das, Selim Gulesci, Imran Rasul, and Munshi Sulaiman. 2013. "Can Basic Entrepreneurship Transform the Economic Lives of the Poor?" SSRN Scholarly Paper ID 2266813. Rochester, NY: Social Science Research Network. http://papers.ssrn.com/abstract=2266813.

Banerjee, Abhijit, Shawn Cole, Esther Duflo, and Leigh Linden. 2005. "Remedying Education: Evidence from Two Randomized Experiments in India." Working Paper 11904. National Bureau of Economic Research. http://www.nber.org/papers/w11904.

Banerjee, Abhijit, and Esther Duflo. 2011. *Poor Economics: A Radical Rethinking of the Way to Fight Global Poverty*. New York: PublicAffairs.

Banerjee, Abhijit, Esther Duflo, Nathanael Goldberg, Dean Karlan, Robert Osei, William Parienté, Jeremy Shapiro, Bram Thuysbaert, and Christopher Udry. 2015. "A Multifaceted Program Causes Lasting Progress for the Very Poor: Evidence from Six Countries." *Science* 348 (6236): 1260799. doi:10.1126/science.1260799.

Bertrand, Marianne, Dean Karlan, Sendhil Mullainathan, Eldar Shafir, and Jonathan Zinman. 2010. "What's Advertising Content Worth? Evidence from a Consumer Credit Marketing Field Experiment." *Quarterly Journal of Economics* 125 (1): 263–305.

"BRAC Uganda Annual Report 2010." 2016. *Issuu*. Accessed April 17. https://issuu.com/brac/docs/brac-uganda-report-2010/14.

"Building Stable Livelihoods for the Ultra Poor | Innovations for Poverty Action." 2016. Accessed April 16, 2016. http://www.poverty-action.org/publication/building-stable-livelihoods-ultra-poor.

Cohen, Jessica, and Pascaline Dupas. 2010. "Free Distribution or Cost-Sharing? Evidence from a Randomized Malaria Prevention Experiment." *Quarterly Journal of Economics* 125 (1): 1–45. doi:10.1162/qjec.2010.125.1.1.

"Demonstrating How Low-Cost Randomized Controlled Trials Can Drive Effective Social Spending." 2015. Coalition for Evidence-Based Policy. http://coalition4evidence.org/wp-content/uploads/2014/12/Request-for-Proposals-2nd-year-of-competition-Dec-2014.pdf.

"Deworming: A Best Buy for Development." 2012. J-PAL Policy Bulletin. Abdul Latif Jameel Poverty Action Lab. https://www.povertyactionlab.org/sites/default/files/publications/2012.3.22-Deworming.pdf.

"Evaluating the Teacher Community Assistant Initiative in Ghana | Innovations for Poverty Action." 2016. Accessed April 19, 2016. http://www.poverty-action.org/study/evaluating-teacher-community-assistant-initiative-ghana.

Gertler, Paul, Sebastian Martinez, Patrick Premand, Laura B. Rawlings, and Christel Vermeersch. 2011. *Impact Evaluation in Practice*. Washington, D.C.: The World Bank. http://siteresources.worldbank.org/EXTHDOFFICE/Resources/5485726-1295455628620/Impact_Evaluation_in_Practice.pdf.

Glennerster, Rachel, and Kudzai Takavarasha. 2013. *Running Randomized Evaluations: A Practical Guide*. Princeton: Princeton University Press.

Glewwe, Paul, Michael Kremer, and Sylvie Moulin. 2009. "Many Children Left Behind? Textbooks and Test Scores in Kenya." *American Economic Journal: Applied Economics* 1 (1): 112–35. doi:10.1257/app.1.1.112.

Glewwe, Paul, Michael Kremer, Sylvie Moulin, and Eric Zitzewitz. 2004. "Retrospective vs. Prospective Analyses of School Inputs: The Case of Flip Charts in Kenya." *Journal of Development Economics* 74: 251–268.

Goldacre, Ben. 2010. *Bad Science: Quacks, Hacks, and Big Pharma Flacks*. 1st American ed. New York: Faber and Faber.

Green, Donald and Alan Gerber. 2012. *Field Experiments: design, analysis, and interpretation*. New York: W.W. Norton.

Gugerty, Mary Kay. 2009. "Signaling Virtue: Voluntary Accountability Programs Among Nonprofit Organizations." *Policy Sciences* 42 (3): 243–273. doi:10.1007/s11077-009-9085-3.

Gugerty, Mary Kay, and Michael Kremer. 2008. "Outside Funding and the Dynamics of Participation in Community Associations." *American Journal of Political Science* 52 (3): 585–602. doi:10.1111/j.1540-5907.2008.00331.x.

Hannah, Rema, Esther Duflo, and Michael Greenstone. 2016. "Up in Smoke: The Influence of Household Behavior on the Long-Run Impact of Improved Cooking Stoves." *American Economic Journal* 8 (1): 80–114.

Harris, Phillip, Joan Harris, and Bruce M. Smith. (2012). "Standardized Tests Do Not Effectively Measure Student Achievement." in *Standardized Testing*, edited by Dedria Bryfonski. Detroit: Greenhaven Press. At Issue. Rpt. from "Chapter 3: The Tests Don't Measure Achievement Adequately." The Myths of Standardized Tests: Why They Don't Tell You What You Think They Do. 2011. 33–45. Opposing Viewpoints In Context. Web 23 Sept. 2013.

Haskins, Ron, and Jon Baron. 2011. "Building the Connection Between Policy and Evidence." NESTA. http://coalition4evidence.org/wp-content/uploads/2011/09/Haskins-Baron-paper-on-fed-evid-based-initiatives-2011.pdf.

"History, Pratham." 2016. Accessed April 19, 2016. http://www.prathamusa.org/about-us/history.

Iyengar, Sheena, and Mark Lepper. 2000. "When Choice Is Demotivating: Can One Desire Too Much of a Good Thing?" *Journal of Personality and Social Psychology* 79 (6):995–1006. https://doi.org/10.1037/0022-3514.79.6.995.

"Joseph Kony Captures Congress' Attention - Scott Wong - POLITICO.com." 2016. Accessed April 18. http://www.politico.com/news/stories/0312/74355_Page2.html.

Karlan, Dean. 2005. "Using Experimental Economics to Measure Social Capital and Predict Financial Decisions." *American Economic Review* 95 (5): 1688–1699.

Karlan, Dean. 2014. "Here's How to Determine If That Charity Is Worth Your Dollars." *Los Angeles Times*, December 18, sec. Op-ed. http://www.latimes.com/opinion/op-ed/la-oe-karlan-charitable-giving-20141218-story.html.

Karlan, Dean, and Jonathan Zinman. 2011. "List Randomization for Sensitive Behavior: An Application for Measuring Use of Loan Proceeds." *Journal of Development Economics* 98 (1): 1–75.

Karlan, Dean, and Jacob Appel. 2011. *More than Good Intentions: How a New Economics Is Helping to Solve Global Poverty*. New York: Dutton.

Karlan, Dean, and Jacob Appel. 2016. *Failing in the Field: What We Can Learn When Field Research Goes Wrong*. New York: Princeton University Press.

Karlan, Dean, Melanie Morten, and Jonathan Zinman. 2015. "A Personal Touch: Text Messaging for Loan Repayment." *Behavioral Science & Policy* 1 (2): 25–32.

Karlan, Dean, Robert Osei, Isaac Osei-Akoto, and Christopher Udry. 2014. "Agricultural Decisions after Relaxing Credit and Risk Constraints." *Quarterly Journal of Economics* 129 (2): 597–652.

Karlan, Dean, and Jonathan Zinman. 2010. "Expanding Credit Access: Using Randomized Supply Decisions to Estimate the Impacts." *Review of Financial Studies* 23 (1): 433–464.

Karlan, Dean, and Jonathan Zinman. 2011. "Microcredit in Theory and Practice: Using Randomized Credit Scoring for Impact Evaluation." *Science* 332 (6035): 1278–1284. doi:10.1126/science.1200138.

Levine, Carlise, Tosca Bruno van Vijfeijken. 2016. "Measuring International NGO Agency-Level Results." Interaction. https://www.interaction.org/sites/default/files/ALR_WhitePaper_FINAL_0.pdf.

J-PAL and IPA. 2015. "Where Credit Is Due." J-PAL and IPA Policy Bulletin. Abdul Latif Jameel Poverty Action Lab and Innovations for Poverty Action.

"Mexico: WHO Statistical Profile." 2015. World Health Organization. http://www.who.int/gho/countries/mex.pdf?ua=1.

Miguel, Edward, and Michael Kremer. 2004. "Worms: Identifying Impacts on Education and Health in the Presence of Treatment Externalities." *Econometrica* 72 (1): 159–217.

Montresor, Antonio, David W. T. Crompton, Theresa W. Gyorkos, Lorenzo Savioli, and World Health Organization. 2002. "Helminth Control in School-Age Children : A Guide for Managers of Control Programmes." http://www.who.int/iris/handle/10665/42473.

Morten, Jerven. 2013. *Poor Numbers: How We Are Misled by African Development Statistics and What To Do About It*. Ithaca, NY: Cornell University Press.

"NextGen Donors." 2013. Johnson Center for Philanthropy, 21/64. http://www.nextgendonors.org/wp-content/uploads/next-gen-donor-report-updated.pdf.

Ogden, Timothy N., ed. 2016. *Experimental Conversations: Perspectives on Randomized Trials in Economic Development.* Cambridge, MA: MIT Press.

Orwell, George. 1946. *Animal Farm.* New York: Houghton Mifflin Harcourt.

Osunami, Steve, and Ben Forer. 2016. "Atlanta Cheating: 178 Teachers and Administrators Changed Answers to Increase Test Scores." *ABC News.* Accessed February 2. http://abcnews.go.com/US/atlanta-cheating-178-teachers-administrators-changed-answers-increase/story?id=14013113.

"Paris Declaration and Accra Agenda for Action – OECD." Accessed April 16, 2016. http://www.oecd.org/dac/effectiveness/parisdeclarationandaccraagendaforaction.htm.

Podcasts, and Middle East & Africa. 2016. "To Increase Charitable Donations, Appeal to the Heart – Not the Head." *Knowledge@Wharton.* Accessed April 16. http://knowledge.wharton.upenn.edu/article/to-increase-charitable-donations-appeal-to-the-heart-not-the-head/.

Prakash, Aseem, and Mary Kay Gugerty. 2010. "Trust but Verify? Voluntary Regulation Programs in the Nonprofit Sector." *Regulation & Governance,* February. doi:10.1111/j.1748-5991.2009.01067.x.

"The Price Is Wrong." 2011. *Bulletin.* Cambridge, MA: Abdul Latif Jameel Poverty Action Lab. https://www.povertyactionlab.org/sites/default/files/publications/The%20Price%20is%20Wrong.pdf.

Russo, Edward J., and Paul J. H. Schoemaker. 1992. "Managing Overconfidence." *Sloan Management Review* 33 (2): 7.

Sandefur, Justin, and Amanda Glassman. (2015). "The Political Economy of Bad Data: Evidence from African Survey and Administrative Statistics." *The Journal of Development Studies* 51 (2): 116–132.

"Types of Malnutrition | WFP | United Nations World Food Programme - Fighting Hunger Worldwide." Accessed April 23, 2016. https://www.wfp.org/hunger/malnutrition/types.

"United Nations Millennium Development Goals." Accessed April 16, 2016. http://www.un.org/millenniumgoals/bkgd.shtml.

"Vaccines Are Effective | Vaccines.gov." 2016. Accessed April 19, 2016. http://www.vaccines.gov/basics/effectiveness/.

Van den Steen, Eric. 2004. "Rational Overoptimism (and Other Biases)." *American Economic Review* 94 (4): 1141–1151. doi:10.1257/0002828042002697.

Weiss, Carol H. 1998. *Evaluation: Methods for Studying Programs and Policies.* 2nd ed. Upper Saddle River, NJ: Prentice Hall.

"What We Do." *Evidence Action.* Accessed April 23, 2016. http://www.evidenceaction.org/.

"World Development Indicators | World DataBank." Accessed April 18, 2016. http://databank.worldbank.org/data/reports.aspx?source=2&country=MEX&series=&period=.

"World Health Organization | Moderate Malnutrition." *WHO.* Accessed April 19, 2016. http://www.who.int/nutrition/topics/moderate_malnutrition/en/.

INDEX

Note: Page numbers followed by '*f*' and '*b*' refer to figures and boxes.

Agaba, Collins, 202, 205, 207, 208
Albendazole, 217
amount of services provided, as proof of
    impact, 16–17
anchoring
    definition of, 275
    and measurement bias, 125–126
assumption-based counterfactuals,
    103–104
assumptions
    definition of, 40 *b*, 275
    identification of, in theory of change,
    31, 40–42, 53, 77–79, 78 *f*
attribution bias, 93
backward mapping, in development of
    theory of change, 31

Bashar, Abul, 170, 171, 174
BBB Wise Giving Alliance, 257
before-and-after comparisons, as
    measurement of impact, 4–5, 16,
    17–19, 102–103, 233, 238 *f*, 240
bias
    definition of, 92–93, 275
    from external factors, 93
    feedback data and, 193
    in impact evaluation, 92–95
    randomized control trials and, 95
    types of, 93–95
    in user reviews of nonprofits, 257–258
    See also measurement bias; social
    desirability bias
BRAC (Building Resources Across
    Communities)
    BRAC Dairy, 167–168
    commitment to monitoring and
    evaluation, 167, 168
    history and mission of, 167
    microfranchise model of, 167, 168
    operations in Uganda, 168–169
    separate units for monitoring and
    evaluation, 168, 178
    sustainability focus of, 167–168
BRAC monitoring unit
    actionable data collected by, 168, 178
    branch-level resentment of, 173, 178
    long chain of command in, 179–180
    revolving monitoring by, 169–170, 178
BRAC Poultry and Livestock Program
    goals of, 169

monitoring of program
    effectiveness, 170
theory of change, incentives for CLPs
    as key element in, 22 *b*, 166, 167 *b*,
    169, 173
BRAC Poultry and Livestock Program,
    and Community Livestock
    Promoters (CLPs)
    active status, monitoring of, 170–173,
    171 *f*, 175 *f*
    false reporting by, 172
    feedback survey of, 171, 171 *f*, 173–
    174, 176 *f*–77 *f*, 179, 180
    as individual entrepreneurs, 166
    interviews of, 166
    role of, 169
    supervision of, 169
    training of, 169
    verification of activity reported by,
    140, 171–172
BRAC Poultry and Livestock Program,
    monitoring of CLP incentive
    effectiveness, 11, 166, 170–173, 171
    f, 175 *f*
    and actionable data, collection of, 174,
    178–180
    additional data needed in, 180
    analysis of data, 173
    benefits of, 22 *b*
    case analysis, 178–180
    changes to program based on, 174–175
    false reporting by CLPs, 172
    feedback survey of CLPs on, 171, 171 *f*,
    173–174, 176 *f*–77 *f*, 179, 180
    need for credible, actionable data,
    166–167, 167 *b*
    reports on, 174, 175 *f*–77 *f*, 179
    unaddressed problems identified
    in, 180
    verifying of CLP reported activity, 140,
    171–172
Brest, Paul, 253
Bulayev, Boris, 147, 149, 150, 155, 159,
    162, 163

Campbell Collaboration, 108
CART principles, 6, 10
    broad applicability of, 12–14
    as common language for donors and
    organizations, 246, 253

learning from data
  culture of learning and inquiry
    necessary for, 87–88, 179
  as goal of monitoring, 22, 66–67,
    69, 70 b, 71–72, 74, 76, 79, 80, 84,
    87–88, 263
  as predictor of nonprofit success, 261
  responsibility for, 4
Lepper, Mark R., 27 b
list randomization, 125
Living Standards Measurement Survey
    (World Bank), 134
logical checks in data entry tools, 141
logic model. See theory of change
look-back period, and measurement
    error, 126, 128
Lopez, Teresa, 227, 228, 229
Lord's Resistance Army (LRA), 200–201

Mali, measuring effectiveness of hygiene
    campaigns in, 18–20, 18 f
malnutrition, types of, 122
Martinez, Sebastian, 115
Massachusetts Institute of Technology
    (MIT), and impact evaluation for
    Indian tutoring program, 91
matching, in impact evaluation, 100
Matovu, Jackson, 61 b, 181–182,
    184–188, 192–194
measurement bias, 123–125
  common forms of, 125–126, 127 b
  definition of, 124, 124 b
measurement error
  common causes of, 126–129
  definition of, 124
mere measurement effect, 125, 275
metrics. See indicators
Mexico, nutrition deficits in, 229. See
    also Programa Integral de Nutrición
    (PIN); Un Kilo de Ayuda
microcredit programs
  feedback data, inaccuracies in, 75
  and impact evaluation, 16–17, 20
  repayment rates as primary
    monitoring goal for, 196
  See also Finance for Life program
Miguel, Edward, 213
Miguel, Tom, 99
Ministry Watch, 257
monitoring

actionable data for learning and
    improvement as goal of, 22, 66–67,
    69, 70 b, 71–72, 74, 76, 79, 80, 84,
    87–88, 263
  collection of unused/unusable data, as
    common error, 61 b, 67, 69, 182 b,
    188–189, 196–197
  types of data to be monitored, 23,
    69–77, 77–85, 265 b
  See also activity monitoring;
    engagement data; feedback data;
    financial data; targeting data
monitoring and evaluation system
  activity monitoring as key
    component of, 22
  CART principles as guide to creating,
    15, 24, 29
  challenges of creating, 15
  increasing demand for, 7–8
  necessity of, 6
  resources for construction of, 264, 265
    b, 273n2 (chap. 10), 277–278
  time required to develop, 200 b
  See also CART principles
monitoring and evaluation system,
    right-fit
  characteristics of, 24–25
  as Goldilocks-type challenge, 5–6, 9
  need for, vii–viii, 3–5
monitoring and evaluation system,
    wrong-fit
  as pointless drain or resources,
    vii–viii, 3–5, 9, 20
  types of, 8–9
More Than Good Intentions
    (Karlan), 9
Morton, Melanie, 184

Namugongo Good Samaritan
    Project, 148
Nansubunga, Joan, 153, 154
NFA. See Nutrition for All
Niger, measuring effectiveness of
    hygiene campaigns in,
    18–20, 18 f
non-program factors
  evaluation of, in theory of change,
    42–43, 51
  inability to isolate, as signal to rethink
    value of outcome data, 43

Nutrition for All (NFA) [hypothetical NGO]
  and desired outcome, clear definition of, 120
  evaluation of assumptions connecting activities to outputs, 77–79, 78 *f*
  and identification of essential data, 52–53, 54
  and indicators, finding of, 134
  and metric (indicator), clear definition of, 120, 122
  mission of, 32–33
  and overconfidence, dangers of, 43–45
  right-size monitoring, development of, 77–85
  theory of change, steps in defining, 33–43
  unit of randomization in, 97
  See also theory of change

observer bias, 123, 127 *b*, 275–276
Okello, Patience, 166, 171–172
operational evaluations
  as alternative to impact evaluation, 21 *b*
  Un Kilo de Ayuda switch to, 21 *b*
Oportunidades (Mexican social assistance program), 232
opportunity costs of data collection, 28, 58, 60, 61 *b*, 86, 95
organizations
  definition of, 5, 276
  and impact evaluation, demand for, 7–8
  large-scale, as area for future work, 264–266
outcomes
  alternative explanations for, in theory of change, 36, 37, 39, 43, 82, 83
  clearly defined, importance of, 163
  data on, as distinct from targeting data, 73
  definition of, 37 *b*, 276
  easily-measured, deceptive simplicity of, 80–82
  establishment of, in theory of change, 36–37
  evaluation of assumptions connecting outputs to, 40, 41–42, 42 *f*

impact as change in vs. counterfactual case, 19 *b*, 19, 23
  inability to isolate non-program factors as signal to rethink value of, 43
  incorrect use of data on, 8–9
  increased calls for measurement of, 7–8
  mapping of, in theory of change, 36–37
  monitoring of, for targeting purposes, 82
  vs. outputs, importance of distinguishing between, 31, 35–36, 37–39, 178, 208–210
  See also Educate! Experience, desired outcomes in; impact
outputs
  vs. activities, 35
  critical, identification of, in theory of change, 47, 70 *b*, 72
  definition of, 35 *b*
  evaluation of assumptions connecting activities to, 40–41, 41 *f*, 77–79, 78 *f*
  evaluation of assumptions connecting to outcomes, 40, 41–42, 42 *f*
  identification of, in theory of change, 34–36
  monitoring of, 51, 71–72
  vs. outcomes, importance of distinguishing between, 31, 35–36, 37–39, 178, 208–210
overhead ratios, as gauge of charity effectiveness, 68, 257, 274n2 (chap. 15)

Paris Declaration on Aid Effectiveness, 7
Pay for Success (PFS) model, 249–253
  and adjustments to contracting practices, 253
  advantages and disadvantages of, 250–251
  evaluation costs of, 250, 251
  implementation issues in, 251–253
  increasing use of, 249
  and monitoring and evaluation, need for, 252–253
  and output/outcome to be compensated, 249
  risk aversion and, 250–251, 252
  three models for contracts in, 252

performance-based contracts. *See* Pay for Success (PFS) model
personal information, and data privacy, 28, 142, 266
Philanthropedia, 257
piloting of data collection instruments, 135–136
PIN. *See* Programa Integral de Nutrición
Pratham, Indian tutoring program of, 90–92, 106–107
predictive validity, 122, 276
Premand, Patrick, 115
pretesting of data collection instruments, 135–136, 193
primary data
definition of, 129
types and uses of, 129–130
prison recidivism, Pay for Success programs to reduce, 249, 251
privacy, as issue in data collection, 28, 142, 266
Programa Integral Nutricion, and impact evaluation
alternative to RCT in, 241
complexity of program and, 234–235
design of RCT for, 235–236, 236–237, 237 *f*
lack of, 229, 234, 240
lack of funding for, 236–237
monitoring improvements deployed in place of, 237
use of anecdotal evidence for, 233, 240
use of before-and-after evidence for, 233, 238 *f*, 240
Programa Integral de Nutrición, data collection by, 227–228, 230–231, 232–233
determining right amount of, 228 *b*
time required for, 229
and tradeoff between actionability and responsibility, 228 *b*, 239–240
program design
rapid-fire (A/B) testing and, 76
responsibility principle in, 60
See also theory of change
program selection bias, 94–95
propensity score matching, 100

quasi-experimental methods of impact evaluation, 100–102, 111

randomization
ethics of, and responsibility principle, 109
as means of creating counterfactual, 20
measurement bias and, 125
randomized control trials (RCTs), 95–99
alternatives to, 20, 100–102
appropriate uses of, 95
balancing cost and benefit of (responsibility principle), 107–111
and bias, elimination of, 95
cost of, 107
cost reduction measures, 111–112
counterfactual creation in, 20, 95
definition of, 20, 95–96
as gold standard for impact evaluation, 95, 272n6 (chap. 6)
limitations of, vii–viii
opportunity costs of, 110
poorly-executed, 95
potential benefits of, 107
sample size in, 97–98, 114
social and ethical costs and, 108–111
spillovers (externalities) in, 98–99, 111
unit of randomization in, 97, 98 *b*, 99, 111, 114
validity of, as issue, 96
rapid-fire (A/B) testing, and feedback data, 76–77
rating systems for nonprofits
broad coverage, importance of, 256, 257, 258
challenges of creating, 255–256
current systems, limitations of, 257–259
need for, 254–255
overhead ratios as, 68, 257, 274n2 (chap. 15)
as prod for improvement, 256, 262
required features of, 256–257
See also impact auditing; Charity Navigator; Charity Watch; charity watchdog; Guide Star
Rawlings, Laura B., 115
RCTs. *See* randomized control trials
recall period, and measurement error, 126, 128
regression discontinuity analysis, 101–102

Experience (Uganda); Finance for
Life program; Invisible Children
UKA. *See* Un Kilo de Ayuda
United Kingdom, and demand for impact
evaluation, 8
United Nations
and demand for impact evaluation, 7
Millennium Declaration, 7
United States government, and demand
for impact evaluation, 7–8
unit of randomization, in randomized
control trials, 97, 98 *b*, 99, 111, 114
Un Kilo de Ayuda (UKA), 227–241
activity monitoring 227–228
and accountability to donors,
demonstration of, 240
feedback and engagement data, need
for, 239
handwashing safe water, and impact
evaluation, 235–236, 241
history of, 229
holistic approach to malnutrition,
229–230
holistic approach to nutrition,
230–232
improvements to actionability, 237
monitoring and evaluation challenge
faced by, 12, 21 *b*
program design, expert advice in,
230, 234

rapid response to failed treatments,
227–229, 231, 232–233, 239
services of, 227, 230–232
switch to operational evaluations, 21 *b*
theory of change, 234–235
uses of InfoKilo system in, 227
See also InfoKilo system; Programa
Integral de Nutrición (PIN)

vaccine distribution, and transportability
principle, 62
validity of measurement
as component of credibility, 25, 50, 85
indicators and, 118, 120–122,
120 *b*, 123
measurement bias and,
123–126, 127 *b*
measurement error and,
124, 126–129
Vermeersh, Christel M. J., 115

Weiss, Carol, 35
Wells Fargo Bank, and perverse
incentives, 88
Willms, Dennis, 182–183
wording, unclear, and measurement
error, 126, 128
World Bank, 134

Zinman, Jonathan, 184